I0834575

IGNATIAN FORMATION

THE INSPIRATION OF THE *CONSTITUTIONS*

# Ignatian Formation

## The Inspiration of the *Constitutions*

János Lukács SJ

Gracewing

First published in England in 2016
by
Gracewing
2 Southern Avenue
Leominster
Herefordshire HR6 0QF
United Kingdom
www.gracewing.co.uk



ISBN 978-1-78182-043-8

Cover design by Bernardita Peña Hurtado

Jesuit insignia by Moranski, Public Domain,
https://commons.wikimedia.org/w/index.php?curid=5596804

Typeset by Word and Page, Chester, UK

## CONTENTS

# ACKNOWLEDGMENTS

Some of the basic insights of this book began to take shape between 2000 and 2002 as I was studying at the Weston Jesuit School of Theology in Cambridge, Massachusetts, USA. Since preparing a Licentiate in Sacred Theology thesis in spirituality coincided with preparing to be a master of novices, I often felt perplexed as I tried to match the principal documents of the Society with my limited yet unforgettable previous experiences as a formator. During the four short semesters I felt truly blessed to be able to count on the experience and generosity of a number of excellent Jesuits who were teaching at the time at the Weston Jesuit School of Theology or at Boston College: Bill Barry, Michael Buckley, George Drury, Howard Gray, Dan Harrington, Jim Keenan, John O'Malley, Ed Vacek and several others companions, scholastics included, who inspired me by informal conversations rather than in an academic setting. In a series of makeshift workshops, J. Carlos Coupeau, who was at the time preparing a doctoral thesis on the *Constitutions*, also shared his insights in an effort to help two would-be masters of novices to grow into the task of introducing others to this great resource of the Society of Jesus.

Many years later, the actual writing of this book was inspired mainly by a series of conversations with Hungarian superiors of various religious orders, initiated by Ed Nemes SJ, and by the joy over the novitiate of the Hungarian province reopening in 2009 after several years of discontinuity. Several fellow Jesuits also reassured me that even in the midst of pressing everyday concerns and apostolic needs, it is worth pondering some of the fundamental questions of our Jesuit lives. I am grateful to many persons who contributed to the slowly evolving text, giving new momentum for it to take shape. Tibor Bartók SJ read the manuscript several times, formulating numerous crucial questions, offering important suggestions, adding clarifying or complementary notes. Two other members of our Province's Ignatian Spirituality Center, Zsuzsa Laczkó SJC and Elemér Vízi SJ also gave very helpful feedback. Besides their support, I also reworked several parts of the text based on comments by Hedvig Viktória Deák OP, Tamás Forrai SJ, Péter Nemeshegyi SJ, Ferenc Patsch SJ, Zsuzsa Rochlitz and the late Mónika Laura Barlay.

I thank Andrea Pólik wholeheartedly for her dedication to translating this text into English. As I revised the translation, most of the corrections that I chose to make concerned my own original text rather than the translation, because the two years that have passed since finishing the original manuscript have brought about slight changes in the way I see the questions treated in this book. I have also chosen to rewrite parts of the book entirely and consequently the English text corresponds more to a second edition than to a simple translation of the Hungarian original.

My mother, Krisztina, a spirited teacher of English, always made it a priority to answer swiftly whenever I turned to her for help. I am also grateful to Sally Rude RSCJ, who, after having spent years in Hungary, moved to Halifax, Canada, but volunteered generously to check the final English text.

Feedback from readers of diverse backgrounds lessened the text's unevenness, but could not smooth it completely. Many contemporary questions remain to be confronted more thoroughly with the Ignatian text, and many results wait to be formulated more accurately. The fact that we try to address issues that have not had a prominent place in contemporary Jesuit spirituality, in the hope that we can go beyond what we are already familiar with, explains these limitations to a certain extent.[1] Readers knowledgeable in theology, psychology or church history will also notice the need for stronger foundations regarding these dimensions. Yet even in the present form of the text, we hope this series of observations will contribute to the ongoing discussions on Jesuit formation and to contemporary efforts to interpret the *Constitutions*.

1 "To take Ignatian studies further, it is obviously not enough to do more of the same activities [...] innumerable studies of the same numbers in the *Exercises* do not necessarily lead to a better understanding of Ignatian spirituality." P. Goujon SJ, "Pilgrims of Research", *Review of Ignatian Spirituality* 40/3 (2009), p. 53.

## ABBREVIATIONS

| | |
|---|---|
| ConsCN C | The Constitutions of the Society of Jesus |
| ConsCN CN | Complementary Norms |
| DEI | Diccionario de Espiritualidad Ignaciana |
| Delib. | The Deliberation of the First Fathers |
| FI | Formula of the Institute |
| SpEx | The Spiritual Exercises |

# Introduction

Jesuit formation restarted in Hungary without much special preparation in 1989, when, after a forty-year-long enforced hiatus under a Marxist regime, the novitiate reopened its gates for new applicants seeking admission. During the early years the number of young applicants was especially high. However, the quick revival expected by many did not happen. Many of those who entered did not persevere, leaving the Society of Jesus unexpectedly during or after their studies. Those remaining had to face not only the real challenges and hardships of the new beginning but also questions about the viability of Jesuit life itself.

After the euphoric early years of restoration, perturbing questions emerged. What is behind the decisions to leave the order? Is it personal inadequacies? Is it lack of fidelity? Or are we who stayed perhaps to blame ourselves? Is it possible that young Jesuits did not receive the necessary support from the Society? Maybe their companions should have cared more about them? Or, rather, should we be happy that only the truly dedicated stay? Do we perhaps simply need to accept realistically the extent to which our modern era is unsupportive of religious life—or indeed, of any form of life that is based on commitment, including marriage?

No answers could be found to these questions; yet gradually it became clear that difficulties did not simply stem from the particular situation in the Hungarian Province. In our contemporary globalized cultures, religious life has to face the same sort of questions the world over. If we are to help Jesuits in formation more successfully, we must go beyond our local questions to broaden our horizon.

During recent decades, the Society of Jesus, as well as other religious orders, has made great efforts to adjust the process of formation to contemporary needs. Recent documents present a balanced synthesis of many efforts and reflections.[1] Besides all the achievements, however, the formation process is still troubled by unanswered questions.[2] In a recent speech, Father General Adolfo Nicolás explained his concerns:

> I am convinced that Saint Ignatius considered that our training was for transformation, not for information. He wanted transformation. [. . .]
>
> My first concern toward formation is: Saint Ignatius takes for granted that something happens in the novitiate, in the juniorate, in philosophy, in regency. Something happens. My concern is: does it really happen? [. . .]
>
> Second: transformation cannot be taught. We cannot just speak about transformation. We can speak about it, but that doesn't help. We have to accompany people who are being transformed. Do we know how to accompany people? That is my concern. [. . .] I am convinced that every Jesuit should be a good spiritual father.[3]

How efficient is Jesuit formation, after all? Those in formation pursue the usual practices of Jesuit life: they pray, do the Examen as a reflection on God's activity in their daily lives, study, participate in the Eucharist and a variety of community programs, test themselves in various pastoral and other services, do the yearly Spiritual Exercises, and so on. As a result of all this, does one actually become capable of living a life that is both happy and fruitful in the service of others? To what extent do the elements of Jesuit formation contribute to helping individuals reach their goal?

This question is intriguing, thought-provoking and relevant, but it is also a daunting one as it touches a multitude of convoluted spiritual, cultural, psychological, pedagogical, practical and other aspects, buried in the inextricable mystery of the human person. Who could ever monitor all the influences that can help or hinder someone becoming a mature and committed Jesuit: subtle calls from God, manifestations of personal growth or immaturity, conversations with fellow companions, casual encounters, personal resolutions, deeply rooted and only slowly

1 See *The Formation of Jesuits: From the Letters of Fr. Peter-Hans Kolvenbach* (Rome: General Curia of the Society of Jesus, 2003).

2 See for example: W. Barry SJ, "Jesuit Formation Today: An Invitation to Dialogue and Involvement", *Studies in the Spirituality of Jesuits* 20/5 (1988), pp. 2–50.

3 Fr. Adolfo Nicolás's speech at the Hungarian Jesuits' Jubilee Province Assembly, Budapest, 7 September 2009.

emerging desires, and so on? The question of what actual transformation is happening during the years of Jesuit formation, and how the process of becoming a Jesuit could be fostered better, is simple and clear. What is less simple and clear, however, is whether this question can be answered at all.

Our Ignatian tradition encourages us to face these questions about Jesuit formation with cautious hopefulness. A few decades ago small groups of Jesuits confronted similar issues concerning not the process of formation as a whole, but the more confined world of the Spiritual Exercises, where accompanying a spiritual process requires practical answers in the midst of similarly perplexing interweaving psychological, cultural and spiritual issues. *What kind of a process does one go through during the days of doing the Exercises, and how can the person be helped in this process?* This question proved to be astonishingly fruitful during the second half of the twentieth century. It has led us back to the practice of the first companions, who gave the Exercises to individuals rather than to groups, allowing us to help our contemporaries more competently in their search for God, and granting us a renewed familiarity with our Ignatian heritage.

Those who seek to help others to do the Spiritual Exercises will find the book of the *Spiritual Exercises* to be an inspiring and relevant read. In the 1950s this small, four-hundred-year-old book began to broaden the perspective of Jesuits, who were accustomed to the long talks of preached retreats—plenty of *information*—that were common in those times. For example, they realized how genuinely accurate the second Annotation of the *Spiritual Exercises* was, namely, that it is more fruitful—more *transformative*—to contemplate an evangelical story directly rather than listening to long elucidations, "for it is not knowing much, but realizing and relishing things interiorly, that contents and satisfies the soul" [SpEx 2].[4] The director of the Exercises should not focus on his talks but rather accompany gently and attentively a process that takes place between God and the exercitant. This method, which in all its "newness" was in fact a return to the practice of St Ignatius and of the first Jesuits, gained popularity in the 1960s, and turned out

4 G. E. Ganss (ed.), *The Spiritual Exercises of Saint Ignatius: A Translation and Commentary* (Chicago: Loyola Press, 1992).

to be eminently helpful for Jesuits and others alike who longed for a deep and personal relationship with God. The Exercises soon gained significance beyond the actual practice of accompanying individuals during retreats, and it began to permeate a variety of apostolic fields as well as everyday Jesuit life.

By comparison, those who seek to help Jesuits more effectively during their formation years often find that the *Constitutions*, the very work that discusses Jesuit formation in detail, seems to be a less helpful guide than the *Spiritual Exercises*. We do tend to emphasize its significance, but this claim can sometimes remain somewhat hollow, since actual references to the text of the *Constitutions* play a relatively modest role in everyday Jesuit formation. It is true that most major topics are covered, especially in the novitiate and in tertianship, and scholarly interest in the text is not lacking either: in recent decades several doctoral dissertations have examined the origins, goals and possible interpretations of the *Constitutions*.[5] It is also true that many Jesuits feel the obligation to become more familiar with the *Constitutions*, encouraged to do so also by the general superiors.[6] Yet most Jesuits—including formators—tend not to turn directly to the *Constitutions* with questions concerning Jesuit life. Contemporary documents, such as the *Complementary Norms*,[7] other recent directives of the Society of Jesus and various psychological considerations seem far more accessible and, if genuine Ignatian inspiration is needed, the familiar book of the *Spiritual Exercises* seems to be more readily at hand.[8]

5 Among recent works, the doctoral thesis of J. Carlos Coupeau SJ is especially noteworthy. It gives a detailed summary of earlier writings as well: J. C. Coupeau, "From Inspiration to Invention: Rhetoric in the Constitutions of the Society of Jesus" (Saint Louis: The Institute of Jesuit Sources, 2010).

6 "Without this book of challenges and reminders, our desire to go forward remains without perspectives and without energy." "Introductory Discourses of Father General, No. 3: On Our Law and Our Life" (7 January 1995), *Documents of the 34th General Congregation of the Society of Jesus* (Saint Louis: The Institute of Jesuit Sources, 1995), p. 278.

7 The *Complementary Norms* summarize the results of recent decades' general congregations. The 34th General Congregation's decision was that the text of the *Constitutions* and the *Complementary Norms* must always be published as one volume.

8 J. Carlos Coupeau SJ sums up Ignatian publications of the past decade that are worthy of a wider interest: J. C. Coupeau SJ, "Ignatian Spirituality Publications

The *Constitutions* might well strike the contemporary reader—accustomed to the freshness and liveliness of the book of the *Spiritual Exercises*—as an outdated text that reflects the rather authoritarian approach of its own age. The difference between our perceptions of the two texts is remarkable, but in our current cultural context we seem to have become accustomed to it to the point of not even asking any more why we experience these two fundamental Ignatian works so differently. Our Ignatian heritage, as we see it today, could be compared to a gorgeous painting, part of which has been restored to its original beauty. Our attention tends to get caught by the cheerful colors and delicate brushwork of the details already cleaned, while we may slowly lose interest in what might still be hidden under the age-old dust and soot.[9] In other words, even the hope might fade that a cathartic reconnection with the *Constitutions* could transform Jesuit formation in a similarly characteristic Ignatian way, as the "new" understanding of the book of the *Spiritual Exercises* in the second half of the twentieth century transformed the practice of giving the Spiritual Exercises.

Can we open the *Constitutions* in the hope of finding there an Ignatian vision of Jesuit formation that will be as inspirational and helpful to us as the Ignatian vision of giving the Spiritual Exercises? Could we expect the *Constitutions* to transform our collective thinking in a similarly genuine way? The affirmative answer that we hope to develop in this book builds on the presupposition that if in recent decades the *Spiritual Exercises* exceeded all expectations in "answering" our questions about how to give the Exercises, it is reasonable to expect similarly practical help from the *Constitutions* regarding Jesuit formation. Our primary goal will be to examine the conditions of and to establish the foundations for such a pragmatic reading of the *Constitutions*.

since 1999", *Review of Ignatian Spirituality*, 40/122 (2009), vol. XL/1 (2009), pp. 58–83. While he lists dozens of papers related to the *Spiritual Exercises*, only a single publication, translated from French, concerns the *Constitutions*. See A. de Jaer SJ, *Together for Mission: A Spiritual Reading of the Constitutions of the Society of Jesus* (Saint Louis: The Institute of Jesuit Sources, 2001).

9 For a more detailed account of the one-sided nature of earlier Ignatian renewal, see J. Lukács SJ, "The Incarnational Dynamic of the Constitutions", *Studies in the Spirituality of Jesuits* 36/4 (2004), pp. 1–45.

The first half of this work aims to lay the foundations for a more thorough analysis of the *Constitutions*. We start by investigating some of the conditions that made possible the renewed interest in the Spiritual Exercises in the second half of the twentieth century and up to today. Why was the book of the *Spiritual Exercises* able to initiate a process of renewal, and why did no similar process happen for the *Constitutions*? Our goal is to consider the current interest in the Spiritual Exercises as a paradigm that can enlighten a better understanding of the *Constitutions*. In three preliminary studies, we examine three decisive factors that contributed to the contemporary reception of the book of the *Spiritual Exercises*, but that seem partly or entirely missing with regard to the *Constitutions*. We look more in detail firstly at the concept of a dynamic of progress, secondly at the compatibility with contemporary anthropology, and thirdly at the reception of some key Ignatian expressions in our contemporary vocabulary of Ignatian spirituality.

Firstly, in the middle of the twentieth century the interpretation of the *Spiritual Exercises* began to focus on the intensive psycho-spiritual process that we commonly refer to today as the "dynamics of the Exercises".[10] In the initial years of the Ignatian renewal, discussions turned around the question of how the Ignatian instructions fostered the development and the deepening of the dynamic of the Exercises, in other words, the exercitant's ever more energetic movement toward God. Contemporary interpretations of the *Constitutions* do not imply a comparable concept. Although a number of commentaries do talk about psychological and spiritual growth in the *Constitutions*,[11] even about "a dynamic similar to that of the Spiritual Exercises" which can be called an "incarnational process",[12] the concept remains less accurate, intuitively less engaging and less loaded with practical consequences

10 "Despite all differences, and the enduring uniqueness of each exercitant, there still exists a fundamental dynamic which is the same for all." A. Lefrank and M. Giuliani, *Freedom for Service: Dynamics of the Ignatian Exercises as Currently Understood and Practiced* (Rome: World Federation of Christian Life Communities, 1989), p. 12.

11 J. O'Malley SJ, *The First Jesuits* (Boston: Harvard University Press, 1993), p. 337.

12 de Jaer, *Together for Mission*, p. 75 and p. 54. See also D. Bertrand SJ, *Un corps pour l'Esprit: Essai sur l'expérience communautaire selon les Constitutions de la Compagnie de Jésus* (Paris: Desclée de Brouwer, 1974), pp. 11–41.

than the concept of the dynamic of the Exercises. For example, discussions about particular details of Jesuit formation often tend to lack explicit references to the concept of a dynamic progression that appears in the *Constitutions*. Our first preliminary study will examine the text of the *Constitutions* for signs of a concept that would be similar to the dynamic of the Exercises but applicable to the formation process of Jesuits as a whole. Can the concept that so successfully facilitated the renewal of giving the Exercises be somehow transplanted into our discussions about Jesuit formation and the *Constitutions?*

Secondly, the *Spiritual Exercises* strike the contemporary reader as being surprisingly sensitive to individual needs, always aiming at what is more helpful to the exercitant. The Exercises usually offer real help to a great variety of exercitants, enabling them to turn toward God, recognize the obstacles in the way, and take steps toward ordering their lives, arriving at both greater freedom and a deeper commitment to Christ. While accompanying the Exercises, we seldom encounter any tension between Ignatian anthropology and our contemporary, psychologically minded approach; on the contrary, the two seem to enrich each other rather convincingly. Those however who try to apply in practice the regulations of the *Constitutions* soon encounter tensions. For example, the many details that emphasize strict obedience can easily evoke an image of God and an anthropology that hardly appeal to us today. Is it at all possible to understand, on the basis of our contemporary understanding of the human being, that obedience does not perpetuate immaturity but can be helpful in becoming an affectively and spiritually mature Jesuit, who is ready to face the manifold challenges of apostolic life with great inner freedom? Our second preliminary study aims to provide elements for bridging the gap that seems to have opened between the anthropology implied in the *Constitutions* and our contemporary way of seeing the human being.

Thirdly, part of the renewal in giving the Spiritual Exercises concerned vocabulary. Many terms originally used by Ignatius could be imbued with meanings that proved to be relevant in our contemporary context. Years or even decades of intense discussions, research and writing turned some of the basic expressions of the book of *Spiritual Exercises*—such as *consolation, desolation, discernment of spirits, first week* and the like—into a terminology that can express well-defined spiritual experiences and make us attentive to a range of ever-changing new experiences. As a result, we can use the very expressions of Ignatius to share our experiences concerning the Spiritual Exercises, which brings us closer to the world of the Ignatian text. Many central expressions of the *Constitutions*, however, still sound ancient and out of date. Few readers of the *Constitutions* would spontaneously say, for example, that "progress in the virtues" [ConsCN C 243][13] is among their primary goals. It is as if some key Ignatian expressions would hinder a practical understanding of the *Constitutions* rather than help it. Therefore, our third preliminary study will look at examples of how some important terms of the *Constitutions* could acquire a fresh, relevant meaning, somewhat like what has already become reality for the terminology concerning the *Exercises*.

The results of our three preliminary studies are then used in a fourth investigation, which summarizes the hermeneutical principles that have governed the interpretation of the *Constitutions* in recent decades. We confirm these principles, and, if needed, modify or complement them in accordance with our findings. Our goal here will be to harmonize the conclusions that we draw from the renewal of giving the *Spiritual Exercises* with the hermeneutical principles that have been established in recent decades for interpreting the *Constitutions*.

The second part of this book analyses the *Constitutions* from two perspectives. First, how does the text reveal a process of transformation in the case of each phase of formation? And secondly, how is this process to be fostered? Possible connections between the world of the Ignatian text and our contemporary concerns will be emphasized. For example, how do the Ignatian directives help to develop and maintain a psycho-spiritual dynamic of Jesuit life during the novitiate and then in each subsequent stage of formation? How do the successive phases of formation serve personal growth and integration? How can psychological "inconsistencies"[14] that are in

13 See J. W. Padberg SJ (ed.), *The Constitutions of the Society of Jesus and their Complementary Norms: A Complete English Translation of the Official Latin Texts* (Saint Louis: The Institute of Jesuit Sources, 1996).

14 L. M. Rulla, *Anthropology of the Christian Vocation* (Rome: Gregorian University Press, 1986), vol. I, p. 479.

opposition to a Jesuit vocation diminish through a Christ-centered development of the personality?

Finally, at the end of this book we examine the contemporary reception of the *Constitutions* as a process of inculturation, seeking to comprehend how the renewed understanding of Ignatian spirituality that began half a century ago could, by studying the *Spiritual Exercises,* become a paradigm for understanding the *Constitutions* today so that both fundamental Ignatian texts continue to bear fruit in the years ahead of us.

As is clear from this brief overview, our attention focuses on those parts of the *Constitutions* that concern formation and the lives of individual Jesuits. We do not consider in detail Parts I and II, which deal with admission and dismissal. We only occasionally mention Parts VII–X, which discuss themes such as the choice of apostolic works, unity among members, the qualities of the Superior General or the preservation of the body of the Society in its well-being—themes which, by the way, seem to be more in the forefront of discussions today. For reasons of simplicity, we continue to use the word *Constitutions,* even if we refer primarily to Parts III–VI, which describe the successive phases of formation. As here used, the term *Constitutions* is meant to include the General Examen, a text written for candidates applying for admission into the Society, and always published together with the *Constitutions* in the proper sense of the word.

We expect the reader to be familiar with the fruits of earlier Ignatian spiritual renewal. Familiarity with the book of the *Spiritual Exercises* and the experience of having made or given the individually guided Exercises will be of great help. Without such background, the *Constitutions* can easily remain impenetrable.[15] Without adequate personal experience, expressions such as the "dynamic of the Exercises" may remain mere abstractions and unfit as a vehicle for understanding the *Constitutions*. Furthermore, familiarity with the Exercises will provide the Christ-centered theological horizon that, in the interpretation of the *Constitutions,* can safeguard from an overly simplistic emphasis on

15 "The Constitutions are unintelligible apart from the experience of making the Exercises." J. Veale SJ, "How the Constitutions Work", *The Way Supplement* 61 (Spring 1988), p. 12.

human action and enable the reader to appreciate the activity of God in Jesuit formation.

Nevertheless, readers unfamiliar with the Ignatian tradition are also likely to come across familiar themes in the pages of this book. Concepts that we label "Ignatian" often correspond to general Christian spiritual tradition.[16] When writing the *Constitutions*, Ignatius carefully studied some of the great Rules of existing religious orders, sometimes borrowing whole phrases.[17] In a way, there is not much that is extraordinary in the writings of Ignatius—as if he were simply offering personalized help for knowing, loving and following Jesus more devotedly as he presents himself in the Gospels. This straightforward focus on the Lord is a characteristic that one should be able to discover in the *Constitutions* as well, even without being expert in Ignatian spirituality.

16 J. M. Ribas SJ, *Los Ejercicios en la Tradicíon de Occidente* (Barcelona: EIDES, 1998).

17 A. Hsü, "Dominican Presence in the Constitutions of the Society of Jesus: A Study of Dominican Influence on the Textual Make-up of the Jesuit Constitutions in Regard to Formation of Novices and the "Rules for the Novice Master", Based on an Unpublished Manuscript of Juan A. Polanco (1517–76)", STD thesis (Roma: Pontificia Università Gregoriana, 1971).

# Part I

# Preliminary Studies

✣ I ✣

# Pathway and Progress in the *Spiritual Exercises* and in the *Constitutions*

## Our Different Attitude toward the Two Principal Ignatian Texts

We do not have an equally lively relationship with our two most important Ignatian sources, the book of *Spiritual Exercises* and the *Constitutions*. The difference is not just that we consult the former more often. It is more notable that we use these two works in different ways. The book of *Spiritual Exercises* is inseparable from the practice of personally guided retreats. We generally consider this text to be one of the best tools for helping fellow Jesuits and others in their search of God. We often feel that we can and need to rely on this text, while in the meantime we keep reflecting on how it can be applied to the particular cases that we encounter. The *Constitutions* are not regarded quite the same way. Although they define the basic principles of Jesuit formation that are still valid today—such as the two years to be spent in the novitiate and the six experiments[1] to be completed during this time—all in all the *Constitutions* can easily strike the reader as an outdated text that relatively rarely becomes a source of inspiration for a formator today.

The difference between the two books becomes clearer if we consider a unique feature that distinguishes the book of the *Spiritual Exercises*.

1 Experiments or testing experiences, also called probations, are activities spent outside the novitiate, such as working in a hospital, teaching children or going on pilgrimage without money. Experiments typically last several weeks and constitute a characteristic feature of the Ignatian novitiate.

When giving the Exercises, the phenomenon that we call "the dynamic of the Exercises" usually soon sets in. This dynamic manifests itself as sequences of experiences with emotional, rational and spiritual dimensions that correspond to the four weeks presented in the book of *Spiritual Exercises,* and provide the inner momentum that drives the exercitant along a journey even in the midst of spiritual trials and hard-to-face realizations. This momentum springs from the innermost being of the exercitant and usually keeps growing in the course of the Exercises. The secret of the Ignatian text is that it incites and deepens a process in which the exercitant becomes more and more able to receive "God's grace" [SpEx 2]. This extraordinary process is what makes the almost half-millennium-old *Spiritual Exercises* invaluable, and this is the reason why familiarity with the four-week structure of the Exercises has become such a powerful constituent of our Jesuit identity. Without the dynamic of the Exercises, this Ignatian text would probably also appear to us as little more than a slightly quaint composition of religious considerations and instructions that hardly resonates with our twenty-first-century concerns.

The difference between the *Spiritual Exercises* and the *Constitutions* can be also explained in a terminology proper to Ignatius: the former text means more to us because of the help it provides for *moving along* a well-defined spiritual pathway. In the text of the *Exercises,* one can easily find expressions that indicate *progress* or relate to the concept of progressing. For example, one should be vigilant when encountering "obstacles to going forward (*ir adelante*) in the service of God our Lord" [SpEx 9], while the person who is deeply immersed in prayer should repose until fully satisfied, "without any anxiety to go on" *(pasar adelante)* [SpEx 76].[2] Persons who are earnestly confronting their sinfulness—who "keep going on" *(van)* in their effort to do so—might be obstructed by the evil spirit "preventing their progress" *(no pase adelante)*". At the same time, they are being helped by the good spirit so that they may "move forward" *(proceda adelante)* in doing good [SpEx 315]. The different "spirits" affect those who are "going" *(proceden)* from good to better and those who are "going" from bad to worse in the opposite

2 The source of the Spanish expressions is the "Texto autografo"; see *Ejercicios espirituales* (Santander: Sal Terrae, 1987).

manner [SpEx 335]. These examples show the variety of expressions in the *Spiritual Exercises* referring to the phenomenon that we generally call today the dynamic of the Exercises.

The strong focus on the experience of "moving forward" in the Exercises influences our Jesuit vocabulary to the extent that we tend to associate expressions like "progress" or "dynamic" quite naturally with personally guided retreats. As we give an account of the time spent in the Exercises, we almost instinctively use the language of traveling: I could "move forward" with the help of a prayer exercise, I was "being led" in a certain direction, an exercitant "came a long way", and so on. Paradoxically, during the time of retreat, we even use the metaphor of a journey for describing those periods where we miss the experience of moving ahead: "I came to a halt", "I cannot see where to go now". This perception of the Exercises contrasts with the static way we tend to perceive Jesuit life, where the terminology of moving ahead usually refers to public events like ordination, final vows or receiving a new mission.[3]

## Similarities in the Two Texts

Based on what has been said above, one could expect to find a large number of linguistic elements referring to the concept of a pathway in the *Spiritual Exercises* but not much of the same in the *Constitutions*. This expectation may be confirmed by an article of P.-H. Kolvenbach, who examines the presence of the metaphor of "a pathway to God" in some of the fundamental Ignatian texts. According to his findings, synonyms of "way" and "path" and even verbal expressions of "moving ahead" are used only in a very general sense in the *Constitutions*, and there is nothing indicating that the author had considered the symbol of a pathway as something significant. Such expressions are rather to be regarded as general Christian terminology, or as referring to Christ himself. In fact, Christ being the Way is such a powerful image that it has to be considered as "taken", and not restricted to Jesuit life.[4]

3 See R. A. Blake SJ, "The First Word . . .", *Studies in the Spirituality of Jesuits* 36/4 (2004), pp. iii–v.

4 "Yet we must say that the *Constitutions* do not give the impression of being consciously constructed or, at any rate, elucidated in terms of a kind of symbolism

Eventually, Fr Kolvenbach identified the verb *discurrir* as the characteristically Ignatian expression that reflects his missionary ardor. This verb—instead of being an abstract or symbolic term—has a direct geographical meaning: going to different parts of the world with the purpose of spreading the Gospel.[5] Expressions that would refer to a dynamic of progress, in the sense of a series of transformative experiences with affective, rational and spiritual dimensions, seem to be missing from the *Constitutions*.

At this point, a more thorough examination of the *Spiritual Exercises* results in a surprising discovery. Words that actually refer to a path, or advancement on it, are rather rare in this text as well. The number of occurrences in the Spanish original barely exceeds the examples already cited. How then can the text of the *Spiritual Exercises* still be so closely tied to the experience of making progress? How does the text refer again and again to the process that we call today the dynamic of the Exercises? As we seek to answer this question, the verb *aprovechar* may grab our attention. This frequent expression is only distantly related to progression, and consequently is mentioned only marginally by Fr Kolvenbach. The word has a variety of meanings such as "taking advantage of", "serving the advancement of", "being useful for", "benefit", "profit", "promote", "progress" or "help".[6] In the Exercises, for example, "exercitants should be given, each one, as much as they are willing to dispose themselves to receive, for their greater help and progress *(más se pueda ayudar y aprouechar)*" [SpEx 18]. An exercitant who "desires to make all

of path. If we are to take as witnesses the words which translate the idea of 'way, path, journey'—namely, the Spanish *vía* and *camino*, or the Latin *via*—we have the impression that the author of the *Constitutions* uses these terms without meaning to focus any particular attention on them. Even today the use of the term 'way' or 'path' is so firmly rooted in the vocabulary of religious language as to make it difficult to compose any text of some length without in fact employing it." P.-H. Kolvenbach SJ, "Via Quaedam ad Deum", *CIS Review of Ignatian Spirituality* 22/3 (1991), pp. 25–45. Also published under the title: "A Certain Pathway to God (Via quaedam ad Deum)", in P.-H. Kolvenbach SJ, *The Road from La Storta: On Ignatian Spirituality* (Saint Louis: The Institute of Jesuit Sources, 2000), pp. 201–22.

5 *Ibid.*, p. 25.

6 "Provecho", in Grupo de Espiritualidad Ignaciana, *Diccionario de Espiritualidad Ignaciana (G–Z)* (Madrid and Santander: Mensajero and Sal Terrae, 2007), p. 1505.

the progress possible *(que en todo lo possible desea aprouechar)*, should be given all the Spiritual Exercises" [SpEx 20]. "Ordinarily, in making them an exercitant will achieve more progress *(más se aprouechará)* the more he or she withdraws from all friends and acquaintances, and from all earthly concerns" [SpEx 20]. "That both the giver and the maker of the Spiritual Exercises may be of greater help and benefit to each other *(más se ayuden y se aprouechen)*", it should be presupposed that every good Christian ought to be more eager to put a good interpretation on a neighbor's statement than to condemn it" [SpEx 22]. "[T]he more one divests oneself of self-love, self-will, and self-interests, the more progress one will make *(tanto se aprouechará)*" [SpEx 189]. The complete inventory would be rather long to quote as the expression *aprovechar* appears thirty-three times in the *Spiritual Exercises*.

Repeated occurrences of the noun equivalent of the verb *aprovechar*, "profit" *(provecho)*, give further weight to the importance of this concept. The rich meaning of the verbal form is especially present in the instructions for Gospel contemplations from the second week on: "reflecting upon myself, I will draw some profit *(sacar algún provecho)*" [SpEx 114, 115, 116]. Here, the meaning of the word *provecho* is close to that of the impersonal form of the verb *(aprovecha)*. For example, the colloquy "will be of great benefit *(mucho aprovecha)*" to the person who desires to obtain the third way of being humble.[7] In contrast with things generally necessary *(debe, es necessario)*, in this case the needs of the person are to be considered, and the "profit" that he or she seeks correlates with the personal needs that emerge in a particular prayer exercise.[8] The profit that one can draw is both intimately personal and inseparable from how

7 *Ibid.*, p. 1508.

8 "Encontramos la categoría de la obligación, de la que dan cuenta habitualmente las formas verbales 'debe', 'es necesario'. La obligación de la que se trata remite, pues, a la regla general que se aplica a todos. Es el caso de la observancia de un mandamiento de Dios y, para todo el que haga los Ejercicios, del respeto a la forma prescita por Ignacio. Hay, por otro lado, lo que pertenece al orden de una exigencia en relación con la situación espiritual de la persona concernida y ligado al el provecho que busca. En este contexto predomina la forma verbal 'aprovecha'. Se trata de consejos orientados a un cumplimiento en relación con la situación concreta de la persona concernida." See "Provecho", in *DEI (G–Z)*, p. 1508.

the person moves along each week of the Exercises.[9]

The dominant usage of the verbal form of *aprovechar* to designate helping someone in the manner that is most suitable to the person's unique situation indicates that Ignatius is not so much interested in an abstract idea of a dynamic of progress as in the act of helping someone's personal advancement. The book of *Spiritual Exercises* does not seek to provide a theoretical explanation for the phenomenon of progressing but rather deals with how the giver of the Exercises can in fact help the exercitant to move forward in the typical situations that the person might encounter.

If, bearing all this in mind, we once again turn to the *Constitutions*,[10] this time looking for occurrences of the expression *aprovechar*, we might be surprised at finding no less than fifty examples. As we shall see later, the vast majority of these can be found in those parts of the text that describe Jesuit formation, such as the General Examen or Parts III and IV. The expression almost always refers to the Jesuit individual, apart from a few exceptions such as when discussing the profit or advancement of apostolic works or laypersons in Part VII. In addition to these come some further occurrences of the nominal form *provecho*. It seems that the expression familiar from the *Spiritual Exercises* also has a dominant role in the *Constitutions*.

The frequent use of the verb *aprovechar* in the *Constitutions* allows us to complement the findings of Fr Kolvenbach significantly. Though "pathway" and other similar expressions are not used in a characteristically Ignatian way, since they have either a general spiritual meaning or refer directly to Christ who is the Path himself, the frequent recurrence of the expression *aprovechar* evokes the vivid image of a person in need of support while advancing on the pathway of Jesuit life. The striking linguistic resemblance between the *Spiritual Exercises* and the *Constitutions* lets one assume that both texts presuppose a dynamic

9 "El 'aprovecharse' ignaciano quiere decir progresar." See "Magis (Mas)", in *DEI (G–Z)*, p. 1166.

10 Among the numerous versions of the original text, the source of the Spanish citations is the latest one, the D manuscript. See S. Arzubialde, J. Corella and J. M. García-Lomas (ed.), *Constituciones de la Compañía de Jesús: Introducción y notas para su lectura* (Bilbao-Santander: Mensajero-Sal Terrae, 1993).

vision of a person constantly on the move, and that a primary aim of both texts is to help foster this progress with means that are most suitable to the current position of the person. The characteristic use of *aprovechar* calls for a re-evaluation of the role of synonyms for "path" and "progress" in the Ignatian text, since it becomes clear that the seemingly general spiritual terminology conceals a powerful Ignatian vision of what can foster progress among the specific conditions of Jesuit life. It looks like the metaphor of progressing is just as indispensable for interpreting the *Constitutions* as it is for understanding the *Spiritual Exercises*.

## Jesuit Life as a Pathway?

The analogy between the *Spiritual Exercises* and the *Constitutions* is quite manifest, but mere analogies can also be misleading. It is worth investigating in more detail how the *Constitutions* and other fundamental writings of the early Society utilize the concept of progress when they speak about Jesuit life.

Unfortunately the *Constitutions* do not define what "progressing" would mean in Jesuit life when not making the yearly Exercises. Does the expression perhaps indicate that prayer exercises can be continued in daily life even when the privileged time of the Spiritual Exercises is over? This assumption comes in handy but it is still not quite clear where one can progress further when one has completed the fourth week in the Exercises. The *Constitutions* offer no direct answers to this question, but the approach of the text is once again familiar from the *Spiritual Exercises*. In both cases, Ignatius sidesteps clear-cut definitions and focuses almost exclusively on practical instructions. He does not explain what the pathway is but rather intends to help one progress on it:

> we think it necessary that constitutions should be written to aid us to proceed better *(mejor proceder)*, in conformity with our Institute, along the path of divine service on which we have entered *(en la vía començada del diuino seruicio)*" [ConsCN C 134].

"Path" as an image of Jesuit life is not an invention of the *Constitutions*: it was a metaphor dear to Ignatius and his first companions. During their intense early deliberations about various future options for the Society, when—as they themselves recounted—"there was a cleavage of sentiments and opinions about our situation" [Delib.[11] 1], their desire to preserve unity among themselves made them search for a path that would be suitable for all of them. They were already familiar with the paradoxical experience of moving along a spiritual pathway in the Exercises: it is both common to all (in accordance with the book of *Spiritual Exercises*), and yet it does not make them uniform (as everyone walks on his own very personal path). They imagined the pathway of Jesuit life to be in a similar manner common to all but still suitable for a great diversity of persons:

> We were in perfect accord in singleness of purpose and intent; namely, to discover the gracious design of God's will within the scope of our vocation. But when it came to the question of which means would be more efficacious and more fruitful, both for ourselves and for our neighbour, there was a plurality of views.
>
> Since we did hold different judgments, we were eagerly on the watch to discover some unobstructed way *(aliquam viam plene apertam)*, along which we might advance *(incedentes)* together and all of us offer ourselves as a holocaust to our God, in whose praise, honor, and glory we would yield our all. [Delib. 1]

It is no wonder, then, that the expression "pathway to God" soon appeared in the Formula of the Institute, a document that introduced the newly formed Society to the Holy Father, and was officially published as a papal bull of approval.[12] The Formula uses this metaphor to describe the relationship between the Institute—the principal writings defining the life of the Society—and the life of individual Jesuits. The nature of the Institute is such that it can be called a pathway (that is, neither a rule in the sense of a law book, nor a collection of spiritual advice). Jesuits must consider it highly important to keep this specificity

11 "The Deliberation of the First Fathers", *Deliberatio Primorum Patrum*, is a Latin document written in 1539 and printed in the first edition of the *Constitutions*. The source of the English citations is J. J. Toner SJ, "The Deliberation that Started the Jesuits: A Commentary on the *Deliberatio Primorum Patrum*", *Studies in the Spirituality of Jesuits* 6/4 (1974), pp. 179–212.

12 "Regimini militantis Ecclesiae", 1540, and "Exposcit debitum", 1550, in *The Constitutions of the Society of Jesus and their Complementary Norms*, pp. 3 ff.

of the Institute before their eyes—only the contemplation of God is more important than this. Their lives should not be governed by mere conformity to the particular directives of the Institute but by the desire to reach their goal through moving ahead on the common pathway according to their individual aptitudes:

> [Whoever wishes to serve in our Society,] let any such person take care, as long as he lives, first of all to keep before his eyes God and then the nature of this Institute, which is, so to speak, a pathway to God (*curetque primo Deum, deinde huius sui instituti rationem, quae uia quaedam est ad illum*), and then let him strive with all his effort to achieve this end set before him by God—each one, however, according to the grace which the Holy Spirit has given to him and according to the particular grade of his own vocation. [FI 1]

The role of the metaphor of the pathway to God is thus to clarify the relationship between the Institute and the daily lives of Jesuits. The founding documents of the Society refer to a specific path, and Jesuits take these references into consideration in order to be able to advance according to their own personal abilities.[13] This unique, characteristically Ignatian perspective establishes a flexible bond between the directives of the text and the ever-changing reality of Jesuit life. Directives are not "simply" to be respected. In specific life situations, Jesuits and their formators are to consider the Ignatian instructions with the same question in mind as they normally pose when engaging in or accompanying the Exercises: what would be most helpful to the person who desires to advance more dynamically on his way to God?

13 The first companions, when interpreting the *Constitutions*, also used the metaphor of a path in order to pull together the many practical details of Jesuit life: "Gil González Dávila, SJ. [in his] *Pláticas sobre las reglas de La Compania de Jesús. Prólogo y edición de Camile M. Abad, SJ.* These are conferences given between 1585 and 1588 when González Dávila was provincial of Andalusia. [...] in part he rises to the heights of spiritual principles [...] and in part he descends to practice, and sets before our eyes 'the road we must travel in order to arrive at the proper end of our vocation'. Alfonso Rodríguez made use of some portions of these conferences in his *Practice of Christian Perfection* published in 1609." I. Iparragueirre SJ, *Contemporary Trends in Studies on the Constitutions of the Society of Jesus: Annotated Bibliographical Orientations* (Saint Louis: The Institute of Jesuit Sources, 1974), p. 22.

Ignatian instructions should thus be interpreted according to the criterion of how they help us to make progress. The *Constitutions* seem to consider this criterion quite obvious, yet emphasize its importance again and again. Random examples from Part III, which deals with the novitiate,[14] illustrate well the absolute priority of a dynamic progression that appears as an outstanding value *per se*, and often serves as the ultimate argument to justify a specific way of proceeding. Progress depends on personal dedication: "They should be taught how to guard themselves from the illusions of the devil in their devotions... by endeavoring always to go forward in the path of the divine service *(andar adelante en la uía del diuino seruicio)*" [ConsCN C 260]. While in probation, acts of "penance" might have to be done, the reason for which being the "spiritual profit" *(aprouechamiento spiritual)* of this exercise [ConsCN C 269]. The utmost purpose of obedience is that "it is very helpful for making progress and highly necessary" *(muy expediente para aprouecharse y mucho necessario)* [ConsCN C 284]. The same is true for acts of chastisement: "all this is in order to proceed with greater light" (*con más lumbre se proceda*) [ConsCN C 300]. The great variety of expressions that refer to *progressing* weave together amazingly diverse elements of life in the novitiate, and serve as a common rule or decisive argument in matters that would otherwise seem unrelated to each other and even insignificant for someone who would not know how these exercises can be helpful for advancing in Jesuit life.

If particular instructions are meaningful because they help to make progress, then consequently the significance of the text's various details can be appreciated only in the light of a clear idea of the entire dynamic of progress in Jesuit life. A particular practice described by the *Constitutions* will appear to be worth applying in the eyes of the formator who has developed a sufficiently thorough vision of the entire Ignatian pathway to God, and who can evaluate the usefulness of the particular practice for a person who is to move forward in a given phase of the pathway. Unfortunately, however, not only does the understanding of the details depend on the understanding of the pathway to God as a whole, but there is also dependence in the opposite sense. Ignatius—as

14 The word novitiate is not used in the text of the *Constitutions*; instead, Ignatius talks about the time of probation *(los que quedan en probación)*.

we have seen—does not explain what the pathway itself looks like; he only gives details about how to help those who want to progress on it. The only way for us to understand the pathway to God as a whole seems to be a careful consideration of the details in the hope that the whole picture will progressively become clearer.

If we need to see the whole picture to understand the details but we are only given the details then we seem to be caught in a Catch-22 dilemma: understanding the details and seeing the whole picture seem mutually dependent. At this point, we might be encouraged by the example of those Jesuits in the 1950s who did not have the understanding of the dynamic of the Exercises that we have today, but still believed that there is more to be found in the Ignatian text than material for preached retreats. They experimented with details of the text, tried to see how particular instructions and insights can become fruitful in the accompaniment of individuals, and in the meantime they engaged in a sustained reflection to understand the dynamic of the Exercises, the big picture of what happens during this privileged time spent in prayer. They understood well that attention to particular details will be necessary to perceive the big picture and vice versa, and they did not consider this situation to be a deadlock, but hoped to discover new depth in Ignatian spirituality by meticulously working their way through both challenges simultaneously. By progressively recognizing the usefulness of previously overlooked details of the text, and at the same time developing an increasingly refined notion of the dynamic of the Exercises, they were able to make undreamed of progress in the understanding of the *Exercises,* meaning both the practice of giving them and the interpretation of the Ignatian text.

An initial piece of information about the pathway to God immediately revealed by the *Constitutions* is that it consists of characteristic phases that differ significantly. Similar to the four weeks of the Exercises, the pathway to God consists of four distinct sections: the novitiate, scholastic years, tertianship and professed life.[15] These four phases are presented in four successive parts of the *Constitutions,* Parts III to VI. Each of

15 Between the four weeks of the Exercises and the four sections of the pathway to God in the *Constitutions* there is a strong parallelism, see J. Lukács SJ, *The Incarnational Dynamic.* Here, these similarities will be less emphasized, since the *Consti-*

these four parts talk in one way or another about progressing as the goal of that phase of Jesuit life, usually immediately in the paragraphs that explain the purpose of the given section. The goal of the novitiate is to "make progress both in spirit and in virtues along the path of the divine service" (*uayan adelante en la uía del diuino seruicio*) [Part III., ConsCN C 243]. Part IV speaks about "the progress in learning and in other means of helping [. . .] fellowmen" (*aprouecharlos en letras y otros medios de ayudar al próximo*) [ConsCN C 308]. During tertianship, the final phase of the formation, Jesuits "apply themselves [. . .] to the school of the heart [. . .] so that when they themselves have made progress they can better help others to progress for the glory of God our Lord (*auiéndose aprouechado en sí mesmos, mejor puedan aprouechar a otros*)" [Part V, ConsCN C 516]. The process of progression does not end when formation in the strict sense of the word ends. A professed Jesuit keeps on advancing, and in no ordinary manner as "it is presupposed that those so admitted will be men who are spiritual and sufficiently advanced that they will run in the path of Christ our Lord (*aprouechadas para correr por la uía de Christo Nro. Sr.*)" [Part VI, ConsCN C 582]. All in all, both the concept of progress and that of helping others' progress are threads running throughout the descriptions of the four phases of Jesuit life, and within this overall dynamic vision, even the succinct description of progressing reveals the unique character of each of these phases. This characteristic fourfold division, as simple yet fundamental as the four-week structure of the *Exercises*, will serve as a framework for our reflections on the Ignatian pathway to God.

From our initial observation that the *Constitutions* offer less help to the contemporary formator than the book of the *Spiritual Exercises* to those accompanying a retreat, we have come to the conclusion that in order to better understand this text, we need to develop a vision of Jesuit life as a dynamic movement toward God. We started by wishing that the *Constitutions* were more easily comprehensible, but the focus has moved to ourselves, the readers of the text, as the *Constitutions* demand us to change the place where we stand. As long as we stay with a static conception of Jesuit life, the answers offered by the *Constitutions*

*tutions* will not be studied in the mirror of the *Exercises* but through the mediation of an anthropological model which can help to interpret the text more accurately.

will not match our concerns and we risk missing the Ignatian vision about Jesuit life that is mediated by the *Constitutions*. The *Constitutions* become accessible to us to the extent that we adopt an image of Jesuit life where the desire of a dynamic progression on a pathway to God is as obvious as the desire to order one's life and find God's will during the special days of doing the Spiritual Exercises.

Our contemporary culture makes us sensitive to the fact that any act of understanding is dependent on its cultural environment. For example, liberation theology has been long reminding us that the Gospels tend to become especially vivid when read in real communion with poor people. Similarly, it is plausible to think that a change of where we stand will help us to understand the *Constitutions* better. Still, the idea that a constant progression should be at the heart of Jesuit life can encounter resistance. For companions of the older generation, this notion might evoke a conception of progression that was so permeated by voluntarism that it seemed better to abandon it altogether. Younger companions might fear the loss of spontaneity in Jesuit life and resent the possibility of an abstract idea of progression getting in the way of seeking God in all things.

To these and other similar objections that are susceptible to expressing preconceptions rather than genuine openness to the Ignatian text, embryonic conceptions of the Ignatian pathway to God will not offer convincing arguments. It might be more helpful to contemplate the familiar dynamic of the Exercises: how do the four Weeks structure open a space of liberty for a person seeking to find God? How is familiarity with the dynamic of the Exercises indispensable in making sense of a great variety of spiritual experiences? How do the Exercises foster a genuine spontaneity, a capacity to be moved by the Spirit of God? Appreciation of the dynamic of the Exercises is probably the best way to set the tone for a better understanding of the Ignatian conception of a pathway to God which should be similarly liberating, similarly helpful in telling real growth from appearances, and similarly useful in disposing ourselves to the grace of God. Only such a conception of the Ignatian pathway to God can promise that a greater familiarity with the *Constitutions* will be beneficial for Jesuit formation.

We have seen that in order to understand the *Spiritual Exercises* better, attention had to be paid simultaneously to the details of the text and to the process as a whole. In the case of the *Constitutions*, a similar strategy seems advisable. This is why in the next preliminary study we develop an initial, sketch-like model of what it might mean to make progress on a pathway to God in Jesuit life. The second half of this book will presuppose this initial model and use it for interpreting specific details of the text. These details will in turn help us to conceive a more accurate representation of the pathway to God as a whole. The analogy with the work that started in the middle of the twentieth century on the *Spiritual Exercises* should sufficiently warn us of the modest dimensions of such an enterprise. From the time when the *Spiritual Exercises* began to attract contemporary attention as a practical source of help in accompanying others, the question of the dynamic of the Exercises remained a central preoccupation for some twenty years. In the case of the *Constitutions*, work of a similar order of magnitude can be expected. Years of well-coordinated research will be necessary before we can develop a sufficiently nuanced and powerful understanding of the dynamic of progress that is implied in the term "a pathway to God". Yet at the same time, the example of the Jesuits two generations before us can assure us that any step in this direction can become beneficial in moving toward a more grace-filled, attractive and fruitful conception of Jesuit life.

✣ 2 ✣

# A Relationship Model of Ignatian Anthropology

## Implicit and Explicit Anthropology

It would be difficult to assess how extensively St Ignatius' vision of the human being affects today's Jesuits as they go about their various ministries. The Ignatian vision presupposes the possibility of a direct, intimate relationship between the human person and God as something self-evident. It attributes great weight to personal freedom[1] and values the freely made vocational and other decisions[2] of persons who have committed themselves to Christ. Ignatian anthropology makes us attentive to the emotional and cognitive dimensions of the human being, to the importance of developing personal talents and abilities, or to the extraordinary possibility of cooperation between God and the human being in everyday life. We also tend to identify most deeply with the Ignatian vision of the human being as we give the Spiritual Exercises. We know that the fruits of the Exercises—insights, affective movements or encounters with the Lord—can emerge because the Exercises have a deeply human character. Many Jesuits share the experience that the Exercises, although deeply embedded in Catholic tradition, can prove to be helpful to Christians of other denominations,

1 M. J. Buckley, "Freedom, Election, and Self-Transcendence: Some Reflections upon the Ignatian Development of a Life of Ministry" in *Ignatian Spirituality in a Secular Age*, ed. G. P. Schner (Waterloo, ON: Wilfrid Laurier Univ. Press, 1984).

2 "La première chose offerte est la liberté ; elle inclut tous les autres dons. [. . .] Elle est le centre et le noyau de l'anthropologie ignatienne, comme celle qui rend possible le don de soi à Dieu." J. Stierli, *Chercher Dieu en toutes choses, vie au coeur du monde et prière ignatienne* (Paris: Le Centurion, 1985), p. 93.

and up to a certain point even to people who do not consider themselves to be devote Christians. At times, we almost wish to offer the Exercises to non-religious people! It is obvious that Ignatius draws on his profound knowledge of the human being as much as on his spiritual experiences. The book of the *Spiritual Exercises* has strong anthropologic foundations that are valid to this day.

Curiously, we tend to identify less keenly with the Ignatian vision of the human being that seems to be expressed in the *Constitutions*. Why does the text seem to contradict insights and assumptions of contemporary psychology that tend to be so obvious for us, for example that autonomy can be more helpful in reaching maturity than obedient submission? Why does Ignatian anthropology not make it easier to use the *Constitutions* for finding practical responses to our modern problems? Why does Ignatian anthropology as we know it not support the deeper understanding of the pathway to God outlined in the *Constitutions*? And why do we perceive the Ignatian vision of the human being as modern when we consider the *Exercises*, but outdated and old-fashioned when we read the *Constitutions*?

Ignatius did not leave behind a systematically developed and detailed anthropology. His ideas need to be reconstructed mainly on the basis of the implicit hints in his writings. This drawback, however, became an incentive for creativity when later generations of Jesuits highlighted and redefined various elements of Ignatian anthropology according to the cultural conditions of their age. Systematic presentations of Ignatian anthropology are therefore susceptible to being culturally biased. For example, "will" is a frequent expression in the *Spiritual Exercises* but some interpretations of "will" in the first half of the twentieth century had more to do with the cultural climate of that time than with the Ignatian vision of the human being.[3] In our contemporary context it is equally possible that Ignatian anthropology suffers from a bias. Since research from the second half of the twentieth century has concentrated mainly on the *Spiritual Exercises*, we take for granted that Ignatian anthropology focuses on questions relevant from this perspective. We see more and more clearly, for instance, that the Ignatian model of the human psyche, the "soul",

3 See "Voluntad", in *DEI (G–Z)*, p. 1787.

can be traced back to two different schools of philosophy, that of St Augustine and that of St Thomas Aquinas (and through him, eventually to Aristotle); we recognize Augustine's thoughts in the threefold structure of the human soul (memory, intellect and will) and identify the Thomist model behind polarities such as body and soul, intellect and will.[4] Our contemporary renderings of Ignatian anthropology imply important achievements; and yet they might be ill-adapted to a better understanding of the *Constitutions*.

The meaning of progress in Jesuit life will be impossible to understand if we limit our focus to topics of spirituality and psychology. Issues of a different nature like community life or intellectual preparation for the apostolic mission will also have to be taken into account. Beyond the already familiar considerations of Ignatian anthropology further elements will be necessary to facilitate the interpretation of the *Constitutions*. This is why we turn to Ignatian anthropological insights implicitly present in the *Spiritual Exercises* but rarely discussed explicitly today. We will call these insights, grouped together, a relationship model of Ignatian anthropology.

## "Spirits" and Motivations

To develop a relationship model of Ignatian anthropology, the discernment of spirits, a cornerstone of contemporary Ignatian spirituality, could be a suitable basis. Discernment evaluates the meaning of spiritual phenomena in the context of the relationship between a human being and God: "Rules to aid us toward perceiving and then understanding, at least to some extent, the various motions which are caused in the soul: the good motions that they may be received, and the bad that they may be rejected" [SpEx 313]. Theoretical and practical aspects of discernment have raised much interest in Ignatian spirituality in recent decades[5] and—quite like in the time of the first Jesuits—the

4 See the chapter "Los elementos antropológicos de los Ejercicios" in J. Melloni Ribas, *La mistagogía de los ejercicios* (Bilbao and Santander: Mensajero and Sal Terrae, 2001), pp. 71–103.

5 See for example: J. J. Toner SJ, *A Commentary on St. Ignatius' Rules for the Discernment of Spirits* (Saint Louis: The Institute of Jesuit Sources, 1982), pp. 82–7

discernment of spirits is recognized as one of the specific characteristics of the Society. Although we tend today to interpret "spirits" as psychological phenomena rather than manifestations of a spiritual world,[6] this has hardly any influence on the *practice* of the discernment of spirits. Genuine Jesuit life needs to be skilled in discernment and in the practical application of Ignatian insights to a whole range of different life situations.

For Ignatius, questions of discernment could not be disconnected from the rest of his observations about the human being. In his *Autobiography*, he recalls how he began to notice movements of the spirits during the lengthy recovery after his serious injury. The question he had was fairly simple: what was the reason for his recurring mood swings? With amazement, he recognized the influence of his readings but also of his daydreaming. From this general question about what was perturbing his soul, little by little he came to perceive how he was pushed farther away from or closer toward God by the different spirits, "one from the devil, the other from God" [Autobiography[7] 8].

Discernment of spirits can thus be placed in the context of more general questions concerning motivations: What kind of influences is the human being exposed to? What kinds of impressions spark human emotions and thoughts? What powers tend to move someone to do or not do something, to do this one thing instead of another?[8] This

and 115–21. It would be difficult to enumerate even the last few years' works published in English, French, Italian, Spanish and other languages. See above: Coupeau, *Ignatian Spirituality Publications*.

6 For a plausible interpretation see L. M. G. Domínguez SJ, "Inordinate Affections in Ignatian Anthropology", in F. Imoda (ed.) *A Journey to Freedom: An Interdisciplinary Approach to the Anthropology of Formation* (Leuven: Peeters Publishers, 2000), pp. 293 ff.

7 *A Pilgrim's Testament: The Memoirs of Saint Ignatius of Loyola*, translated by P. R. Divarkar (Saint Louis: Institute of Jesuit Sources, 1995), pp. 9–10.

8 Such an extended meaning of the discernment of spirits was not unusual at the time of Ignatius. For example, Denys the Carthusian (1402/3–71) did not restrict the use of the word "spirit" to a purely spiritual context: "Spirits are by which we are moved from without, namely, that the visible things are beautiful, the audible things are enjoyable, those odorous are pleasant, those sweet are soothing, the touchable things are to be loved, and the useful things provide help." Hence, when we are touched by the beauty of a landscape, we are, as Denys phrases it, touched by "the

wider context of motivations rarely occupies our attention as we focus mainly on the rules for discernment as outlined in the *Spiritual Exercises* [SpEx 314–36]. This may be the reason why our theoretical knowledge about discernment is sometimes not matched by a sufficiently practical, common-sense understanding of the human being. We may only realize at the moment when a fellow Jesuit suddenly decides to leave the Society that we never had an idea of what forces moved this person. By the time we conclude that discernment is needed, it is very possible that we are too late in trying to help.

Ignatius is aware of the influences that a person is subjected to well beyond the specific rules for discernment. A quick scan of the *Spiritual Exercises* can reveal how this preoccupation is almost omnipresent. Almost every Annotation seeks to strengthen the motivation of the exercitant: for example, someone who can discover the meaning of a Gospel story himself or herself will find more joy in it [SpEx 2]; feelings of contrition must not be urged or forced since real motivations take time to develop [SpEx 4]; generosity toward God is greatly beneficial, and particularly so when expressed explicitly [SpEx 5], and so on. From beginning to end, the desires of the exercitant meet special attention. Certain desires will be intensified: "I should call to mind the contemplation I am about to make in my desire to know better the eternal Word made flesh, so that I may better serve him and follow him" [SpEx 130]. Of other desires the exercitant grows freer: "I ought to find myself indifferent [...] to such an extent that I am not more inclined or emotionally disposed toward taking the matter proposed rather than relinquishing it" [SpEx 179]. Desires stem both from the innermost depths of human existence and from the graces received from God: "one should [...] ask our Lord for the contrary; that is, to have no desire for this office or benefice or anything else unless the Divine Majesty has put proper order into those desires, and has by this means [...] changed one's earlier attachment" [SpEx 16]. Ignatius seems to have been a spiritual master with exceptional sensitivity to human motivations.

spirit of beauty". In "De discretione et examinatione spirituum", *Opera omnia*, 40, 268. Quoted in *Ignatius von Loyola: Bericht des Pilgers, Übersetzt und kommentiert von Peter Knauer SJ* (Frankfurt am Main: als Manuskript gedruckt, 1999), p. 45.

In order to develop a relationship model of Ignatian anthropology that comprises some of the fundamental Ignatian observations about human motivations, we first examine those parts of the *Spiritual Exercises* that offer universally valid insights in this area. We will focus on three major themes of the *Spiritual Exercises*: the Principle and Foundation, the Contemplation to Attain Love, and the meditation on the Two Standards. Our aim is to gain insight through these well-known texts into how Ignatius looked at the mysterious world of human motivations.

## A Fourfold Structure of Relationships

The Christian conviction that the human being is able to connect with God and that praising, reverencing and serving God is the goal and fulfillment of human life [cf. SpEx 23] is the principle and foundation of not only the Spiritual Exercises but also of the Ignatian anthropological vision in general. Such a relationship with God should be considered superior to other, usually important motivations such as the desire for wealth, honor, long life and the like. This statement can perhaps sound somewhat dry at first, but personal prayer during the Exercises can transform it into a deeply rooted, lively source of motivation that is based on gratefulness to God and personal conviction. Our experience with the Exercises helps us to see the extent to which Ignatius regarded this personal relationship with God as an authentic motivational force, something that is comparable to other motivations but is more fundamental, even though the human being cannot own it, but only seek it, ask for it and receive it.

To draw the outlines of an Ignatian vision of motivations, we do not need to evoke all the richness implied in Ignatian texts about the relationship between God and the human being.[9] At this point, a simple metaphorical sketch may be sufficient: for human beings, a window opens through which they can directly connect with their Lord and Creator. This direct connection is reciprocal, and with the intensification of love for God, it becomes more and more apparent through

9 For a detailed monograph on this see Hugo Rahner SJ, *Ignatius the Theologian*, translated by Michael Barry (London-Dublin-Melbourne: Chapman, 1968), pp. 35 ff.

a mutual sharing of gifts. This progression is clearly noticeable in the *Spiritual Exercises*. In the beginning, the direct connection between God and the human being is presented in the First Principle and Foundation rather like an opportunity that is offered for everyone, while in the fourth week it appears to have become a profound experience:

> Two preliminary observations should be made. First. Love ought to manifest itself *more by deeds* than by words. Second. Love consists in a *mutual communication* between the two persons. That is, the one who loves gives and communicates to the beloved what he or she has, or a part of what one has or can have; and the beloved in return does the same to the lover. [Contemplation to Attain Love, SpEx 231]

Salvation is this generous mutual relationship with God. Within this relationship, human beings can approach the goal they had been created for: "Take, Lord, and receive [. . .] all that I have and possess [. . .] Give me love of yourself along with your grace, for that is enough for me" [SpEx 234]. One of the most important yet by no means self-evident aspects of Ignatian anthropology is that the mutual relationship with God can be *unmediated*. The giver of the Exercises ought to "stand by" in a manner that allows "the Creator to deal immediately with the creature and the creature with its Creator and Lord *(inmediate obrar al Criador con la criatura)* [SpEx 15], that is, God and the human person are not connected solely through the sacraments, church ceremonies or other similar means. This conviction of Ignatius—which he had to defend before the inquisition because of its philosophic, dogmatic and practical repercussions—only became an unquestionable treasure of the Society and of the church after the papal approval of the *Spiritual Exercises*.

In addition to the relationship with God, a further set of key relationships appears in the meditation on the Two Standards [SpEx 136–48]. Ignatius, who tends to use words sparingly, explains in an unusually ceremonious introduction how important it is, before making the Election, to be knowledgeable about those areas of life that are likely to be most full of struggles whether in lay or in religious life. The meditation on the Two Standards prepares the presentation of these aspects of human life by emphasizing their decisive importance both for "the enemy of human nature" and for Christ:

> we shall in our next exercise observe the intention of Christ our Lord, and, in contrast, that of the enemy of human nature. We shall also think about how we ought to dispose ourselves in order to come to perfection in whatsoever state or way of life God our Lord may grant us to elect. [SpEx 135]

The meditation itself sets forth a solemn and ceremonial tone as it presents the dramatic battle between Lucifer and Christ our Lord, and, in the midst of this battle, the three "steps" where the decisive fights are fought. On each of the steps, Lucifer exploits phenomena that provoke emotional reactions and urge human beings to think and to act. Christ our Lord in each case persuades us to remain mindful and vigilant about the situation, doing the exact opposite of what Lucifer suggests. The outcome of the struggle hangs on how the human being reacts in the midst of these contradicting voices:

> Consider the address which Christ our Lord makes to all his servants and friends whom he is sending on this expedition. [. . .] In this way there will be three steps: the first, poverty in opposition to riches; the second, reproaches or contempt in opposition to honor from the world; and the third, humility in opposition to pride. [SpEx 146]

What is the anthropology behind the description of the three crucial steps in the meditation on the Two Standards? Beyond the theatrical setup, we see at each step that human beings are exposed to the motivations pushed by Lucifer when developing a relationship with their environment. It is obvious that human beings are not only in relationship with God but also with the world they live in. It is less obvious, however, that the nature of human beings is such that they can connect with their environment in several ways, each being qualitatively different from the other.

The meditation on the Two Standards depicts the human person as if three new windows opened for him or her to the world. Through the first window, the person can connect with things, material goods, and that is where the question of *riches* or wealth arises. The second window opens onto the world of interpersonal relationships: the desire for *honor from the world* can be kindled because human beings are able to immerse themselves in the fascinating, gratifying but often confusing world of interpersonal relationships, and may become inadvertently dependent on the satisfaction that can be gained here. The third window opens onto the world of values, truths and ideals: *pride* is possible because human beings are able to assimilate values, ideals and truths and then spontaneously regard themselves as representatives or accomplishers of these; yet while identification with values, ideals or great causes can release enormous energies to speak out and work for achieving these, it might also cause an idealized perception of self and a narrow perception of others, which translates into despising others and placing oneself above them.[10]

The opportunity to connect with the world in all these ways is a gift of human life, something to be used courageously when seeking to find God: "things on the face of the earth are created for the human beings, to help them in the pursuit of the end for which they are created" [SpEx 23]. As the Contemplation to Attain Love offers at the end of the Exercises a guided tour of the gifts received, it is not difficult to notice the imprint of the four "windows". The starting point is a direct, face-to-face relationship with God: "Here it is to see myself as standing before God our Lord" [SpEx 232], and "I will ponder with deep affection how much God our Lord has done for me, and how much he has given me of what he possesses" [SpEx 234]. Then follow the impersonal creatures: "I will consider how God dwells in creatures; in the elements, giving them existence; in the plants, giving them life; in the animals, giving them sensation" [SpEx 235]. Afterwards come the human beings, others and myself: "[I will consider how God dwells] in human beings, giving them intelligence; and finally, how in this way he dwells also in myself, giving me existence, life, sensation, and intelligence; and even further, making me his temple" [SpEx 235]. At the end, the world of values completes the picture: "I will consider how all good things and gifts descend from above; for example, my limited power from the Supreme and Infinite Power above; and so of justice, goodness, piety, mercy, and so forth" [SpEx 237]. The desire to respond

10 "Vanity [being attached to *honor from the world*] and pride are different things, though the words are often used synonymously [...] Pride relates more to our opinion of ourselves, vanity to what we would have others think of us." J. Austen, *Pride and Prejudice* (London: Dent, 1907), p. 17. First published in 1813 (London/Whitehall: T. Egerton).

to the love received can focus otherwise scattered human actions "to love and serve the Divine Majesty in all things" [SpEx 233]. To live in God's love is to recognize God's gifts everywhere, through whichever "window" one looks at the world, and to have one's motivations ordered in a profound harmony.

Profound harmony in communion with the Lord is a distant hope, while the raw reality of fierce inner conflicts is the inevitable present revealed by the meditation on the Two Standards. The world, while it bestows human beings with a plenitude of gifts, can also seize control over them because the satisfaction involved in the gifts is limited in time and intensity, and quite soon the need for pleasurable things, cherished persons and important projects will return vehemently. Human life can easily become a directionless zigzagging between various attractions that present themselves rather than an ever growing availability to be attracted by God.

The struggle which takes place on the first step is that of the human being connecting with material objects. The attraction, interest and longing from early childhood on for the tangible or metaphorical richness that the material world can offer make it impossible to keep away from this step altogether. It would be impossible to enumerate all the good things that human beings "receive" from the material world: the comfort of a home or even of a hotel room at the end of an exhausting day, the sense of accomplishment after repairing a dripping tap or even the excitement of a computer game, the safety secured by savings in the bank or the sense of freedom embodied by the car in the garage; the beauty of a work of art or the enchantment of contemplating blue mountain peaks, and so on. All that is, however, not given without a price, as the world of material things demands a lot from human beings: abilities, activities, desires and even timetables are in many ways oriented to acquiring or using material things. Talents such as manual skill, technical intelligence, thinking and problem-solving capacity, memory or imagination make human beings competent to face the world of material things. In our simplified model, we find that the logic of "more by deeds" and "mutual communication" is valid to a certain extent even for the "window" that opens to the world of material objects: human beings give a lot of themselves to the material world, and they likewise receive a lot in return—even if they do not consciously reflect on that, and much of this can be driven by concealed motivations. Attraction to "riches" can manifest itself in the possession and use of objects that promise comfort, excitement, aesthetic sensation, safety and the like. There is such complexity in the area of relating to material things that discerning what matches the tactics of Christ our Lord and what comes from Lucifer is far from obvious.

A similar situation arises on the second step, where the choice of worldly honor or reproaches and contempt opens a passage into the world of interpersonal relationships. Much of the joy and satisfaction that one can obtain in this world is through the love, attention, appreciation, acceptance and intimacy received from other persons. What a profound joy, what an intense contentment it is to make the experience—or just simply recall it in our heart—that someone knows and sincerely values us. Human beings receive plenty in the world of personal relationships while they also need to give a lot of themselves. Active participation in the world of interpersonal relationships make demands on us: we take care of others, give personal attention, listen with empathy, express ourselves, show respect, encourage, solve conflicts, and so on. Being active and well absorbed in "mutual communication" with others contributes fundamentally to a sense of life that is full and good. This is why human beings can become profound sources of motivation for each other. A school child, for example, can work hard to earn the look of praise of a beloved teacher, or take foolish risks in order to merit the approval of a peer group. Human beings are encoded by nature to have a longing for the appreciation and admiration of others, and it is once again hard to distinguish between legitimate and excessive needs here. This is a promising field for interference from Lucifer, and Christ our Lord surely knows how high the stakes are as he instructs his disciples how to engage in the battle on this second step.

On the third step, we see human beings inspired by values that incite them to think and to act. Values make up the third major source of human motivations. Those who embrace values and also experience themselves as valuable will—contrary to those caught in the battle of the second step—not depend on the good opinion of others: feelings of self-worth are not defined by others' thoughts or feedback. Even while working in isolation, not being understood by anyone, a person can be reinforced by the conviction that his life is meaningful because he is committed to clear values and ideals, because he has created something valuable or beautiful, or because he has consecrated his life to an ideal that he holds dear. Sufficient independence from others' opinions is even a precondition for creating a work of art or leading a group, being a parent, acting as a manager or as a superior of a religious community while remaining faithful to a cherished set of values. To please everyone, to comply with others' expectations would compromise the very values and the common good that is at stake. Those who attach importance to values often experience a certain sense of satisfaction—at least as long as they fulfill their roles. They live with a certain poise and dignity, fight their fights with great inner strength as they believe in accomplishing the goals that they see clearly. Thus, a mutuality of communication can become realized on this third step, too, between the human being and the world surrounding him. Those giving the best of themselves, their knowledge, skills and love in order to act according to the values they have appropriated and to change the world for the better can discover an extraordinary source of motivation and a formerly unknown sense of self-worth. Such individuals may, however, become entrapped in this perception of reality when they succumb to pride. An overly strong focus on goals and ideals tends to go together with a biased perception of reality and the multiplication of blind spots; through idealizing oneself, one might grow insensitive to one's own needs, and become inclined to see others solely as contributors or hindrances to the next achievement. Just as in the previous steps, once again it is extremely difficult to differentiate what is from God and what only appears as good yet is no longer in accord with the Gospels.

To summarize: the three steps described in the meditation on the Two Standards direct our attention to three primary sources of motivation in human life: material goods, other human beings and values. Each of these can provide significant satisfaction so that human life can be, up to a certain point, "carried" by each of them. Yet, these three motivational sources, magnificent and abundant as they are, offer only a rather ambivalent support. Each represents only one aspect of the created world and none can give the rich sense of harmony and fulfillment that one can taste through the Contemplation to Attain Love. Lucifer seduces through the sense of power, joy, safety and the rest that these three sources of motivation can promise. He can "set up snares and chains" [SpEx 142] to the extent that he is able to accustom humans to being dependent on the satisfaction that the world can provide in these three ways. Christ our Lord insists that freedom be preserved in each of the three fields, even if the letting go of attachments is not pleasant [cf. SpEx 146]. The extent to which human beings are exposed to the world they live in—at times almost defenseless with regard to whatever happens within the threefold relationship with their environment—explains that there is a lot at stake. Freedom in the Lord is not a mere spiritual sentiment but the result of receiving the gift of salvation while being put to the test in a variety of ways so that lasting transformation can take place in the depths of the personality.

At each of the three steps, the question remains: are there any criteria? What falls under the category of necessary security and what is excessive wealth? How to tell an innocent need for human support from a disordered craving to be honored? How can purposeful work for clear goals be distinguished from the proud ambition to set everything right? Ignatius does not provide any readily applicable answers. What he gives instead is a powerful vision of the reality of the human condition that must be well known in order to be able to discern what leads to freedom in Christ and what leads to being paralysed by seemingly good choices. He also shares his conviction that true freedom in the Lord will only be a reality if the desire for it is as powerful as the human motivations that Lucifer can grab and distort.

The *Exercises* offer much help in bringing about the new motivational force that can reliably carry our human existence and help us find freedom in Christ. Successive exercises face us again and again with the person of Christ, and—especially during the second week—Christ is shown as someone who is concerned about how human beings communicate through the three "windows" opening onto the world. For example, the Contemplation of the Kingdom [SpEx 91–8] depicts Christ as a leader with an important cause that can spark the fervor of persons who are eager to act upon great values and ideals. As for the second window, one is invited to engage in personal, intimate conversations with Christ ("properly speaking, in the way one friend speaks to another" [SpEx 54]), and develop an "interior knowledge" of Our Lord [SpEx 104]. Finally, the example of the binaries [SpEx 149–56] or the consideration of the third way of being humble [SpEx 167] give orientations for dealing with material things. Yet the main thrust of the gradual transformation that happens here is the ever growing attachment to the person of Christ. The grace and the disposition to know Christ intimately, to love him more and more, and to follow him closely is the basis on which previously scattered and discordant motivational forces can be ordered, and gradually submitted to the living relationship with the Lord. Anthropocentric considerations reach their limits here: the ultimate source of human freedom and strength is God, and the question of how particular individuals can find this source belongs to their unfathomable personal mystery.

The relationship model of Ignatian anthropology as presented above offers a way of seeing the human being as a creature open to four major motivational sources: God, values, other persons and material things. The advantage of this simple model is that it enables us to see how human beings are embedded in their environment, as creatures who must struggle both for meaningful connections with the world and the freedom from attachments to it, thus developing their unique way of giving and receiving, of engaging in mutual communication. Human personality is fundamentally structured by the need to engage in these four "worlds" and by the fourfold openness to the environment that sustains human life. Openness to the world is a gift and a potential for growth, but also implies vulnerability since personal freedom, joy and the capacity to love can diminish when individuals become prisoners of a proud identification with the values they profess, of their need to be prized by others, or even of seemingly indispensable material conditions. The call to serve Christ is a call to enrich and form the four fundamental aspects of the personality in a way that the personality becomes increasingly integrated through an active and focused relationship with the person of Christ.

Despite its simplicity, the fourfold relationship model complements Ignatian anthropology with a dimension that tends to be neglected by contemporary research, and sheds light on important characteristics of Jesuit life understood as a pathway to God. More specifically, it can be useful for a preliminary description of the process of transformation that Jesuit formation aims at bringing about. Hence we now turn our attention to sketching out a "roadmap" of Jesuit life to get a first impression of the Ignatian pathway to God as a whole, one that can be later refined in accordance with the *Constitutions*. For the sake of comparison however, we will first discuss two other possible "pathways", lay and monastic life. As we will see, the common feature of these different paths is the progressive ordering and harmonizing of deep human motivations.

## Lay and Religious Paths of Life

The relationship model of Ignatian anthropology shows that the pain of an unfulfilled life is often caused by the contrasting influences that reach us through the four "windows" that we open onto the surrounding world. For example, I would like to give time to God but my mind is busy with things to do at work, so I spend barely any time in prayer. I would like to support someone in need but I must also think of my own financial security. I am affectively nourished by a relationship with an attractive colleague, but I am aware of being responsible for my family and so I do not wish to divorce. I would like to speak up in harmony with my convictions but I do not dare to risk my livelihood. According to our simplified Ignatian model, life's joys and satisfactions tend to arise from the four fundamental motivational sources, conflicts develop when motivations crash, and pain indicates their loss. Human life gains strength and momentum when motivations are successfully harmonized, or at least when the most important one gets obvious priority over the others. Our life story is generally an expression of a dynamic compromise between various motivations, based on which we shape our own fate with more or less freedom and creativity.

Over the course of life, dominant motivations keep changing, and subsequent phases of life can even be characterized by the specific motivation that tends to become dominant in that phase. While each human being is unique, certain common patterns can be recognized and consequently some of the general characteristics of human life as a transformative process can be described.

Traditional cultures used to impose a rather inflexible course of lay life: basic motivational forces that correspond to the four "windows" were expected to become determinant in a fixed order. Those who came of age (for example, by some ritual of initiation that marked the end of the protected and privileged years of childhood) were supposed to fulfill socially recognized roles in an ordered way that brings to mind the order of the three steps of the meditation on the Two Standards. The first life task was to secure one's living according to what was customary in the given culture, for example by developing the skills for agricultural work. Success in this area entitled young people to courtship and marriage, where the desire for intense interpersonal relationships could be lived out. With the birth of the children, the responsibility to govern the family in the spirit of a personally appropriated set of values could become a major source of joys and anxieties. A life centered on God, mainly free of the previous burdens, was often the fate of the elderly and the "wise", as a well-merited reward at the end of their lives.

Such clear-cut life phases are hard to recognize in modern societies. All the more surprisingly, when Abraham Maslow studied the motivation system of psychologically healthy people, he summarized his findings—nowadays represented in a pyramid—by means of a system of human needs very similar to the ones just discussed.[11] According to Maslow's theory, human life is driven by deeply rooted inner needs such as basic physiological needs, a need for safety, love and belonging, esteem and self-actualization. Each of these needs holds a dominant position among human motivations as long as it is not fulfilled in a satisfactory way, giving way to the next level of the pyramid when that pressing need gains dominance. The main aspects of this theory—which is widely diffused in modern popular psychology even though it is not supported by much experimental data—can be easily correlated with the steps of the Ignatian model. One can recognize not only the similar traits between the safety–intimacy–esteem triad and the three steps of the meditation on the Two Standards but also the striking resemblance of experiences of contemplative prayer with the "peak experiences" that Maslow describes at the height of personality development.[12] It seems that human life is predisposed to develop according to a hierarchy of needs, corresponding to the three Ignatian steps, even in constantly evolving modern societies where superficial trends easily obfuscate more profound human needs.

11 A. Maslow, *Motivation and Personality* (New York: Harper, 1954).

12 G. G. May, *Will and Spirit: A Contemplative Psychology* (San Francisco: Harper & Row, 1982), p. 58.

The pathway of monastic life is structured somewhat differently. Life conditions in the monastery are designed in a way that the "windows" that correspond to the three steps are rather narrow. The gates of the monastery filter the persons and objects that might be encountered and also the values that one might live for. In the meantime, a high quality of mutual communication can be ensured on all three levels by the greater intensity of attention, based on the principle known from the *Spiritual Exercises*: "what fills and satisfies the soul consists, not in knowing much, but in our understanding the realities profoundly and in savoring them interiorly" [SpEx 2]. Within the monastery, the environment—material things, people and values alike—can be freely arranged in order to help the relationship with God as well as possible. This is why the monastic environment consists of aesthetically pleasing objects that help to remain recollected, carefully chosen people and purposefully collected, valuable literature in the library. In contrast to lay life, the fundamental motivational forces are not meant to be ordered through successive phases of development but through the unambiguous primacy of the relationship with God which is sufficiently explicit and powerful to integrate the threefold structure of relations with the "world". This is the anthropological foundation upon which a monastic community culture is built, where the wisdom, the human qualities and the constant attention of the superior—along with easy access to prayer, personal accompaniment and other spiritual resources—can foster the further purifying of motivations and the transformation toward inner peace, spiritual freedom and ever deeper love. Naturally, even the most thoughtfully arranged environment cannot replace freely made personal human decisions, without which there is no progression in monastic life or elsewhere.

The pathway to God as it is envisioned in the Institute of the Society of Jesus differs from both the path of lay life and that of monastic life because a Jesuit must be able to connect with his environment freely even when outside the walls of a Jesuit house. When considering the material, "temporal" goods, the *Constitutions* emphasize practical dexterity (in kitchen work, for example) and the need to preserve the inner freedom inherent in poverty, while delegating much of the actual work in this area to the brothers (temporal coadjutors). On the level of human relationships, apostolic life requires Jesuits to develop the interpersonal skills that include ease in moving around in a variety of social milieus without fear and anxiety, the ability to gain the trust of people, a capacity to adapt to others, empathy, compassion, respect and the rest. As for values and ideals, Jesuits must be able to interpret complex events in the light of the Gospel and act purposefully in order to bring about Gospel values that can permeate apostolic works and communities. In the midst of all their occupations, Jesuits cannot give themselves over to be carried by the satisfactions that the "world" can offer: "the Society's members may not accept [recompenses] from anyone other than God our Lord; and it is purely for his service that they ought to do all things" [General Examen, ConsCN C 4]. A Jesuit who is active in the world can only remain "a human instrument united with God" [cf. ConsCN C 813] to the extent that he preserves his inner freedom and remains sensitive to movements of the Spirit: "dispose [. . .] according to your will. Give me love of yourself along with your grace, for that is enough for me" [SpEx 234].

Thus, Jesuit life can be lived according to the Institute of the Society if—beyond the suitability examined upon admission—the major motivations of the Jesuit are structured and ordered before the actual beginning of the apostolic life in such a way that he can live from the Father's love and preach the Gospel in close companionship with Jesus. Formation has to bring about a profound transformation of the individual motivational system so that the divergent motivating forces can be integrated in a personality able to persist in focusing on the service of God even without the support of a monastic environment. Such transformation is the goal of the pathway to God drawn by the *Constitutions*, and this is the aspect of Jesuit formation that needs the wise and firm support of superiors who are knowledgeable about the *Constitutions*.

To complete the picture, we might attempt to understand what happens in a "decadent and not quite reformed" order, such as the one which St Ignatius considered joining after his studies in Barcelona: "When thoughts of entering an institute came to him, then he also had the desire to enter a decadent and not quite reformed one (if he were to be a religious) so that he would suffer more in it" [Autobiography 71]. Such an order, although references to God would probably not be missing when presenting its life and its mission, cannot support its members in the process of the profound transformation that religious life requires them to go through. Reasons can be numerous. The order might have lost the ability to guide its members toward a personal relationship with and a committed service of God, or it might show only a momentary glimpse of the beauty and richness of such life. If this happened, secondary reasons for joining the order might come to the forefront: in poor societies, for example, material security or the opportunity for a better education and a more meaningful life; in an individualistic society, the promise of community; in a world of shaken values, a romanticized longing for a perfect life. As a "decadent" order can only be of weak assistance in the purification of mixed initial motivations, immature forms of behavior can be expected to solidify, and the abilities that can support a joyous and meaningful religious life might not develop. To have given up life in the world without resolutely following the path of religious life can therefore become equal to falling between two stools. The result is a frustrating life heavily laden with strenuous inner tensions, a life that can only be maintained within the frame of the three religious vows through lesser or greater compromises. At times important projects or the emotional closeness of a loved person, or these two things together, become the ultimate source of joy and satisfaction, and thus the object of attachment. Apostolic life might suffer from a decreased intensity of "mutual communication", while depressive lack of motivation or obsessive activism may emerge. Interpersonal relationships within the community are likely to become burdensome. In any case, the transparency of a life dedicated to God that can attract to the community new candidates with an authentic vocation will be seriously endangered.

## Contributions from the History of Spirituality and Psychology

As we have taken a brief look at different paths of life, we can notice how the relationship model of Ignatian anthropology, even at a rather simple level of elaboration, casts light on some basic objectives of Jesuit formation. Our model proves to be useful, but we must avoid equating Ignatian anthropology with a simplified, schematic model. Contributions from the history of spirituality and from the area of psychology can supply a number of further details confirming that we are dealing with solid elements of Ignatian anthropology that remain valid and even essential in a contemporary context.

The background of the three steps of the meditation on the Two Standards in the history of Christian spirituality is the recurring topic of the "threefold lust": "the lust of the flesh, the lust of the eyes, and the pride of life is not of the Father but is of the world" [1 Jn 2:16]. In early Christianity, monks understood the three vows as a conscious effort to fight the three powerful forces of sexuality, desire for comfort provided by material goods, and pride, so that they could remain open to the love of God. St Thomas Aquinas, whose works, according to the *Constitutions,* were to be known by the Jesuits—"in theology there should be lectures on [. . .] the scholastic doctrine of St Thomas" [ConsCN C 464]—explains the religious vows without the exaggerations of the early ascetics: "it is in renouncing these [three things] altogether, as far as possible, that the evangelical counsels consist".[13]

Another very similar description of the most powerful forces that affect the human being is given by St Thomas when he explains that the devil tempted Jesus in the same way as he had done with Adam, the first man. When recounting the motivations that are most vulnerable to the devil's influence, this other description also talks about material riches and pride, but sexuality is replaced by vainglory.[14] In these two different perspectives on the three main spiritual battlefields, two battlefields—the temptation of wealth and that of pride—look the same, but in the case of interpersonal relationships, there is a perhaps surprising shift of focus from sexuality to vainglory.

Ignatius puts forward this second interpretation of the "threefold lust" in the meditation on the Two Standards. He was undoubtedly influenced by the Spanish culture of his time, which valued good reputation and honor, *fama,* to the point that it was worth killing for. Still, Ignatius' choice has important potential, since in the area of interpersonal relationships he puts emphasis on something more subtle than mere sexuality: vanity can be quenched not by the satisfaction

13 St Thomas Aquinas, *Summa Theologiae,* I–II, q.108 a.4.

14 St Thomas Aquinas, *Summa Theologiae,* III, q.41 a.4.

of a powerful basic instinct but through the very existence of another person. Other persons can cause contentment or deep pain through their capacity to formulate an opinion and express—by words and deeds—respect, appreciation, or even admiration on the one hand, and rejection, refusal or even hostility on the other. The rich world of interpersonal relationships, unduly underestimated in the history of western cultures, received proper attention in Ignatius' anthropology. The emphasis on interpersonal relationships suits our modern cultural awareness well, too, although we would perhaps prefer to complement "vainglory" with the desire for intimacy, another way of longing for comfort offered by another person but potentially including sexual attraction as well.

The relationship model of Ignatian anthropology shows strong parallels with a number of recognized psychological theories, even though the Ignatian model is more ontological than psychological in its character, since the relationship with the world within which the human being is embedded precedes psychological phenomena. We saw that the levels of Maslow's pyramid of motivations not only correspond with the Ignatian steps but also develop in the same order. Jean Piaget,[15] when studying the cognitive development of children, found that between characteristic developmental stages the thinking of children goes through a sudden change in quality, arising from the at least partial resolution of a key developmental conflict. Inspired by Piaget's work, Lawrence Kohlberg[16] examined the development of moral reasoning—a specific area of thinking—from childhood to mature adulthood. His description of the three main levels of moral development also correlates with Ignatius' steps (a child's "pre-conventional" moral reasoning is centered on the self, disregarding others' feelings and needs; "conventional" morality is based on feelings of interpersonal conformity and social acceptance; "post-conventional" or "principled" morality realizes ethical principles and values). At first sight, similarities with Erik Erikson's[17] model of

15 J. Piaget, *The Construction of Reality in the Child* (New York: Basic Books, 1937/1954).

16 L. Kohlberg, *Essays on Moral Development, Vol. I: The Philosophy of Moral Development* (San Francisco: Harper & Row, 1981).

17 E. H. Erikson, *Childhood and Society* (New York: W. W. Norton & Co., 1950).

psychosocial development seem less apparent but in fact the later life stages described by Erikson do lend themselves to comparison with the three Ignatian steps. Interesting links can be found beyond the theories of developmental psychology as well. The transactional analysis model of Eric Berne[18] explores unintentionally recurring "games" that constitute characteristic patterns in human relationships. His explanation is based on the definition of three ego states, which are quite different from the relationship model of Ignatian anthropology but still offer several thought-provoking parallels. Emerging results of research on multiple intelligences (such as defining the EQ or emotional intelligence and SQ or spiritual intelligence as sets of abilities different from the IQ) can also be seen as the identification of human skills and potentials apt for relating to other persons and to values that can make life meaningful, beyond the traditionally privileged IQ that applies to understanding inanimate things. All in all, several contemporary theories enable us to understand certain possible aspects of the Ignatian model better, including its relevance for our contemporary concerns in Jesuit formation.

A further interesting contemporary parallel to the fourfold relationship model of Ignatian anthropology can be recognized in the formula that surfaced in twentieth-century ecumenical discussions. Based on the witness of Scripture texts, the main functions of early Christian communities could be summarized under the following Greek headings: *diakonia* (fair distribution and proper use of material goods), *koinonia* (community building, interpersonal relationships), *martyria* (uncompromised profession of the Christian teaching, of the values that define the community), *leitourgia* (service and glorification of God).[19] These functions can be understood today as before as the main dimensions of the mission of the church beyond denominational differences. A particular Christian community or church can be considered authentic and healthy if it is capable of covering these areas and can maintain an organic unity of these four fields.

We can conclude that the fourfold relationship model of Ignatian anthropology is closely connected to quite a few essential insights of both the history of spirituality and modern psychology. It can bring the

18 E. Berne, *Games People Play* (New York: Grove Press, 1964).

19 Cf. Ac 2:42.45–7a.

spiritual and anthropological wisdom that was once treated under the question of the threefold lust to our contemporary understanding of Jesuit life and of Christian life together. The three steps of the meditation on the Two Standards, when understood as an insightful account of the subjective experience of the human being, can help to avoid not only a naïve mixing of the realms of spirituality and psychology but also a sterile separation of the two. In fact, the Ignatian model helps us to identify a range of psychological theories as potentially useful, albeit only partial, elements of a more comprehensive anthropology that can also integrate the relationship with God as a fundamental reality of human life. Inversely, the ambition of contemporary schools of psychology to define various "sub-parts" of the self could help one to discover behind the three steps of the Two Standards references to a "materialist self", an "interpersonal self" and a "value-oriented or principled self", all three distinct from the "true self" that can thrive in a living relationship with God. Such an extension of Ignatian anthropology, by explaining what dimensions or aspects of the personality need to be integrated in the course of achieving maturity, could fructify contemporary discussions about Jesuit formation, where personal integration tends to have prime importance, sometimes without convincing clarity about what exactly that means in theory and in practice.

Pointing beyond the immediate goals of this book, the relationship model of Ignatian anthropology may even contribute to the development of a "metapsychology", that is, a vision of the human being that can serve as a framework for linking psychological theories that currently tend to be isolated from each other.[20] Reflections about religious life can, as happened in former times, reveal insights about the human being that may become fruitful in helping others who live in contexts very different from ours.

20 "While it can be pretended that this division of labor [between various psychological models and traditions] is an appropriate consequence of the separate tasks to which each theory is best suited, the fact remains that no whole theory of personal functioning will be possible in the absence of some higher order psychology in which to integrate the wisdom of each. Lacking such a metapsychology, both academic research and clinical practice are less than they might be". In R. Kegan, *The Evolving Self: Problem and Process in Human Development* (Cambridge: Harvard University Press, 1982), p. 14.

✠ 3 ✠

# Some Ignatian Expressions in a Contemporary Context

Ignatian terminology was enriched, revived and made relevant for contemporary use by the renewed understanding of the Spiritual Exercises in the second half of the twentieth century. Expressions like consolation, desolation, discernment, the four weeks of the Spiritual Exercises and many others have become indispensable in maintaining a meaningful relationship with the almost half-millennium-old Ignatian text, in understanding each other over questions of detail and in introducing new generations of spiritual directors to the Ignatian way of giving the Spiritual Exercises. A better contemporary reception of the *Constitutions* will have to be prepared by similar work on Ignatian vocabulary, in a way that Ignatian terms are not only clarified in reference to each other but also tested against the concerns and preoccupations that Jesuit formation is facing today. In what follows, we attempt to place three expressions—help, capital sins and virtues—into a contemporary context. In each of these three cases, our approach will be very limited, since we only focus on some aspects that seem useful for reading the *Constitutions*.

## To Help

As we have seen earlier, the *Constitutions* barely discuss progress outside the context of helping it to happen. Accordingly, the idea of helping is not only referred to through the rich meaning of the verb *aprovechar* but also explicitly by the word "to aid" *(ayudar)*:

> we think it necessary that constitutions should be written to aid us to proceed better, in conformity with our Institute, along the path of divine service on which we have entered *(que ayuden para mejor*

*proceder conforme a nuestro instituto en la vía començada del diuino seruicio)"* [ConsCN C 134].

The objective of helping one proceed better is characteristically Ignatian, yet it raises questions for today's reader. To help is not easy, and to accept help is not easy either. The sheer volume of the *Constitutions* might also instill a furtive doubt: Where is that highly respected inner freedom in Ignatian spirituality when hundreds of paragraphs present our list of duties? Are we ever going to perceive the help offered by *Constitutions* as real, actual help?

Ignatius himself helped in many different ways. While he was in Manresa, he "busied himself helping in spiritual matters certain souls who came there looking for him" [Autobiography 26]. We can call this kind of help *spiritual* help as it meant listening to others' questions, interpreting spiritual experiences or suggesting certain specific methods or practice. This help was directed to spiritual matters, that is, in such cases Ignatius did not change the external circumstances among which the person seeking help lived. Rather, he helped people to conduct themselves properly in the given circumstances and to make the best possible decisions according to their free will.

Another possible way of helping is to change the *circumstances* that determine the life of a person or group but are beyond their control. Ignatius gave an example of such help during the time when he returned to his native land. He saw to it that the poor were provided for officially and regularly, he changed the public opinion about the cohabitation of unmarried couples and he introduced the practice of ringing the church bells to indicate prayer times so that praying become a community affair [Autobiography 89]. Another example of changing the life circumstances of those in need of help—much later, and in a much more refined way—was the foundation of schools. By creating a powerful intellectual and moral environment, Jesuits helped the education of young Jesuits, and then that of other youths as well.

These two ways of helping, spiritual help and the changing of circumstances, can also be combined, as happens in the monastery. Monks can not only relatively easily access spiritual help but also live in a milieu that can be fine-tuned by a charismatic founder or superior, who can quite freely determine the material, social, intellectual and liturgical environment that he or she considers the most suitable for helping the members of the community. The thick walls of the monastery create a space that is protected from the outer world not only in a physical sense but also in the interpersonal and the intellectual dimensions of life. Monks enter into contact with a consciously and carefully shaped environment day after day, and the purpose of this "world" of monastic life with all its simplicity and beauty is to help those who want to consecrate their lives to the praise and service of God. The thick walls of the monastery are meaningful because they assist the personal progress of the monks toward God; the doors can be closed more tightly or be opened wide in accordance with this objective.

The personally accompanied Exercises, as an especially characteristic form of Ignatian help, also combines the two methods of helping. Like a mini-monastery, this help simultaneously modifies the environment (*what* is encountered by and requires adjustment from the person), and secures spiritual assistance (*how* to make the best possible decisions). Both ways of helping are presented in the *Spiritual Exercises* as early as in the introductory explanations ("to aid *(para ayudarse)* both the one who gives [the Exercises] and the one who is to receive them" [SpEx 1]). An example of changing the outer circumstances is when Ignatius urges the person's withdrawal and separation from relatives and friends [cf. SpEx 20].[1] Spiritual help is offered through the advice that "the persons who do the Exercises will benefit greatly by entering upon them with great spirit and generosity toward their Creator and Lord" [SpEx 5].

Upon examining more deeply how the "mini-monastery", the harmony of the two methods of helping, becomes a reality in the Spiritual Exercises, we make a striking discovery. The path of the Exercises, which we tend to think of as one of our most beautiful experiences of freedom, is often lined with surprisingly strong walls, walls not made of stone but of the "tough" words of the person who accompanies the Exercises. Exercitants enter an environment that is greatly restricted even without the stone walls of the monastery: they cease to commu-

1 "An environment to facilitate the movement toward God is offered by Ignatius in the additional directions [77–86]." M. Cowan CSJ and J. C. Futrell SJ, *Companions in Grace: A Handbook for Directors of the Spiritual Exercises of Saint Ignatius of Loyola* (Saint Louis: The Institute of Jesuit Sources, 2000), p. 10.

nicate not only with their relatives but also with others residing in the retreat house; reading is limited or even reduced to nothing; one is submitted to a relatively strict daily schedule; one might even be told to spend more time or less time outdoors, and so on. The "world" of the exercitants is limited even further as they agree to focus their attention on a particular Scripture passage throughout the entire length of one or more prayer times, while they might even be asked to refrain from turning the pages of the Bible so that they do not "wander away" from the "place" that is considered most suitable. A surprising number of restrictions seem to be necessary until a space of personal freedom is created where the exercitant can engage in a generous and attentive encounter with a well-defined part of the "surrounding world", that is, the short text of a Scripture passage given for meditation. This is how a firmly established environment can provide the preconditions for deep mutual communication by creating a safe and undisturbed place where assimilation and understanding can take place and a free personal response can emerge. The very best of one's attention, intellect and all other abilities can be "given" to the biblical story, when it becomes possible to receive something meaningful with an open heart, "to draw some profit" [SpEx 114] from the story. The outer circumstances—though in no way can these substitute for what can only emerge from the inner freedom of the exercitant—thus play a key role in facilitating high-quality mutual communication that can, through encountering a biblical text, also become an encounter with God.

As we can see, the *Spiritual Exercises*, where so many contemporaries experience freedom in the Spirit, keep the exercitant within surprisingly strict limits by means of instructions from the giver of the Exercises. In the text of the *Exercises*, these instances can be recognized through the frequent appearance of the imperative as infinitive, instructions being phrased as if they were matter-of-fact descriptions of what one will do. Thus, in the Exercises, the role of the monastery's stone walls is taken over by the accompaniment that happens according to the *Spiritual Exercises* and is based on mutual trust. The giver of the Exercises adapts Ignatian instructions and pronounces them, while the exercitant accepts that these instructions will frame the "world", the "reality" to be encountered during the following day. This ongoing cooperation is vital for progressing in the Exercises:

> When the one giving the Exercises notices that the exercitant is not experiencing any spiritual motions in his or her soul, such as consolations or desolations, or is not being moved one way or another by different spirits, the director should question the retreatant much about the Exercises: whether he or she is doing them at the appointed times, how they are being made, and whether the Additional Directives are being diligently observed. The director should ask about each of these items in particular. [SpEx 6]

As we can see, Ignatian help implies a paradox barely understandable by anyone who has not experienced it in person. The retreatant agrees voluntarily and even with a certain ease to undergo restrictions that greatly limit what he or she can do. Why are these restrictions not perceived as intolerable chains on one's personal freedom? It is because the person most of the time knows and feels as evident that all these restrictions are intended to offer genuine help as they create a protected space for progressing more resolutely. Without such restrictions—set up in accordance with the dynamic of the Exercises and matched by appropriate spiritual help—the exercitant could not have the experience of making spiritual progress within a relatively short time.

Experiences of progression may include the astonishing or moving experience of the presence of the living God, the increase of trust, insights explaining hitherto incomprehensible or seemingly mutually exclusive phenomena, or a growing sense of freedom and love. The experience of making progress tends to motivate a person more deeply than thoughts and emotions. It can even persist in the absence of intense emotions or clear thoughts, and in this sense it is related to consolation. Consolation also arises from a deeper level than emotions or thoughts, as it can be born in the midst of painful emotions and without a clarity of understanding [SpEx 316]. Experiences even remotely related to progress can sometimes be as significant as the explicit growth in devotion, inner freedom and love. For example, having discovered why one had been stuck or even "quite simply" the emergence of a profound longing for progression are signs of progress themselves and tend to bring about consolation. The experience of making progress and a sense of its goodness beyond all doubts tend to kindle a desire for further progression. This is how the dynamic of advancing can develop and gain momentum, enabling the exercitant to "cope with" the two dimensions of Ignatian help.

Familiarity with the Ignatian conception of helping can allow one to describe more accurately how the *Constitutions* can be expected to help progress in Jesuit life. Thus the *Constitutions* place restrictions in order to create and maintain a protected space, according to the characteristics of each section of the pathway to God. They also provide help in making good decisions that surge from personal freedom. Restrictions and inner freedom, properly adjusted circumstances and spiritual support concur when helping occurs in the Ignatian way, through familiarity with the pathway to God. Progressing on the pathway to God will then be full of challenges yet it will in fact lead toward growing personal freedom and love, and the experience of moving forward will be accompanied by a sense of joy and growing peace even in the midst of being put to the test spiritually or psychologically. If we want the *Constitutions* to be of help in the routine of Jesuit formation, we need to grasp the word *help* in the entire richness of its Ignatian interpretation. Just as we do already when giving the Spiritual Exercises, we need to develop a vision of Jesuit formation where help is understood according to its double aspect as in a "mini-monastery"; that is, spiritual help can go along with a trusting cooperation between formators and Jesuits in formation that aims at setting up and maintaining the environment within which progress can be made efficiently.

Help in the Ignatian sense of the word implies the appropriate use of authority. Consequently the understanding of the *Constitutions* as well as the Ignatian character of Jesuit formation depend on a cultural environment where authority is understood within the context of helping progress to take place. In most parts of the world, such a culture has become a reality in the case of giving the Spiritual Exercises, where the acceptance of authority is an obviously helpful dimension of being accompanied. In the meantime, accepting and using authority in Jesuit formation tends to remain a sensitive affair. In some parts of the world, authoritarian conceptions and practices make it difficult to look at the good of the individual who is trying to make progress. In other cultures, a liberal interpretation equates the use of authority with the limitation of individual freedom. Both conceptions can prevent the *Constitutions* from becoming understood and fruitful in daily Jesuit life. Those in formation will be better helped, in the Ignatian sense, when not merely the necessity of using authority but also its purpose, manner and prerequisites become more obvious to formators and Jesuits in formation alike.

## Capital Sins

Capital sins are barely discussed in Ignatian retreats these days, even though the *Spiritual Exercises* mention them in the Annotations [SpEx 17] and also when explaining the First Method of Praying: "With regard to the seven capital sins [. . .] the subject matter here consists of the sins to be avoided" [SpEx 244]. Ignatius seems to consider the recognition of capital sins to be an advisable exercise of self-knowledge before beginning the Exercises and probably even afterwards, by means of the First Method of Praying.

In line with our objective, we examine the capital sins as phenomena that influence or motivate the behavior of the human being. We do not delve into the history of spirituality to research the contribution of John Cassian and St Gregory the Great to establishing the classic list of seven capital sins (anger, avarice, sloth, pride, lust, envy and gluttony). We do not discuss the moral evaluation of capital sins, nor the amount of damage they cause. (On the latter, sins that destroy the natural environment could be probably considered more severe.) We do not seek to be thorough and complete in our approach. Rather we intend to explore how capital sins might be seen and understood—according to the literal sense of the expression—as typical sources of sins. The term *capital* which tends to be associated with "most important" comes in fact from the Latin *caput*, "head", and points out the "source" from which sins flow, as in the expression "head of the river".[2] Capital sins are not "grave sins" in the sense of implying full knowledge and deliberate consent.[3] Rather, they are primary inclinations of the human personality which the early church Fathers called seven "spirits", or simply "thoughts"

2 *Catechism of the Catholic Church*. 2nd edition, revised in accordance with the official Latin text promulgated by Pope John Paul II. Published by the United States Conference of Catholic Bishops, 2000. §1866.

3 See "Péchés capitaux", in *Dictionnaire de Spiritualité*, vol. XII (Paris, Beauchesne, 1984), col. 853.

*(logismoi)*.[4] For the sake of staying close to the Ignatian text, we will keep the expression "capital sins" even though a different term, such as "sources of sins", might be a more fitting choice today.

Although capital sins may affect the human being with a seemingly irresistible power, the meditation on the Two Standards does not count them—with the exception of pride—amongst the most important spiritual battlefields between Lucifer and Christ. While the relationship model of Ignatian anthropology deals with motivations that put a person in contact with his or her environment, capital sins are rooted within the human being. An outburst of anger, for example, usually serves the alleviation of inner tension, if only temporarily; and the same can be said about lust, a relief from tension through (the fantasy of) an ecstatic fusion with another's body. Both can soothe, for example, the anxiety caused by feelings of loneliness or a sense of worthlessness. Capital sins, as opposed to the motivational forces of the Ignatian relationship model, serve the short-term needs of the individual rather than the more substantial issues that are realized by means of interacting with the surrounding world.

Yet, if we keep searching for a way to apply the Ignatian relationship model to capital sins, we find an unexpected answer: capital sins correspond to behaviors that might well be of good use when the individual tries to establish a connection with surrounding reality, *but only in the case of children. Anger* and fierce opposition might be "legitimate" and necessary tools of communication for toddlers who are in the process of extricating themselves from the parental symbiosis, strengthening their own independent self—even if parents do not always appreciate such aims. *Lust,* the enactment of a craving for intimate union with another person, evokes the fundamental need of the newborn baby for the alleviation of loneliness through not yet sexualized physical connection in a close, loving relationship with the mother or an attachment figure, be it parent or caregiver, because only within such a relationship can basic trust, the prerequisite of all later trust or sense of security, develop. Breastfeeding is a good example of such an intimate physical contact, but it also illustrates how feeding does not simply mean adequate nutrition for a baby but also a way of

4 *Ibid.*, col. 854.

soothing all sorts of tensions and anxieties, since satisfying the returning fits of hunger of a baby or toddler not only results in physiological comfort but also deepens the bond between mother and child. In the case of a grown-up, the immediate satisfaction of the appetite can enjoy similar priority, but that would be the equivalent of *gluttony*. Babies' need for idle rest is a precondition of their healthy development; only later can this same behavior receive a moral evaluation as *sloth*. If we look at *avarice* without moral judgment, seeing it merely as a fierce and inconsiderate attachment to cherished personal "treasures", we can easily identify this behavior as that of a toddler clinging to a favorite teddy bear in order to cope with the separation anxiety during the occasional absence of his or her mother. A young child's *envy* also plays a role in the development of the self by means of competitive interpersonal relationships. Likewise, something we would habitually deem *pride* is in a toddler's life an experience of his or her worthiness and self-esteem: a developmental need so essential that no decent pedagogy can do without engaging it in some way.

Along these lines, if we do not regard capital sins as moral categories but rather see them as typical forms of behavior, we may recognize that young children's "cute" or at least quite natural behavioral patterns all play a role, at various early stages of human development, in the emergence of the fundamental functions of the self. In the life of a grown-up person, however, these same behaviors are considered to be immature, inadequate expressions of motivations that evoke the childhood of the person. In our relationship model, capital sins can be said to refer to the vitally important "window" that opens onto the world for children. When a newborn begins to grow in a symbiotic unity with the mother or parents, behaviors that correlate with capital sins become vital tools in maintaining a connection with the surrounding environment, providing the means that meet the needs of the undeveloped self in order to ensure further development.

In the case of grown-ups, these patterns of behavior can become "capital sins", expressions of evil inclinations or impulses. Their powerful nature is explained by the fact that they have become habitual, useful and established patterns of behavior and may even have turned into a "survival strategy" if the child has had to cope with fear, anxiety, failure, the terror of feeling insignificant and the like. Upon praying about capital sins ("I will call to memory all the sins of my life, looking at them year by year" [SpEx 56]), one might encounter serious difficulties as to whether "full knowledge and deliberate consent", or rather instinctive desire for relief from familiar or even subconscious anxiety and pain, describes them more adequately. In any case, capital sins, if they remain dominant in adult life, point toward an enduring vulnerability, a childlike but misplaced longing for security, intimacy, appreciation, ideally peaceful environment, and so forth. Patterns of behavior that once were meant to function as "windows" onto the world begin to distort the perception of reality, make the person self-centered, withdrawn and estranged from oneself, others and God. Capital sins cripple mature mutual communication and can impair the advancement on the path of growing freedom and love. The path of liberation from capital sins is also that of increasing maturity. As the coercing power of capital sins diminishes and inner freedom becomes stronger, immature patterns of behavior either disappear or become parts of the personality of a mature individual, adequately serving mutual communication. Anger, for example, might then function as energy put to use for the protection of personal ideals and values and sexual desire can become an expression of mutual marital love or even as a metaphor for the burning love of God.

Our reflections on the capital sins started from the acknowledgement that they seem to be poorly integrated into contemporary Ignatian spirituality. One can understand that compared to other, more developed or more immediately attractive models of self-knowledge, the simple mention of the seven capital sins or the awareness of their importance throughout the history of spirituality does not elicit much contemporary attention. We can now conclude that if the Ignatian pathway to God is considered in its reality as a dynamic of progression that includes the dimension of human maturity, then capital sins become worthy of attention for several reasons. Firstly, the reference to capital sins complements the relationship model of Ignatian anthropology with a dimension that can be rather significant both in the subjective experience of self and in the dynamics of Jesuit communities. Looking at this dimension by means of the capital sins can help to integrate a range of phenomena into our understanding of the progression on the way to God which could otherwise be easily ignored. Secondly, the interpretation of capital sins in a contemporary context of personality development can help us to see the strong link between our current emphasis on the need for human maturity in Jesuit life and the Ignatian insistence on recognizing "evil inclinations" [ConsCN C 265, 423] and dealing suitably with temptations. Such a well-defined connection between the areas of psychology and spirituality can enable us to rediscover the relevance of some of the instructions of the *Constitutions* in our days and to integrate these more thoroughly into the practice of Jesuit formation. Thirdly, awareness of how capital sins constitute an element of Ignatian anthropology can help us to understand that the Ignatian vision considers weaknesses of the personality in a rather similar way as desolations. They need to be recognized and named as such, and one should be active in resisting them, but activity does not mean focusing on them [SpEx 319]. Instead, at a time of desolation one focuses on exercises that include prayer, meditation and examination of oneself, and when facing the influence of capital sins, one should focus on striving for virtues: "to avoid the faults [springing from the capital sins] better, a person should propose and strive by holy exercises to acquire and retain the seven virtues contrary to these sins" [SpEx 245]. What has been acknowledged as a disordered reality receives due attention but then attention shifts toward the acquisition of new, previously unknown patterns of thought and action, with the aim of establishing these as habitual and consistent ways of proceeding. This Ignatian instruction further confirms our intuition that capital sins are related to manifestations of the immature personality and that instead of ignoring or trying to directly "fight" these, progress can be made by the development and consolidation of mature patterns of behavior. This is the reason why another recurring expression of the *Constitutions*, "virtues", seems to merit discussion among the examples of Ignatian terminology waiting to be explicated in a contemporary context.

## Virtues

As we have seen, the *Constitutions* declare that the goal of the novitiate is to advance along the path of God "in spirit and in virtues" [ConsCN C 243]. Considering how vital the subject matter of virtues is in the

Ignatian works,[5] it is rather striking that the expression did not play a noticeable role in the Ignatian spiritual renewal during the second half of the twentieth century, and even today it sounds awkward in discussions that deal with Ignatian spirituality or Jesuit formation.[6] Virtue ethics, which itself went through a renewal during recent decades,[7] barely, if at all, influenced Jesuit formation, even though its application sparked interest in the fields of education and in the management of businesses and NGOs alike.[8] This could mean that our contemporary rendering of Ignatian spirituality lacks a dimension that could foster the understanding that the *Constitutions* aim at: a profound transformation of the human motivational system in order to make it the bearer of freedom that is found in the Spirit.

Virtues might well be disregarded today because of the moralizing or voluntarist school of spirituality that the word evokes. Terms like "striving for virtues" can bring to mind the idea of an impersonal, mechanical, joyless effort rather than a delightful progression in the Spirit. Restoring the term "virtue" for everyday use might not be viable in the immediate future. From the perspective of a dynamic conception of Jesuit life as a pathway to God, however, it seems to be inevitable to talk about virtues, because they can empower us to directly and effectively support the dynamic of progress, somewhat like what we do while accompanying the Exercises. A vision of Jesuit formation with a place for virtues can cover the gap between our ideal of formation that values human maturity and the exercises proposed by the *Constitutions*.

Dictionaries define *virtue* as a habitual and firm disposition, a conduct that is good in some way, an established character trait that enables the human being to practice good with a certain ease. A tactful, persevering, well-read, prudent, generous or in other ways virtuous Jesuit will be more effective in his apostolic mission and will find more joy in community life than a companion who is less "advanced" in virtues.

5 See "Virtudes", in *DEI (G–Z)*, pp. 1774–8.

6 J. F. Keenan, "Catholic Moral Theology, Ignatian Spirituality, and Virtue Ethics: Strange Bedfellows", *The Way Supplement* 88 (Spring 1997), pp. 36–45.

7 See for example: W. C. Spohn, *Go and Do Likewise: Jesus and Ethics* (New York: Continuum, 1999).

8 One inspiring, even though somewhat simplified and not explicitly Christian initiative, is The Virtues Project, www.virtuesproject.com.

Virtues are usually acquired through practice, that is, purposeful and repeated acts, but theologians also note that sometimes—especially in the case of the three "theological" virtues [cf. SpEx 327], faith, hope and charity—it is more just to see them as gifts of grace. Virtues are highly important for Ignatius. When he describes the desirable qualities of the Superior General, he only ranks familiarity with God as higher: "the second quality is that he be a person whose example in all the virtues will be a help to the other members of the Society" [ConsCN C 725].

The Ignatian vision of virtues is not quite the same as that of dictionary definitions. It is deeply rooted in the *Spiritual Exercises*, and many references in the text provide help for a more exact understanding. Virtue is a quality that deserves special attention when contemplating the life of Christ our Lord. By way of our inner perceptions, one can experience virtue as pleasant, sweet:

> By the sight of my imagination I will see the persons, by meditating and contemplating in detail all the circumstances around them, and by drawing some profit from the sight [. . .] I will smell the fragrance and taste the infinite sweetness and charm of the Divinity, of the soul, of its virtues, and of everything there, appropriately for each of the persons who is being contemplated. Then I will reflect upon myself and draw profit from this. [SpEx 122–4]

When a virtue becomes attractive during contemplations, its personal appropriation and development must be asked for in the prayerful conversations that follow the contemplation, just as it is the case in regard to other graces:

> Attention should be called to a matter which was partially explained before. In the colloquies we ought to converse and beg according to the subject matter; that is, in accordance with whether I find myself tempted or consoled, desire to possess one virtue or another, or to dispose myself in one way or another. [SpEx 199]

> When the prayer is finished, one should turn to the person to whom it is directed and ask for the virtues or graces for which greater need is felt. [SpEx 257]

Virtues can be acquired and retained through "holy exercises". Unlike the graces received in the Exercises, virtues cannot be received through merely exposing oneself to God in a prayer exercise but need to be practiced in order to become integrated into the personality: "to avoid the faults [springing from the capital sins] better a person should propose and strive by holy exercises to acquire and retain the seven virtues contrary to these sins" [SpEx 245]. To note the significance of virtues in everyday life, consider how they are the building material of the person's inner fortress that protects against temptations: "the enemy of the human nature prowls around and from every side probes all our theological, cardinal and moral virtues. Then at the point where he finds us weakest and most in need in regard to our eternal salvation, there he attacks and tries to take us" [SpEx 327]. Finally, among all virtues the most essential three are those very ones to which Christ our Lord wants to lead us in the meditation on the Two Standards. As we have seen, these are poverty, the ability to bear reproaches or contempt, and humility: "from these three steps they should induce people to all the other virtues" [SpEx 146].

Virtues, according to the *Spiritual Exercises*, are thus first-hand gifts of God, like other graces. By means of careful discernment and practice, that is, purposeful acts flowing from discernment, these gifts can be received fully. Progress in virtues means that graces received in the Spiritual Exercises as well as attributes of Christ that were noticed and asked for in prayer gradually turn into personal traits. The graces received during the Exercises are "fragile" and might become "lost" after the retreat. Virtues that emerge through the contemplation and assimilation of various attributes of Christ, however, seem to be able to "make up for" competencies that would be necessary for a more integrated apostolic life yet were not part of one's upbringing. Progress in virtues means that the graces received bear fruit in a resourceful, reliable, creative and integrated personality, suitable for apostolic life and carried by a deep humanity together with a deep spirituality.

The significance of virtues in the Ignatian vision can hardly be overemphasized. As we have seen, the assimilation of virtues is first of all a task of the novitiate: novices should "[apply] themselves to the pursuit of the true and solid virtues" [ConsCN C 260]. Yet the special attention to virtues is not at all limited to the novitiate. Quite the contrary: the quality of apostolic life is at stake. Virtues are "the means which unite the human instrument with God and so dispose it that it may be wielded well by his divine hand" [ConsCN C 813]. The assimilation of virtues is one of the basic Ignatian practices on the way of reaching personal maturity that can sustain a fruitful apostolic life:

> Thus it appears that care should be taken in general that all the members of the Society devote themselves to the solid and perfect virtues and to spiritual pursuits, and attach greater importance to them than to learning and other natural and human gifts. For these interior gifts are necessary to make those exterior means efficacious for the end which is being sought. [ConsCN C 813]

Reintegrating the use of virtues into a contemporary Ignatian spirituality and Jesuit formation does not necessarily imply a more frequent usage of the word, or even extra sessions about the history and the philosophical background of this concept. The basic information that is to be found in the *Spiritual Exercises* and the *Constitutions* would of course have to be better known, and the intimate relationship between the practice of prayer and virtues should be more explored. Yet Ignatius seems to insist on addressing the reality that the word conveys, that is, the values that can be expressed by way of talking, interacting with each other, going about when working or while reposing, and also the insight that no moving forward on the pathway to God that is Jesuit life is possible without acquiring the human capacities that allow these values to be expressed. A formation culture that can develop a vocabulary rich in virtues can be helpful in maintaining a dynamic of progressing, a sense of being on the move, a hope that change is possible, and it can highlight what is at stake in prayer, while offering non-aggressive yet relatively unambiguous means for shaping the life of a community.

The *Constitutions* do not make clear which particular virtues are to be acquired. There is a detailed enumeration of the necessary qualities of the Superior General [ConsCN C 723–35], the second quality being "that he be a person whose example in all the virtues will be a help to the other members of the Society" [ConsCN C 725]. The texts list charity, genuine humility, freedom from inordinate affections, circumspection in speaking and many other personality traits that sum up a rather descriptive profile. The list is worth studying because the characteristics also apply to Provincials and other superiors [ConsCN C 811] and, as commentators point out, probably portray the ideal Jesuit as depicted by Ignatius.

Novices, however, are not confronted with such a list of virtues. There is no list in Part III of the *Constitutions*. Only obedience and poverty are pointed out specifically, and to these we might add some implicit virtues that are required by various exercises, for example those that are contrary to a capital sin, such as diligence or generosity. In the end, we do not see a list, and the reason is most probably that the only true model is the person and the teaching of Christ. The desire and the need for particular virtues must be born in the personal prayer of the superior and of the members of the Jesuit community, as a result of prayerful encounters with the Gospel, evaluations of everyday experiences, feedback from others, and so forth. To focus the attention on one virtue or another is a matter of discernment, and one of the roles of spiritual direction is to help such discernment: "they will tell [...] all their virtues, with a pure desire to be directed if in anything they have gone astray" [ConsCN C 263]. Virtues authenticate and foster the personal progress on the Ignatian pathway to God just as graces authenticate and foster the dynamic of the Exercises.

✠ 4 ✠

# Hermeneutical Principles

The common objective of the preliminary studies above, each covering rather different topics, was to lay the groundwork for a more deeply rooted contemporary reception of the *Constitutions*. Although complex issues were treated only briefly, it has still been possible to summarize a number of theses that can orient our further explorations:

1. The *Constitutions* will hardly become more relevant in our everyday life unless we can grasp how they foster a dynamic of human and spiritual progress, which in turn is referred to in the text by the terminology of helping to advance on a pathway to God.
2. The dynamic of Jesuit life will remain a merely abstract concept unless Ignatian spirituality and contemporary insights about the human being can be integrated so as to promote a development of contemporary Ignatian anthropology. The Ignatian pathway to God implies an anthropology that emphasizes the relationship with God yet integrates other fundamental dimensions of human life, and is thus potentially capable of bridging the gap between the realm of spirituality and that of contemporary psychology.
3. The *Constitutions* will remain difficult to comprehend until the contemporary relevance of some key expressions can be brought to light, rendering the Ignatian vocabulary more suitable for addressing contemporary formation issues.

All three statements concern the interpretation of the *Constitutions,* and therefore it will be useful to clarify how they relate to the principles of interpreting the *Constitutions* as established by earlier Ignatian scholarship. The critical examination and, if necessary, rephrasing of these principles will help us to avoid the risk of engaging in a mere "spiritual conversation" with the text[1] that would be based on

1 Coupeau, *From Inspiration to Invention,* p. 79, see also the whole excellent

unsupported presuppositions and a flawed methodology. We present six basic hermeneutical principles, based partly on research conducted in recent decades and partly on the results of our preliminary studies.

## Pathway and Progress

The first hermeneutical principle is that Parts III to VI of the *Constitutions*—the sections that discuss Jesuit formation and the personal life of Jesuits with final vows—is a text for giving practical help to those responsible for formation and to Jesuits themselves about advancing in Jesuit life, that is, making progress on a pathway to God according to the Institute of the Society. The expression "pathway to God" remains to be explicated in greater detail, which presupposes a more intimate familiarity with the text and a more attuned attention to the dynamic of Jesuit life. We assume that the text, when better understood, will make Jesuit formation more helpful for those in formation, and that the opposite will also be true: what proves to be helpful in the practice of formation will shed light on the text itself. The relationship between the *Constitutions* and the "dynamic of the Jesuit life" is thus analogical to the relationship between the text of the *Spiritual Exercises* and the already familiar dynamic of the Exercises.

Consequently, the practice of Jesuit formation is the privileged terrain for interpreting the *Constitutions*, since that is where first-hand experience of progress on the pathway to God can be gained. This hermeneutical principle does not seem to have received sufficient attention in the recent past. J. Carlos Coupeau notes that earlier commentaries concentrated mainly on the historical origins of the *Constitutions*, but he "wishes to move beyond" historical studies in his book so as to give priority to how readers "engage the text in light of their own experience".[2] This hermeneutical shift is both reinforced and further clarified by our preliminary studies. To interpret the text in the light of the experience of the reader is indeed necessary, and the reader's experience must extend to a well-defined reality, the practice of Jesuit formation and awareness of its unique dynamic of progress. This is the particular perspective

section on the history of the interpretation of the *Constitutions*, *ibid.*, pp. 1–80.

2 *Ibid.*, pp. 79–80.

that can bring about a new quality of understanding just as such an understanding emerges when the reader of the *Spiritual Exercises* has personal experience of its spiritual dynamic, either because of having done or—what is even more helpful—having given a personally directed retreat.

The *Constitutions* will thus be considered to be a *handbook* that deals with the fostering of a particular spiritual and psychological process of growth, in many aspects analogical to that of the *Spiritual Exercises* that fosters a characteristic spiritual dynamic.[3] As we will see later, this definition does not mean to deny the partial validity of the more common view that whereas the *Exercises* deal with individuals and spirituality, the *Constitutions* treat organizational and institutional issues. The Preamble of the *Constitutions* explains that before issues concerning the entire apostolic body, the question of the progress of individuals has to be dealt with: "what occurs first in the order of execution pertains to the individual members, in regard to their admission, progress *(aprouecharlos)* and distribution into the vineyard of Christ our Lord; it is from this consideration that we shall begin" [ConsCN C 135].

A further consequence of the first hermeneutical principle is that it can be considered as an answer to the question about the literary genre of the *Constitutions*. Earlier research repeatedly raised the question of the right approach to this text. Is it meant to be read as a legal text, or as spiritual or "wisdom"[4] literature? Do general hermeneutical principles of literary "classics" apply to it, so that one should let the text "speak for itself" as a rhetorical piece?[5] All these approaches are justified, and even necessary to a certain degree, yet in the case of Parts III–VI, they must be seen as subordinated to the "handbook genre". The varying of styles indicates a concern to use a range of suitable linguistic tools in order to be of help to individuals desirous of progress in Jesuit life.[6]

3 S. Decloux SJ, "Las Constitutiones, 'Manual de formación'", *Manresa* 66 (1994), pp. 19–34.

4 H. Gray SJ, "What Kind of Document?", *The Way Supplement* 61 (Spring 1988), pp. 22–40.

5 This is J. Carlos Coupeau's starting point, *From Inspiration to Invention*, p. 80.

6 "Careful analysis of [up to six different] strata reveal that paragraphs contain a treasure embracing much more than commands: they show the purpose of the prescriptions, the spiritual principle, the attitude, the situation, the content, the

## Mystagogy

A second hermeneutical principle indicates that the purpose of the *Constitutions* is mystagogy, that is, to introduce the person who starts his Jesuit life journey into the mystery of the Holy Trinity.[7] Recently, José M. Rambla[8] applied this expression to the *Constitutions*, thus rephrasing the conviction, repeatedly expressed by commentaries, that cooperation with God's activity should be considered to be at the heart of the *Constitutions*.[9]

The three divine persons, although not always consistently distinguished, are mentioned throughout the text. "God our Creator" and "our Creator and Lord" are the most frequent references. In particular, Part X, which according to Maurizio Costa is a key to interpreting the entire *Constitutions*, explains how "the means which unite the human instrument with God" [ConsCN C 813] are of primary importance for the Society in attaining its objective [see ConsCN C 812–14],[10] and how "natural means which equip the human instrument of God our Lord" can be put to use so that "we may cooperate with the divine grace" [ConsCN C 814].

The person of Christ is the pathway through which this objective can be reached. To follow Christ closely in as many details of his life as possible, and even to have the desires that he had, are the best means to prepare oneself for Jesuit life:

> to how great a degree it helps and profits in the spiritual life *(ayuda y aprouecha en la vida espiritual)* [...] to accept and desire with all

means, and the method, all intermingled". This is how J. C. Coupeau summarizes the essay by Ignacio Iparraguirre (*Orientaciones para la vivificación de la letra*), see *From Inspiration to Invention*, p. 56.

7 "Las Constituciones: son una iniciación (o mistagogía) análogas a los Ejercicios." See J. M. Rambla SJ, "El hombre de las Constituciones como prolongación del hombre de los ejercicios", *Manresa* 70 (1997/4), p. 359–72.

8 *Ibid.*, p. 363. The expression is applied to the *Spiritual Exercises* by J. Melloni, *La mistagogía de los Ejercicios* (Sal Terrae: Bilbao-Santander, 2002)

9 J. de Guibert SJ, *The Jesuits: Their Spiritual Doctrine and Practice* (Chicago: Loyola University Press, 1964), p. 147.

10 M. Costa, *Legge religiosa e discernimento spirituale nelle Costituzioni della Compagnia di Gesù* (Brescia: Paideia Editrice, 1973). Cited by Coupeau, *From Inspiration to Invention*, p. 57.

> possible energy whatever Christ our Lord has loved and embraced. [...] They [the candidates] desire to resemble and imitate in some manner our Creator and Lord Jesus Christ, by putting on his garb and uniform, since it was for our spiritual profit *(por nuestro maior prouecho espiritual)* that he clothed himself as he did. For he gave us an example that in all things possible to us we might seek, with the aid of his grace, to imitate and follow him, since he is the way *(la vía)* which leads men to life. Therefore the candidate should be asked whether he finds himself with such desires, which are so salutary and fruitful for the perfection of his soul. [General Examen, ConsCN C 101]

The Holy Spirit is shown to be eliciting the desire to grow in charity and in love and to be giving shape to these desires. The Preamble to the *Constitutions* explains that the mysterious work of the Spirit precedes the help that the *Constitutions* themselves will be able to give: "What helps most toward this end must be, more than any exterior constitution, the interior law of charity and love which the Holy Spirit writes and imprints upon hearts" [ConsCN C 134, see also 219, 414, 624, 697–701]. In the background of the text, we can thus recognize the Trinitarian mysticism of Ignatius[11] and the familiar image of a God who continues to labor for the good of the human being [cf. SpEx 236]. To attribute the progress on the pathway to God to human effort rather than the initiative of God would be to misinterpret the *Constitutions*. Jesuit life is to be seen as inspired by the Holy Spirit to move toward God even though one is not always consciously aware of this; this is rather like what is sometimes the case while doing the Spiritual Exercises.[12]

Our preliminary studies reinforce the hermeneutical principle of mystagogy, and urge its more consistent application. The point is not simply to treat the *Constitutions* as a text of spirituality as opposed to a legal work.[13] Precisely the mystagogical character of the text explains that even though numerous parts of the *Constitutions* are suitable for personal meditation,[14] many Jesuits who do try to read them with a

11 de Guibert SJ, *The Jesuits*, pp. 50 ff.

12 *Ibid.*, p. 571.

13 "our presentation of the *Constitutions* [...] envision[s] a Spirit-infused reading ('de type sapientiel')." de Jaer, *Together for Mission*, p. 4.

14 W. A. Barry SJ, *Our Way of Proceeding* (Saint Louis: The Institute of Jesuit Sources, 1997).

desire for spiritual profit end up admitting a lingering sense of a lack of satisfaction. The *Constitutions*, like the *Spiritual Exercises*, is first and foremost not a spiritual reading but a work of mystagogy, meaning that it contains mainly a *methodology* of how to help others and oneself on the pathway to God. Writings of spirituality and theology make an impact on the reader through reading and meditating the text; the *Constitutions* do not exclude this but make an impact first of all by means of a series of exercises. The most suitable way to discover the meaning of the *Constitutions* is by engaging with the exercises and the dispositions presented by the text.

Mystagogy means that the person whose role is to help the progression has a similar position to that of the giver of the Spiritual Exercises. In both cases, a triple relationship develops between God who initiates and drives the progression, the person who "progresses" toward God, entering more and more deeply into the mystery of God, and the facilitator, or leader,[15] who helps the progression. This person—the giver of the Exercises, the Novice Master, superior, or spiritual director—has to consider the relationship that unfolds between God and the progressing person in order to be able to help. The *Constitutions* as a handbook of mystagogy can thus be expected to explicate the particular responsibilities of the Jesuit in formation and that of the formator, much as the *Exercises* explain what can depend on the exercitant and what should happen in the accompaniment; for example, when the director should be more active and when it is more advisable to remain in the background.

Mystagogy, because the initiative of God is primary, demands constant discernment, and the facilitator of the progression has a special responsibility in this discernment. Since the person who is making progress is normally exposed to the various "spirits" helping or opposing the progression, the facilitator's role in finding clarity is indispensable. A formator who knows the characteristics of the various sections of the Ignatian pathway to God can help to discern realities as different as enthusiasm for an apostolic ideal, unconscious need to conform to others, dull routine without spiritual liveliness, fear of failing an exam,

15 Etymologically, mystagogy is the action of conducting (*agein*) a person who has been initiated (*mystes*).

or the intention to serve and love God. The clarity that can result from such distinctions is as fundamental to progressing in Jesuit life as it is during the *Exercises*.

The principle of mystagogy is so significant that it can help in assessing the reception of the *Constitutions* at a given moment of history. If Jesuit life develops according to the dynamic of progression on the pathway to God as conceived by the *Constitutions*, then any Jesuit who desires that "through him God our Lord may be glorified and served" [ConsCN C 595] will tend to recognize with genuine gratitude how the *Constitutions* have helped to foster his progress toward his goal.

## Incorporation

The first two hermeneutical principles for interpreting the *Constitutions* were introduced by way of analogy to the *Spiritual Exercises*. The analogy, however, has its limits. While the Exercises last for thirty days at most, Jesuit life can be expected to last for decades. While the Exercises can be given in a carefully chosen environment, the context of Jesuit life can change constantly. Jesuit formation and Jesuit life cannot be regarded as a lifelong retreat since the spiritual dimension is constantly challenged by other important aspects of preparing for, or being engaged in, apostolic life. Furthermore, while both texts aim to foster personal progress, this is not the only objective of the *Constitutions*.

The pathway to God, as the Institute of the Society conceives it, differs fundamentally from the path of the Spiritual Exercises since, apart from a greater spiritual awareness and increased familiarity with the persons of the Trinity, progressing in Jesuit life also implies being rooted in the reality of a community, adopting a way of proceeding, and becoming integrated into an institutional Society that has its own apostolic purposes. This is a third hermeneutical criterion for interpreting the *Constitutions*: we can call it the principle of incorporation. Commentaries often note how the principle of incorporation is reflected in the *Constitutions*' very structure, which was unique at the time: as opposed to earlier Rules for religious communities, the text is not organized by major topics but according to the successive phases of formation, which correspond to the consecutive stages of incorporation into the Society's apostolic body.[16]

If we consider Jesuit formation as a process of incorporation, we may sense a certain inevitable compromise between two conflicting interests, one being the progression on a personal spiritual path and the other the engagement in the mission of the institutional Society. Some doubts may even remain about the *Constitutions* favoring the institutional perspective of the Society at the expense of the needs of the individual. Whether such doubts are there or not, in an individualistic cultural environment that is quite skeptical about institutions, the reception of the *Constitutions* could be considerably harmed by the implicit presupposition that the help offered to the individual person (as by means of the *Spiritual Exercises*) is in contrast to an institutional approach (as represented by the *Constitutions*). Incorporation as a hermeneutical principle needs to be given a contemporary explication that takes this sensitivity into consideration.

In the text of the *Constitutions*, two recurring metaphors refer to the two realities, the individual and the institutionally organized apostolic community. One of these metaphors is *progressing on a pathway*, which we have already discussed, and the other is the *body*, the body of the Society at the service of God. Like the metaphor of the path, the body as a metaphor also originates in the times prior to the Society's birth, in the conversations of the first companions deliberating their collective future:

> in as much as our most kind and affectionate Lord had deigned to gather us together and unite us, men so spiritually weak and from such diverse geographical and cultural backgrounds, we ought not to split apart what God has gathered and united; on the contrary, we ought day by day to strengthen and stabilize our union, rendering ourselves one body with special concern for each other, in order to effect the greater spiritual good of our fellow men. [Delib. 3]

God's recognized intention and the greater benefit of souls require the group to remain united. In accordance with this, the *Constitutions* include among the goals sustaining the unity and health of the apostolic body, and the metaphor of the body is given as much weight as that of

16 See for example: F. Roustang, "Le Corps de la Compagnie" in *Christus* No. 51 (Juillet 1966), pp. 332–45.

progress. Whereas the *Deliberation* indicated a possible—or perhaps inevitable—tension between these two aspects, the *Constitutions* aim to articulate their relationship:

> Moreover, while the consideration which comes first and has more weight in the order of our intention regards the body of the Society as a whole *(lo que toca al uniuersal cuerpo de la Compañía)*, whose unity, good government, and preservation in well-being for the greater divine glory are primarily in view, nevertheless, in as much as this body is made up of its members, and what occurs first in the order of execution pertains to the individual members, in regard to their admission, progress *(lo que toca a los particulares, assí en admittirlos como en aprouecharlos)* and distribution into the vineyard of Christ our Lord, it is from this consideration that we shall begin. [ConsCN C 135]

Thus, the *Constitutions* do not talk about opposing goals only to be reconciled through some strained compromise but rather about two goals that mutually presuppose each other. The primary objective is the well-being of the body of the Society, and therefore it is imperative that each member get the best possible help in his personal progress. Personal progress, on the other hand, comprises growth and freedom in all dimensions of life, and therefore it is beneficial for the individual to belong to the Society that fosters interpersonal relationships, commitment to substantial values and, above all, an intimate relationship with God. As we will see, at various stages of the formation process the development of this mutually beneficial relationship between the individual and the community has to be verified and considered as a condition for moving to the next phase. Thus in the *Constitutions*, we find no evidence that while the *Spiritual Exercises* help individuals, the *Constitutions* would abandon the good of the individual and have a preference for the institutional and organizational needs of the apostolic community. Likewise, we would be wrong to look for a conception of a personal progress that would be purely spiritual, without implying the relationship with others, especially with Jesuit companions, or the passion for the apostolic mission of the body of the Society.

Personal progress and incorporation into the apostolic body are so intimately associated with each other that upon entering, this characteristic of the Society of Jesus has to be consciously approved. Jesuit life is for him "who judges his incorporation into this Society to be conducive to the greater divine glory and more salutary for his own conscience" [General Examen, ConsCN C 98]. Progress in accordance with the Institute of the Society means more ease with finding God in all things, greater inner freedom in Christ and a deeper sense of readiness to accept a mission as an "incorporated" member of the Society. Incorporation as a hermeneutical principle means that the two interconnected objectives of the *Constitutions*, helping individual progress on the pathway of Jesuit life and sustaining the apostolic body of the Society for the greater glory of God, mutually presuppose and reinforce each other.

## Human Maturity

Growth in human maturity does not seem to appear among standard interpretational criteria of the *Constitutions*. This is understandable since in the past, ever-changing psychological trends and simplified theories about human growth often hindered rather than helped the reception of the rich human and spiritual heritage of the Ignatian—or, more generally speaking, Christian—tradition. Still, with a contemporary mindset, one cannot bypass the question whether the pathway to God as presented in the *Constitutions* is also a way toward greater human maturity.

The *Constitutions*, although a fundamental document of the Society of Jesus that relies on the authority of St Ignatius, would be impossible to interpret with the tacit or explicit assumption that its regulations oppose growth in human maturity. Particular details of the text will be only understood to the extent that they can be seen as contributing to human maturity. A conception of religious life that is satisfied with "giving up the world" for the sake of Christ, and never asks the question of how the strenuous yet real growing opportunities offered by the world—such as starting a family, raising children, assuming career responsibilities and the like—will be replaced in Jesuit life, would hardly contribute to an interpretation of the *Constitutions* that contemporary companions would find helpful.

The *Constitutions* address the issue of personal maturity in the context of the individual's suitability for Jesuit life, which requires a great variety of human abilities. The development of personal, intellectual and spiritual capacities to their fullest potential makes it possible for members to work fruitfully in the mission of the Society: "it has seemed to us necessary, or at least highly expedient, that those who will enter the Society [i.e. make final vows], be persons of good life and sufficient learning for the aforementioned work" [ConsCN C 308]. Framing the question of human maturity as a hermeneutical criterion is thus not simply a contemporary cultural requirement but is also in accordance with the Ignatian text. Our preliminary studies confirm and consolidate this emphasis by helping to dissociate the concept of human growth from arbitrarily chosen psychological theories. By means of the relationship model of Ignatian anthropology, human growth can be conceived as being solidly rooted within Ignatian spirituality as an obvious dimension of the Ignatian vision of the human being. Accordingly, the interpretation of the Constitutions is valid to the extent that it fosters human maturity as much as possible, as understood within the framework of Ignatian anthropology.

The principle can thus be formulated simply but requires a more detailed explanation because, by referring to the relationship model of Ignatian anthropology, it implies the simultaneous realization of several objectives.

1. The *Constitutions* help to diminish the power of immature forms of thinking and behavior—as in capital sins—so that these can be gradually replaced by mature behavioral patterns or virtues.

2. Help is given to develop competencies which enable a Jesuit to connect with his environment, relating not only to God but also to objects, persons and values according to what is necessary for an apostolic vocation to the Society.

3. The *Constitutions* help candidates remain free, "indifferent" [SpEx 23] with regard to the three basic motivational sources that the "world" can offer, by providing support to diminish disordered attachments. In order to achieve this, Jesuit formation prepares the individual for the potential absence of satisfactions from the "world" by fostering growth in the virtue of poverty, by helping candidates to endure "reproaches or contempt"—including the lower-degree form, the lack of appreciation from others—and by helping them to develop humility.

4. Help is provided so that the "true self" that develops in a personal relationship with and service of God can integrate the other dimensions

of personality, and consequently the person can live a life that is contemplative even while active. This is how the four basic dimensions of the human personality can remain active, even in demanding and complex situations, as a coherent and integrated whole, directed toward the greater glory of God and the benefit of human beings, while remaining open to experiences of consolation that can sustain a Jesuit life fully committed to mission.

## The Parts and the Whole

The voluminous text of the *Constitutions* does not fully match the self-imposed criterion of being "complete [...], clear [and] brief" [ConsCN C 136], and its understanding was hindered from the outset by details that did not seem to be particularly significant, important or universally valid. Commentaries thus tend to emphasize the principle that specific details should be interpreted in the light of the entire text,[17] and that any reasoning narrowly built upon a particular detail but not consistent with the *Constitutions* as a whole is invalid. This simple hermeneutical principle is implied in the text itself: "The purpose of the Constitutions is to aid the body of the Society as a whole and its individual members [...], being singly and as a whole conducive to the purpose just stated" [ConsCN C 136]. The understanding of the meaning of particular details is to be sought in their correlation with the entire text.

This hermeneutical principle is without doubt necessary, but it is not very practicable, because the relationship of a detail to the whole can be difficult to determine. For example, if this principle were to be applied to the *Spiritual Exercises*, the question could arise whether midnight meditations [SpEx 72] correspond to the purpose of the Exercises as a whole, namely, ordering one's life, seeking and finding God's will and attaining the salvation of the soul [SpEx 1]. One might remark that the salvation of the soul can be well attained without midnight prayer exercises, and therefore this detail could be considered as an instance of excessive asceticism that has no contemporary

17 See for example: R. Jurado SJ, "La Formación en la Compañía de Jesús según las Constituciones. Finalidad y métodos" in *Manresa* vol. 55 (1983), p. 172.

relevance. Only someone sufficiently experienced in actually doing or even giving the Exercises will be able to respond that midnight meditations can be truly helpful in certain situations since they can intensify the dynamic of the first week and foster the reception of the graces that had been asked for. Consequently, the concrete detail of the text—the instruction concerning the midnight meditation [SpEx 72]—does indeed serve the purpose of the Exercises as a whole, but this convergence between the detail and the entire text remains hidden unless one develops a fine awareness of the dynamic of the Exercises. Particular details of the *Constitutions* likewise risk remaining meaningless for those unfamiliar with the dynamic of progression in Jesuit life. Unless we recognize how specific details can actually contribute to the ultimate goal, we will probably underestimate their significance and neglect them. Interpreting details in the context of the whole is therefore a legitimate principle, although a superficial application of this principle can easily lead to unfounded conclusions.

As a consequence of our preliminary studies, we can offer a more exact and more practically useful definition of the hermeneutical principle concerning the details and the text as a whole: *particular details of the Constitutions serve the purpose of fostering a dynamic of progression which implies fairly well-defined criteria to be met at the end of each phase of the pathway to God.* Accordingly, the argument that a particular exercise—for example in the description of the novitiate—should not be implemented because it does not correspond to "real" Jesuit life is hermeneutically flawed. It is true that specific details might seem negligible or perplexing in the perspective of the ultimate objective of the *Constitutions*. These very elements can nevertheless still be significant within the unique context of the novitiate, since they can intensify a dynamic of progression, and help bring forth the fruits anticipated and hoped for during this time of probation. The central metaphor of the pathway enables us to consider not only the final destination but also the milestones and the special characteristics of each phase, rather like when giving the Spiritual Exercises. On this condition only can one discern whether in a particular case an Ignatian instruction can be expected to be helpful or not.

## Fundamental Ignatian Works as One Œuvre

Many of the above principles, which should clarify the presuppositions that will be at work when in the second part of this book we explore more closely the text of the *Constitutions,* assume that the understanding of this text is intrinsically linked to that of the *Spiritual Exercises.* This assumption may provoke the question whether our criteria comply with contemporary philosophical hermeneutics. Will the countless references to the *Exercises* not move our attention away from the *Constitutions,* which is to be studied as an original work for its own sake? Do the *Spiritual Exercises* not constitute a hermeneutical key that is external,[18] preventing the reader from entering the unique world[19] of the *Constitutions* without prejudices, relying on his or her own personal experiences?

Our preliminary studies make it clear that the experience of the reader must take a central role in the interpretation of the *Constitutions,* and must include especially an experience of a dynamic of progression in Jesuit life. This assertion is in line with the general hermeneutical principles of interpreting a literary work. Difficulties emerge when the unique genre of the *Constitutions* is taken into consideration, because, as we have seen, one faces something like a hermeneutical circle: understanding the text presupposes a certain familiarity with a dynamic of progress in Jesuit life which in turn presupposes familiarity with the text of the *Constitutions.* References to the *Exercises* serve first of all to demonstrate this particular hermeneutical challenge. In the case of the Exercises we are already accustomed to the fact that some familiarity with their dynamic will be necessary in order to begin to understand the

18 This is a critical remark made by J. Carlos Coupeau, questioning one of those interpretations that are based on the *Spiritual Exercises:* "Iparraguirre preferred the *Spiritual Exercises* to the *Constitutions* as an external hermeneutical key". Coupeau, *From Inspiration to Invention,* p. 56.

19 "For what must be interpreted in a text is a *proposed world* which I could inhabit and wherein I could project one of my ownmost possibilities. That is what I call the world of the text, the world proper to *this* unique text." See "The Theory of Interpretation" in P. Ricoeur, *Hermeneutics and the Human Sciences: Essays on Language, Action and Interpretation* (Cambridge: Cambridge University Press, 1981), p. 142.

Ignatian text. A deeper understanding can follow when insights taken from the text are applied in practice, and having evaluated its practical usefulness, one can go back to the text again. This is how the horizon[20] of the reader of the text can be enlarged through an encounter with a major piece of St Ignatius's writing. In a similar way, the *Constitutions* can be expected mainly to talk to the reader who is already somewhat acquainted with the Ignatian pathway to God. We can assume that such a reader will discover new meaning in the *Constitutions* in an abundance as impressive as that encountered by the reader of the *Spiritual Exercises* who is ready to regard his experience of accompanying others in the light of the Ignatian text, and the text in the light of the experience made by listening to people talk about their prayer.

Without sufficient experience of a dynamic of progress according to the pathway to God, the experience of the reader can hinder rather than foster the understanding of the text. For example, the crisis of Christianity in Western cultures can give rise to nostalgia for more disciplined former times which in turn can make the *Constitutions* appear to be an ascetic methodology for training Christ's soldiers who go to spend their lives in "complete obedience" [ConsCN C 284]. Those, however, who have a perhaps unconscious longing to break free from a rigidly regimented childhood environment may be inclined to hear only one part of a sentence of the *Constitutions*: "what helps most [. . .] must be, more than any exterior constitution, the interior law of charity and love which the Holy Spirit writes and imprints upon hearts" [ConsCN C 134]. Such caricatured extremes illustrate the prominent role that personal experience plays in the interpretation of the *Constitutions*. They can help explain why, especially at an early phase of the process of interpretation, when a sufficiently refined understanding of the concept of a dynamic progress in Jesuit life has not yet emerged, "external" sources of information and of experience can be valuable, especially when parallels are as abundant as in the case of the *Spiritual Exercises*.

Therefore, as a sixth basic hermeneutical principle, we affirm that the text of the *Constitutions* is to be regarded as a constitutive element of a corpus of fundamental Ignatian writings. *Essential Ignatian sources such*

20 H.-G. Gadamer, *Truth and Method* (London: Bloomsbury Academic, 2013), originally published in German as *Wahrheit und Methode* (Tübingen: Mohr, 1960).

*as the Spiritual Exercises or the Autobiography will not be considered as hermeneutical keys that are external to the Constitutions.* In the case of the *Spiritual Exercises*, the majority of commentaries accept this principle,[21] and in the case of the *Autobiography*, we have the testimony of the first companions. When Ignatius finally agreed "to narrate all that occurred in his soul until now", Jeronimo Nadal, whose mission it was to put the *Constitutions* into effect by visiting Jesuit communities around Europe, concluded that "the Father could do nothing of greater benefit for the Society than this, and that this was truly to found the Society".[22] The spirit of the Society is carried by the totality of the essential Ignatian works. They complement one another, and references within this circle of writings can be seen, from a hermeneutical perspective, as references to a single literary *œuvre*.

21 A. M. de Aldama SJ, "¿Los ejercicios espirituales son el alma de las constituciones?" in *Recherches Ignatiennes Communications*, III /1, (1974).

22 Introduction by Louis Gonçalves da Câmara, 1, 4.

# Part II

# *The Constitutions* as a Handbook of Formation

Having spelled out some of the presuppositions of a fruitful contemporary interpretation of the *Constitutions,* we can move on to the consideration of a number of relevant segments, section by section and at times paragraph by paragraph. Remaining close to the Ignatian text while taking into consideration later adaptations will be facilitated by the fact that each clarification, modification and abrogation to the *Constitutions* approved by general congregations is either indicated in notes or has become a part of the *Complementary Norms.* Our exploration of the text will focus on the question of how Jesuits can be helped to advance on the Ignatian pathway to God, and what growth, what kind of transformation can be expected during the years of formation. We hope to remain focused on this overall perspective, yet develop details sufficiently in order to put some color on the sketch that we have established earlier about the Ignatian pathway to God.

We do not try to leave aside those passages that challenge our current ways of thinking or proceeding in formation matters. At times, our preliminary studies can help to make sense of these details of the Ignatian text. Quite often, however, the text only says that a particular practice is important for some reason. In such cases there is much room for creativity as to the actual embodiment of the given practice in a contemporary cultural context and its reinterpretation with the purpose of providing real help to those concerned. In the following chapters, we include some of these passages in the hope that the reader will ask the question "But how can one do that in a contemporary cultural context?" Such questions will hopefully prepare the way for an exchange of best practices among formators, and illustrate the hermeneutical principle that we have explored above: understanding the *Constitutions* will be greatly promoted when those actually applying the Ignatian instructions can begin to exchange their experiences, thus enlightening the interpretation of particular details of the text, as has been our approach to the *Spiritual Exercises* for the past fifty years.

✢ 5 ✢

# Part III of the Constitutions: The Novitiate as a Probation

## Preconditions

Part III of the *Constitutions* begins the description of the first phase of Jesuit life with a brief yet surprising reference to Part I, which discusses admission to the novitiate. It implies that those who have been admitted can be considered as called by God to join the Society: "with regard to the admission of those whom God our Lord calls to our Institute by giving them suitable ability for it" [ConsCN C 243]. Ignatius, who seemingly adopts the approach of his time, appears to ignore the cautious and realistic contemporary question as to whether a particular candidate is really and truly called by God or whether some other motivations could have been at play. Could we indeed be sure, after a successful admission process, that "God our Lord calls [the candidate]", simply because he appeared to have the necessary qualities for becoming a Jesuit and thus his application to the Society has been approved? Can a candidate's vocation be said to be from God simply because he appears to have all the prerequisites for being a good Jesuit?

The question is misleading because it implies an abstract conception of a vocation, that is, it presupposes that the vocation to be a Jesuit is something like an attribute or an entity that someone either does or does not receive from God. Such an understanding of a vocation would be difficult to verify upon entrance—even though the most clearly impedimental character traits would obviously stand out—since it would refer to something "deeper" than what a couple of conversations and psychological tests could reveal. In the context, however, of Jesuit life regarded as making progress on a pathway to God, a perceived call to the Society which has been approved after an examination process can be compared analogically to beginning the Spiritual Exercises. The surprising link between being called by God and having the ability to be a Jesuit can thus become a quite helpful and practical insight concerning the mysterious reality of a religious vocation.

The analogy between the Exercises and the Ignatian pathway to God can inspire one to regard a person entering the novitiate in the same way as someone who is just beginning the Spiritual Exercises. In the case of the Exercises, there is no sure way to tell whether a person will be able to proceed until the end of the fourth week. Seemingly well-qualified candidates for the Exercises can end up running into insurmountable obstacles or can become content with having done the first or the first two weeks, while others might receive unexpected graces that, astonishing even the giver of the Exercises, prove to be immensely helpful for their advancement. Once a person has been admitted to do the Exercises, the proper question is not whether his or her choice to do the Exercises was inspired by God or some other cause played a role. The question that will be more helpful is how the person can best dispose himself or herself to meet the Lord, who will not fail to be there for him or her during the privileged days of the Spiritual Exercises.

The analogy with the Exercises also emphasizes that having suitable abilities is all the more important before the actual beginning of the progression. The Spiritual Exercises are not for everyone, and Jesuit life is not for everyone either. Just like other spiritualities, both presuppose specific personal abilities. Candidates for the Spiritual Exercises should be carefully examined about "their age, education and ability" [SpEx 18]. If the necessary qualities seem to be lacking, it will be more beneficial to provide help in other ways: "it is preferable to give such a one some [. . .] light exercises" [ibid.]. Likewise, as to candidates to the Society, "much thought should be given so as to admit only those who possess the qualifications required for this Institute, for the divine glory" [ConsCN C 144]. Candidates received in the Society must "not only be tested for a long time before incorporation into it but also be well known before they are admitted to the probation" [ConsCN C 190]. In both cases, the beginning of the actual progression will have to depend on the discernment of someone who knows the individual in question well, but who is also knowledgeable about the dynamic of progression that will be proposed to the person. This person, who also takes into consideration the opinion of others in the case of admission to the Society, will have the right perspective for saying whether good progression can be expected. The person, however, who is about to begin the Exercises or Jesuit life can already be intensively stirred by different spirits, and experience doubts and fears mingling with trust in God and the desire to proceed. In this sense, the informed opinion of one or several unbiased persons can correspond more to the reality of what can be expected to happen than the opinion of the person himself who, at the onset of a spiritual dynamic, does not yet have the clarity of vision that can be trusted to appear later on as the very fruit of having been engaged in a dynamic of progression.

An important indicator of what can be expected when beginning to progress according either to the *Exercises* or the *Constitutions* is how strongly the person desires to go forward and whether he will be ready to engage in what is being proposed to him: "exercitants should be given, each one, as much as they are willing to dispose themselves to receive, for their greater help and progress" [SpEx 18]. According to the *Spiritual Exercises,* someone who does not have a strong desire to seek God, "a person who wants help to get some instruction and reach a certain level of peace of soul" [ibid.], should not be made to enter the dynamic of the Exercises but should instead receive some other kind of help that is more appropriate for his or her disposition. Likewise, the *Constitutions* emphasize that only those who truly desire to do so should begin to follow Christ in the Society of Jesus: "Therefore the candidate should be asked whether he finds himself with such desires, which are so salutary and fruitful for the perfection of his soul" [General Examen, ConsCN C 101]. Candidates should be helped to go beyond abstract considerations about their vocation by paying attention to their desires with respect to Christ. The desire to follow Christ, even though it may well coexist with an awareness of personal weaknesses or even with not such holy motivations, will be a more reliable sign of a personal vocation than fears and doubts about the future or a superficial enthusiasm: "Where through human weakness and personal misery the candidate does not experience in himself such ardent desires in our Lord, he should be asked whether he has any desires to experience them"

[ConsCN C 102]. This question must be discerned by the candidate, but once it has been faced, and the necessary qualities are seen to be present, the candidate can be considered apt for entering a dynamic of progression according to the Institute of the Society.

Vocation, then, has two dimensions. The first can be discerned before beginning the progression in Jesuit life, while the second emerges during the actual experience of progression. The first is a matter of an initial choice based on discernment and sanctioned by the Provincial, who has the right to admit a candidate, while the latter is a matter of being satisfied with what one discovers while progressing. In other words, the first dimension of vocation discernment is everything up to the final decision to be admitted to the Society, while the second is the confirmation of this decision. Confirmation, by definition, can only happen after an initial decision that has been taken seriously, trusting that God will be present for the individual who has decided to engage himself in the dynamic progression that is Jesuit formation. The *Constitutions* do not encourage a conception of the novitiate that focuses on the question of having a vocation or not, but they do lay great weight on confirmation, which explains why novices are consistently referred to as "those in probation" *(los que están en probación)*. Once the novitiate has begun, the right question to ask is whether the probation will confirm the initial decision, which is considered as a response to the calling of God.

The concept of discerning Jesuit vocation as a two-step process, composed of an initial decision made before entering and a subsequent confirmation, can be illustrated by what we do quite naturally when giving the Spiritual Exercises. Once the Exercises have begun, the accompaniment does not focus on whether God is calling the person to do the Exercises. Even if the person happens to have serious doubts during the first days, the giver of the Exercises will trust the initial discernment and help the person to get moving, to become engaged in the Exercises in such a way that he or she can begin to receive the graces that will give sufficient confirmation of the goodness of the original decision. Only such trust in God's initiative and in the initial decision to begin will reveal those sources of grace that are likely to give abundant confirmation once actual progress begins. The expectation that "the Creator and Lord himself should communicate himself to the devout soul" [SpEx 15] can become reality in this second phase, which comes after the initial decision. Only in retrospect can one definitely say that the inspiration to do the Exercises had come from God, and that the initial feelings of doubt and fear were probably inevitable but not indicative of what would happen during the days of actually advancing according to the dynamic of the Exercises. Those who, despite their fears, focus on God, and begin the Exercises "by entering upon them with great spirit and generosity toward their Creator and Lord" [SpEx 5], are likely to make progress and to experience—although perhaps among difficult realizations and only temporary consolations—the new sources of "God's grace" [SpEx 2] that become accessible to them and manifest themselves in previously unknown ways.

A young Jesuit who has been accepted into the Society is to be regarded as being called by God "to our Institute" in a similar way. Only by considering the novitiate as a time of confirmation can the person entrust himself to God with the openness that is necessary for discovering new sources of grace and motivation. If a novice were encouraged to maintain a prolonged attitude of discernment even after beginning the novitiate, saying that it is uncertain whether God is calling him to be a Jesuit, he would run the risk of not committing himself fully to actually making progress on the Ignatian pathway to God, thus avoiding the only possible and realistic way of having his initial choice to enter confirmed or refuted. This is how the two years of probation can reveal, quite paradoxically but in much the same way as the first week of the *Exercises*, whether an initial inspiration to enter a proposed spiritual dynamic which had been examined and taken seriously as coming from God is in fact confirmed by the reality of progression. It is the actual experience of moving forward that can be evaluated in retrospect: have the changing and more or less intense spiritual experiences justified the efforts and the perseverance that had been necessary to cross harsh deserts or just survive the gloomy times of more ordinary desolations? An affirmative answer will mean that the person sees his vocation to Jesuit life as confirmed.

Considering those in the novitiate as being called by God does not justify in any way the imposition of a moral obligation that they stay even though they do not want to. Quite the contrary, the moral obligation weighs on the shoulders of the person who is accompanying the process: if, during an extended period, there are no signs of confirmation of the initial decision, the novice has to be dismissed. If, for example, a novice is "unable or unwilling to submit his own judgment" [ConsCN C 216] even despite patient help, then—as we will see—the dynamic of progress will not take effect, and confirmation of the initial decision will not be possible. Clear distinction between a decision made before entering the novitiate and confirmation during the time of the probation allows the question of confirmation to be taken as seriously as that of the decision. Enduring signs of inability to progress or unwillingness to do so are to be evaluated as a sign that the vocation to Jesuit life is not being confirmed—rather as similar signs in the first week of the Exercises are understood as indications that the person has not received the graces that would allow him fruitfully to enter the second week. In fact, the actual capacity to progress and the appearance of its fruits in the life of the individual and in the community gives a more accurate prediction concerning future stages of Jesuit life than a general sense of the human or even spiritual maturity of the person.

Beside the suitability and the desire of a candidate, a genuine calling is thus characterized by the onset of a dynamic of progression according to the pathway to God. Hence the imperative to empower those who are in formation to make progress, which is practically a synonym for "preserving" them in their vocation:

> also due consideration and provident care must be employed toward preserving in their vocation those who are being retained and tested in the houses or colleges and toward enabling them to make progress both in spirit and in virtues along the path of the divine service *(y en el aprouecharlos, para que de tal manera uayan adelante en la uía del diuino seruicio en espíritu y virtudes)*, in such a manner that care is also taken of the health and bodily strength necessary to labor in the Lord's vineyard. [ConsCN C 243]

The many criteria that help to determine someone's suitability for Jesuit life are partly listed in the General Examen [ConsCN C 1–131], and partly in Part I. We will not examine these in detail because that has been done elsewhere.[1] Instead, we ponder the question of obedience,

1 See for example: B. O'Leary SJ, *Sent into the Lord's Vineyard: Explorations in the Jesuit Constitutions* (Oxford: The Way, 2012), pp. 24–54.

which has to be raised before admission because it is related to the ability to enter a dynamic of progress according to the *Constitutions*: "for the candidate's own greater spiritual progress (*por mayor prouecho spiritual*) he should be asked whether he is willing to be entirely obedient in everything which has been stated and explained here" [General Examen, ConsCN C 90; see also ConsCN C 57, 60, 63 etc.]. Progress, just as in the *Spiritual Exercises*, depends on the free and trusting cooperation between the person who desires to advance and the person accompanying him. This relationship implies a dimension of authority which is justified by its usefulness for advancing.

In the first phases of the pathway to God, obedience is thus at the service of personal spiritual progress. This statement is far from being evident for someone with a contemporary mindset, who may associate obedience with wildly differing conceptions and practices, including clearly unhealthy ones. For clarifying the role of obedience in personal advancement, the analogy with the *Spiritual Exercises*, which presupposes a trusting yet unequal relationship of accompaniment, can prove to be useful. At the beginning of the Exercises, the person giving the Exercises must reach a certain "intuitive conviction"[2] that the exercitant is truly committed to keeping regular prayer times and to respecting the instructions about prayer. A similar relationship with an authority person—in this case, mainly the superior—is essential for the onset of Jesuit life as a dynamic progression: "It is very helpful for making progress and highly necessary (*es muy expediente para aprouecharse y mucho necessario*) that all devote themselves to complete obedience" [ConsCN C 284]. The analogy with the *Spiritual Exercises* also highlights the responsibility of the person whose role it is to help the progression by means of a relationship that entails obedience. A superior cannot act arbitrarily but only in the spirit of the Ignatian text and with ongoing discernment that always seeks the good of the persons who are to make progress. Such conformity with the Ignatian text is an obvious prerequisite as we give the Exercises, and a Jesuit formator works within a similar framework. Additional elements of

2 See for example: J. Tetlow SJ, *Choosing Christ in the World: Directing the Spiritual Exercises of St. Ignatius Loyola According to Annotations Eighteen and Nineteen* (Saint Louis: The Institute of Jesuit Sources, 1989), p. 12.

the analogy are the necessity to communicate the Ignatian instructions empathetically yet firmly, according to the criterion of helpfulness, as well as attention to and careful discernment of the fruits that can be expected when actual progression is made. That is how a trusting relationship of obedience can create the conditions, in accordance with the mystagogical objective, of making progress toward more profoundly knowing God and conforming oneself to the will of God. Contemplation in action, the ability to be active while aware of God's activity, can be greatly promoted by such a well-defined relationship not only between the person doing and the one giving the Spiritual Exercises, but also between a novice and his superior:

> [They should maintain] interior reverence and love [for the superior], [. . .] even though things are commanded which are difficult and repugnant to sensitive nature [. . .], regarding the superior's will and judgment as the rule of their own so as to conform themselves more completely *(más al iusto conformarse)* to the first and supreme rule of all good will and judgment, which is the Eternal Goodness and Wisdom. [ConsCN C 284]

Obedience in the novitiate is highly valued yet not idealized by the *Constitutions*. Obedience is both the intention and the ability to hear the words of the superior and to act upon them. As it happens that exercitants do not immediately modify their approach or daily schedule in order to take account of every instruction that was given to them, Jesuit formation also regards obedience as an area where growth is possible if an empathetic, consistent but not rigid superior maintains an appropriate milieu to which novices are expected to adjust themselves. Obedience is a virtue, that is, there is room for progressive advancement, and it is to be "exercised" [ConsCN C 286] through conscious practice that is rooted in prayer.

Beyond the many parallels between the *Spiritual Exercises* and the *Constitutions* at the moment of beginning a dynamic of progression, there is also a key difference. The *Spiritual Exercises*, by definition, focus on a purely spiritual progression, while the first phase of Jesuit life includes another dimension as well: "provident care must be employed [. . .] toward enabling them to make progress both in spirit and in virtues" [ConsCN C 243]. The novitiate cannot be reduced to growth in the relationship with God. Progress is to be made in several dimensions, in line with the relationship model of Ignatian anthropology. These dimensions appear, quite remarkably, one after the other in Chapter 1 of Part III of the *Constitutions* ("The preservation pertaining to the soul and to progress in virtues"), and this Chapter—especially its first half—can even be seen as structured according to the four dimensions of the relationship model of Ignatian anthropology: relationships, material things, values, and relationship with God. Relying on this working hypothesis, we are now going to explore the transformation that takes place during the two years of the probation that make up the novitiate, as well as the proposed means of fostering it.

## Interpersonal Relationships

The first concern of the *Constitutions* when describing the novitiate is how to give good help with regard to interpersonal relationships [ConsCN C 244–50]. First of all, an environment needs to be created that is suitably safe and advantageous for personal progress. For this purpose, interpersonal relationships are significantly restricted in the case of those who might strongly influence novices, either because they easily offer support and consolation, or because they demand attention and care. The desire for interpersonal relationships with family members, friends, and to a certain degree even with fellow novices and friendly Jesuits who live in the house runs into firm Ignatian boundaries:

> In regard to the soul, it is of great importance to keep those who are in probation away from all imperfections and from whatever can impede their greater spiritual progress *(de quanto puede impedir su mayor prouecho spiritual)*. For this purpose, it is highly expedient that they should cease from all communication by conversation and letters with persons who may dampen their resolves; further, that while they advance along the path of the spirit *(caminando en la uía del spíritu)* they should deal only with persons and about matters which help them toward what they were seeking when they entered the Society for the service of God our Lord. [ConsCN C 244]

Rules concerning interpersonal relationships do not only apply to correspondence but also to relations inside and outside the house. The instructions themselves, similar to those of the *Spiritual Exercises*, are phrased adamantly, but the way of communicating these instructions is subject to the discernment of the superior. This paragraph and subsequent ones encourage the consideration of the good of the individuals often and in various ways: "it is highly expedient", "the superior should consider", "on some occasion", and so on. Nevertheless, the environment for progressing in the novitiate needs to remain firmly established. All things considered, when novices are not in experiments, their relationships with externs are almost as restricted as during the thirty-day Exercises.

The restriction of interpersonal relationships in the novitiate does not put all human contacts on hold with the unique purpose of creating a favorable environment for a face-to-face relationship with God, as happens in the case of the Spiritual Exercises. Although protected space for prayer remains important, novices find themselves in an environment where they rely on each other in manifold ways and consequently mutual interactions tend to create an intense and sensitive community dynamic. How one behaves becomes highly significant; unresolved conflicts, for example, are likely to demand a lot of attention and may drain emotional energies, so that interpersonal issues cannot be treated in isolation from the question of personal progress. Novices need to be given practical advice that enables them to make the best possible decisions in matters subject to their own personal freedom. The *Constitutions* provide a set of detailed, step-by-step instructions packed into one succinct paragraph.

As with the *Spiritual Exercises*, where preparatory prayers, "preludes" [SpEx 46], help one to enter the personal encounter with God with an open and well-disposed heart, there is an equivalent of a prelude for entering the world of interpersonal relationships: "All should take special care to guard with great diligence the gates of their senses (especially the eyes, ears, and tongue) from all disorder, to preserve themselves in peace and true humility of their souls" [ConsCN C 250]. The preparation demanded for personal encounters is the preservation of the peace of the soul. Reducing the number of stimuli that directly affect the senses is presented as an important means of initial support. In the sheltered environment of the novitiate—just as while doing the Exercises—the person who aspires to make progress is responsible for a certain deliberate orderliness. He is the one who must "take special care" to keep out those streams of information that would perturb inner peace. This is, of course, a rather rudimentary level of maintaining the peace of soul since, as we know from the Spiritual Exercises, merely reducing the amount of incoming information does not guarantee inner peace in itself. On the contrary, passing an extended period of time in such an environment may cause inner tensions and all kinds of inner streams of thought all the more perceptible. Still, this first step generally proves to be very helpful on the way to discovering inner peace as a gift from God.[3] Peace of the soul in the Ignatian vocabulary is a common attribute of the many possible forms and degrees of consolation: "finally, under the word consolation I include [...] every interior joy [...] bringing [the soul] tranquility and peace in its Creator and Lord" [SpEx 316]. Just as the early experiences of consolation in the Spiritual Exercises prepare the way for receiving a profound and lasting peace coming from God ("you, Lord, have given all that to me [...], that is enough for me" [SpEx 234]), the practice of striving to preserve inner peace in the novitiate prepares the way to become a Jesuit whose interpersonal relationships are firmly grounded in a state of inner peace and consolation.[4]

Inner peace is to be paired with "true humility of [the] soul", which is not to be confused with repeated manifestations of humility and subordination; this latter in itself would indicate a troubled soul rather than inner freedom. Humility is rather the virtue that, on the third step of the meditation on the Two Standards, enables one to avoid pride [SpEx 146]. A novice with true humility of the soul can discern the instances when his personal pride begins to spoil the way he perceives interpersonal relationships and reacts to others. He can enter relationships with sufficient awareness of self to enable him to avoid impediments to fruitful and nourishing relationships, such as self-justification, rivalry, the construction of an overly idealized self-image, or inadvertently despising others, even if these phenomena are disguised

3 See "Pacificar", in *DEI (G–Z)*, pp. 1391–9.

4 "This inner peace (significantly linked with humility), the source of the peace that we radiate and communicate to others, is synonymous with what Ignatius means by consolation." B. O'Leary SJ, "Peace and Reconciliation" in *Review of Ignatian Spirituality* 128, vol. XLII, issue 3 (2011), p. 23.

as defending specific values or ways of being or doing. In a community where outside relationships are restricted, members tend to become sensitive to the reality of interpersonal relationships between each other, and maintaining inner peace in such a context becomes a significant spiritual challenge.

Without humility, the peace of the soul remains fragile because inner realities like anger or resentment can remain unnoticed and still exert a powerful influence: whether bursting out or remaining suppressed, they whittle away both the inner freedom and the capacity to experience consolation.[5] Humility is also fragile without the peace of the soul. When the conscientious examination of oneself, supposedly a sign of humility, is not accompanied by the peace of the soul that can be found in a living relationship with God, it can deteriorate into a scrupulous, irritated and unfruitful self-analysis, eventually generating hostility toward others, which in turn undermines real humility. Inner peace and true humility of the soul only provide a firm base for entering the world of interpersonal relationships if the two can mutually foster each other.

Over time, the instances when the soul becomes disquieted and troubled even though one strives to maintain inner peace and true humility become meaningful in a special way. Those who find themselves exposed to the restricted but real world of the novitiate, which is unavoidably characterized by the quality of interpersonal relationships, are likely to begin by blaming others as they face group dynamics that include lack of sensitivity, inadequate communication, lack of positive feedback from others, seemingly intolerable habits, and even positive qualities that cause rivalry, since all these phenomena can give rise to disturbing feelings and thoughts that work against inner peace. A sincere and regular practice of the Examen should help to move away from this initial perception of blaming others—perhaps by considering the image of the speck and the plank [Mt 7, 5]—toward recognizing and identifying those disordered tendencies in oneself that are triggered by the behavior of Jesuit companions. Such moments lead to a

5 The connection between awareness of self and experiencing consolation is explored in the chapter titled "Helping a Person Notice and Share with the Lord Key Interior Facts", in W. A. Barry and W. J. Connolly, *The Practice of Spiritual Direction* (San Francisco: Harper, 1982), pp. 65–79.

deeper knowledge of self and, if one remains in the context of seeking the presence of God, then these new insights tend to be accompanied by feelings of pain, confusion and shame, as well as an alternation of desolations and consolations that are typical during the first week of the Spiritual Exercises. Trying to seek inner peace in the novitiate thus introduces one to the spiritual struggle of seeking God while being embedded in a web of potentially upsetting interpersonal relationships.

One of the first challenges in beginning Jesuit life according to the Ignatian pathway to God lies in applying what one has learned throughout the thirty-day Spiritual Exercises to the ordinary conditions of the novitiate, in a place that is still protected but much less optimally fine-tuned to foster a relationship with God than the "mini-monastery" that could be temporarily created for the purpose of doing the Spiritual Exercises. This exercise of trying to maintain inner peace and humility allows habitual obstacles that stand in the way of harmonious and mutually nourishing interpersonal relationships to surface, even if they had been ignored or repressed before. The acknowledgement of such inclinations or personality traits and the recognition of the ways they make one vulnerable to desolation will make it possible to progress in the novitiate by means of what one has learned from doing the Exercises. The objective of "disposing our soul to rid itself of all its disordered affections" [SpEx 1] is not merely a spiritual objective any more but an actual precondition for common life lived in spiritual freedom and according to the Gospel during the first phase of the Ignatian pathway to God.

The transformation demanded by the *Constitutions* thus begins by establishing a direct link between the relationship with God, who is the source of inner peace, and interpersonal relationships within the "world", which demand to be approached with inner peace. The gradual establishment of this organic connection between two fundamental dimensions of the human personality indicates the beginning of a progression that implies a dimension of growth in human maturity. A Jesuit whose reactions to others are not determined by raw, "unredeemed" emotions, moods and ideas—such as impatience, disappointment, anger, fear, boredom, scorn or the projection of some anxiety or unresolved injury—but rather by the intention to preserve inner peace and to seek consolation may find that his speech, behavior and even his meta-communication become both more conscious and more personal. To make progress in this direction means taking further steps on the Ignatian pathway to God toward a more integrated personality: "to show [peace and true humility of their souls] by their silence when it should be kept and, when they must speak by the discretion and edification of their words, the modesty of their countenance, the maturity *(madureza)* of their walk, and all their movements, without giving any sign of impatience or pride" [ConsCN C 250]. Acts emerging from a peaceful soul reflect maturity. If peace is not misunderstood as a motionless apathy but as flowing from the presence of the Lord, then the Ignatian "prelude" about striving for peace of soul and humility introduces one to the firm base on which human maturity can begin to develop. Maturity stems from the experience familiar from the Spiritual Exercises: when the soul is calm and at peace in God, one can see more clearly and also say, do or avoid things with a certain ease and confidence that would otherwise not be possible or would require great strain and effort. At such times, one feels stronger, freer, more attentive, more genuine and more in command of one's competencies, whether talking or doing something; in other words, one experiences oneself as more mature. For someone who uses the time of probation well, the practice of speaking or behaving in a way that expresses inner peace of soul can become a habit, and the beginning of the Ignatian pathway to God can prove to be an extraordinary opportunity for personal growth.

Inner peace is not always given and at times may seem hopelessly far away. In such cases, the Ignatian rule of seeking inner peace by spiritual means rather than by what might come through the senses remains valid. The intention to seek the "service and praise of God" [cf. SpEx 20] that has been so advantageous during the Exercises will continue to be helpful in the novitiate: "All should strive to keep their intention right, not only in regard to their state of life but also in all particular details" [ConsCN C 288]. Personal dedication to move forward on the pathway to God, together with discernment that finds support in the accompaniment, can help to move through dark moments until freedom can begin to emerge and peace of soul can be found again. Such prioritizing of the relationship with God exposes areas of lack of freedom in the personality. Just as desolation in prayer makes one prone to give oneself over to distractions, desolation in community life makes one prone to seek relief in interpersonal relationships. The perhaps unconscious desire to fill inner emptiness—an unavoidable experience for those who live the spiritual life—can easily distort interpersonal relationships if it results in expectations being projected onto fellow community members. Such expectations cannot be fulfilled, since desolation by definition is a possible trait of the relationship with God; one cannot expect to receive from the "world" what can only be received from God. The insistence on peace of soul before entering human relationships does not mean, of course, that one is not supposed to leave the chapel until consolation has returned in full vigor; it is very possible that this ideal state of the soul will not be reached soon. It is even possible that talking to others can help to restore inner peace: the soul might be troubled, for example, because one has not said something that would have been important to say, or because one has closed in on oneself and healthy interpersonal relationships have been blocked. Still, the absence of peace of soul calls for an ongoing awareness of what happens in interpersonal relationships, a mindfulness about consolations and desolations that recall the time of doing the Exercises. Depending on one's personality type, there may be countless ways of attempting to fill inner emptiness by means of relationships with others. Community members usually notice quite easily when someone "draws the energy out" of others, but the person in question may need a lot of time and patience before he can acknowledge this tendency and hopefully find some freedom with regard to it.

A hurried reading of the *Constitutions* may make the meticulously detailed Ignatian instructions look like an example of superfluous pedantry presented in an overly pious manner rather than something of practical use. As we have seen, the text mentions silence, the way of talking, facial expression, gait and other movements in general. Are all these details necessary? Is there really no easier and more spontaneous way of relating to others? The meaning of individual details of the text, as we have seen in the preliminary studies, can be expected to be understood on the condition that the reader has sufficient familiarity with the actual dynamic of progress that is implied, and preferably with the accompaniment of the process that the details are meant to foster. In this particular case one can note that all the small details here concern the verbal and non-verbal aspects of interpersonal communication, which remind one of the *Spiritual Exercises,* where good communication with God, especially in the beginning, can also depend on seemingly negligible questions related to posture: sitting, walking, lying face upwards, and the rest can all prove to be helpful during prayer exercises [see SpEx 75–7]. A formator, instead of quickly turning the page, could let himself be inspired by directors of the Exercises who sometimes confirm that such meticulously detailed instructions can indeed play a crucial role when, for example, after a period of desolation, they are proposed to the person doing the Exercises and the person begins to pay attention to them. The same may well be the case when novices need to be helped to find a way out after a period of non-communication or other tension in interpersonal relationships.

The following instructions have to do directly with interpersonal relationships, and refer even more evidently to the *Spiritual Exercises*: "In all things they should try and desire to give the advantage to the others, esteeming them all in their hearts as if they were their superiors and showing outwardly, in an unassuming and simple religious manner, the respect and reverence appropriate to each one's state" [ConsCN C 250]. Giving the first place to another person requires a disposition that recalls, in the *Spiritual Exercises,* the fundamental attitude of giving the leading role to God: "to ask God our Lord for the grace that all my intentions, actions, and operations may be ordered purely to the service and praise of the Divine Majesty" [SpEx 46]. Both exercises demand stepping out of one's self-centeredness, even though in the case of human beings it is a question not of service and praise but respect and reverence that is "appropriate to each one's state". To give up self-centeredness implies becoming sensitive to the other person, but also entails becoming vulnerable. Such vulnerability could, of course, be abused—for example, by those who endlessly take advantage of others' goodwill—in a way that destroys the Ignatian exercise of trying and desiring to give the advantage to others. At this point, the text does not talk about setting healthy boundaries: in the novitiate, it is the superior whose attentive discernment creates the reasonable and fair circumstances in which renunciation for the sake of others can be safely practiced.

The word reverence (*reverencia*) also calls the *Spiritual Exercises* to mind. The *Constitutions* attribute a similar significance to reverence in human relationships to what the *Spiritual Exercises* do when teaching to pray. Reverence in prayer enables one to move from mental representations that are useful for comprehending the created world—or, to some extent, God ("when we are using the intellect to understand" [SpEx 3])—to meeting God as a person: "when we are conversing with God our Lord or his saints vocally or mentally, greater reverence is demanded of us" [ibid.]. The everyday meaning of reverence, without this adjustment brought about by the specific connotations in the Exercises, could make the emphasis on reverence and respect in the *Constitutions* appear to be the obligatory submission in front of a person of authority, or even more pejoratively, a way to express a lack of love ("I do not love you much but I try to respect you nevertheless"). In the Ignatian vocabulary, respect or reverence is a constitutive dimension of love. It includes a readiness to serve others and to relate to them without prejudices, fully open and attentive to their presence.[6] Reverence in an interpersonal relationship brings forth the distinctive quality that is absent when we use objects or relate to human beings merely in function of their usefulness for our own needs. In this sense, reverence constitutes the threshold that marks the entry to the world of interpersonal relationships properly speaking. The reverence that one appropriates while trying to approach the living God becomes the basis for approaching human beings as well.

Initial superficial ideas or even prejudices about God and God's word ("I already know this Gospel text, there is nothing new in it") can be overcome, in the Spiritual Exercises, by means of patiently persisting in the prayer exercises. Initial superficial ideas, judgments and even prejudices about others in the novitiate ("I know what you are going to say and I am not impressed") can be overcome by similarly patient and persistent application of the Ignatian instructions among the ordinary conditions of community life. Reverence can thus progressively become a consistent attitude that fosters the maintenance of a characteristic quality of interpersonal relationships in the community. Reverence, as it becomes habitual, lays the foundation of a style of communication that conveys security, evokes trust and goes beyond appearances, thus becoming increasingly personal.

6 "Acatamiento-reverencia", *DEI (A–F)*, pp. 77–9.

Such "re-learning" in the area of interpersonal relationships requires time and a focused, prayerful atmosphere. It is also a school of self-knowledge and an occasion for facing limitations of the personality that would otherwise remain unattended to. This delicate yet indispensable transformation at the beginning of Jesuit life is probably one of the reasons for the apparent paradox that the preparation for an active, apostolic life—even though it includes experiences outside the novitiate [see ConsCN C 64–71]—begins among almost monastic circumstances. It is true that, unless the two dimensions of Ignatian help, the creation of a favorable environment and adequate spiritual support in personal accompaniment, mutually support each other well, the restrictions demanded by the *Constitutions* are likely to favor regression rather than growth. Without adequate spiritual support and a personal persistence in moving forward on the Ignatian pathway to God, the novitiate can soon appear as a childish environment without real challenges and responsibilities, a period of Jesuit life where there is little excitement and not much at stake. With adequate support, however, and with sufficient clarity about how to progress, the graces received in prayer can begin to work together with ever new insights concerning self-knowledge toward forming solid human and spiritual foundations for becoming a member of the apostolic body of the Society.

A striking Ignatian remark concludes the detailed set of instructions, promising that as a result of the progress made by means of the requested exercises, God's presence can shine through the world of interpersonal relationships. God, who had been present throughout the way by offering consolation and peace, and thus enabled novices to explore the amazingly rich and challenging world of interpersonal relationships with sensitivity and an open heart, becomes accessible in a new way: "so that by consideration of one another they may thus grow in devotion *(devoción)* and praise God our Lord, whom each one should strive to recognize in the other as in his image" [ConsCN C 250]. The word devotion (*devoción*) indicates a light and elevated condition of the soul that is sensitive and attuned to God. The surprisingly rich meaning of the expression can be traced in Ignatius' spiritual diary, which mentions in close succession expressions like "great devotion", "intense devotion", "a certain warm devotion, glowing as it were", "impulse to devotion and tears", and so on.[7] The term, dated as it may sound today, plays such a central role in the writings of Ignatius that many other expressions can be said to "converge on it".[8] Towards the end of the *Autobiography*, the brief account of the years in Rome indicates that devotion is closely related to what we understand today by the term contemplation in action: "he had always grown in devotion, that is, ease in finding God; and now more than ever in his whole life. Every time, any hour, that he wished to find God, he found him" [Autobiography 99].

As the *Constitutions* surprisingly conclude, if the novices observe the instructions concerning interpersonal relationships, they will change in such a way that each will "thus" be able to recognize God's presence "in the other", experiencing an ever greater devotion. God, who could previously be found mainly in quiet prayer, in movements of the heart or through Gospel stories, can now be also recognized in the world of interpersonal relationships: "consider how God dwells in [. . .] human beings" [SpEx 235].

How can one recognize God in a fellow human being? The *Constitutions*, possibly disappointing those who focus exclusively on the text, do not give a clear answer. Those, however, who read the text with an eye for its practical application may sense here a discretion that is familiar from the *Spiritual Exercises*. In both cases, Ignatian instructions can take one "only" to the doorstep of an encounter with God. Recognition of God, the encounter itself and the transforming power of the encounter remains a personal gift, a mystery that shines out unexpectedly for the person who makes real progress toward God. In the novitiate, the instances of finding God in or through an interpersonal relationship that previously could have appeared to be hopelessly flawed tend to belong to the moments that remain as memorable and genuinely transformative as the most intimate and consoling prayer experiences during the Spiritual Exercises. Listening to personal accounts of such experiences probably provides the most direct keys for understanding the concluding words of the paragraph that gives instructions for entering interpersonal relationships in the novitiate.

7 "Selections from the Spiritual Diary", translated by E. J. Malatesta and G. E. Ganss, In *Ignatius of Loyola: Spiritual Exercises and Selected Works*, ed. G. E. Ganss SJ (New York: Paulist, 1991).

8 "Devoción", in *DEI (A–F)*, pp. 584–7.

To summarize: during the probation that is the novitiate, a powerful community setting and accompaniment by the novice director enables individuals to strive to acknowledge their own shortcomings by means of the Examen, brotherly feedback and other similar practices, relying on spiritual strength nourished by prayer, so that they move forward on a way of healing, maturing and assuming more and more responsibility for themselves. Novices can thus turn toward others with a charity that is more and more reliable, with increasing openness to "mutual communication" and a generosity expressed "more by deeds". The community will less and less be used as a surface for inadvertently projecting psychological difficulties, and—perhaps unconscious—unrealistic expectations to have childhood injuries healed or taken care of. Relationships can become more genuine and free of compulsion, and the community less burdened by immature or self-centered behavior. Games that people play to gain emotional "payoffs"[9] and consequent impasses in community life gradually give way to a new quality of mutual communication.

What does all this mean for our Jesuit communities? The *Constitutions* do not expect candidates to be able straight away to shape their interpersonal relationships in a way that mirrors Gospel values. One of the objectives of the novitiate is to foster a fundamental transformation in this field. Just as in the *Spiritual Exercises,* where the preconditions for engaging in further weeks can be established by making sufficiently good progress in the dynamic of the first week, those who cannot or do not want to make satisfactory progress in the interpersonal—and equally spiritual—dynamic of the novitiate will have no firm foundation for the successive stages of Jesuit life. A healthy sense of progression, human maturity, integration into an apostolic body and competencies necessary for apostolic life will all be wanting. The progress made during the novitiate thus directly influences the future authenticity and effectiveness of apostolic life, as well as the quality of community life in the Society in subsequent years and decades. Concerning the recurring contemporary questions about the quality of Jesuit community life, the *Constitutions* do not offer quick-fix answers, but they do spell out the path of spiritual and human growth in this area, which is to be a deter-

9 See Berne, *Games People Play.*

mining dimension of Jesuit formation. Only Jesuits who are suitably trained in moving forward within this dynamic of growth will be well resourced to find creative answers to the challenges of community life so that the presence of God can shine forth even in the midst of the fragilities of the human condition.

## Material Things

Having discussed interpersonal relationships, the *Constitutions* turn to another dimension implied in the relationship model of Ignatian anthropology, the world of material things [ConsCN C 251–9]. As a transition, the text briefly touches upon two questions, both linked distantly to the subject matter. First, it speaks about eating [ConsCN C 251–2], then it discusses how novices should be engaged in work, that is, how they need to maintain an active stance in relating to their "environment", whether physical, intellectual or spiritual: "Generally, all those who are in good health should be busy with spiritual or exterior occupations" [ConsCN C 253].

With regard to relating to the world of material things, the first objective is once again to create a favorable setting, this time a physical environment that will suitably help the progression. To ensure that concerns relating to material things do not hinder progress, before the actual beginning of the novitiate proper care should be taken of any personal property that should not be disposed of before the final vows [ConsCN C 254–6]. Similarly detailed instructions cover any property donated to the Society at this moment [RA 258]. In both cases, the goal is to create a space of freedom, so that compelling responsibilities in the management of personal goods do not divert the attention that will be necessary for making progress in this decisive first phase of Jesuit life.

Modest material conditions directly support progress along the pathway to God. This statement is understood to be evident for Jesuits who have already made progress and can see in retrospect how the use of material things has been instrumental in helping them toward living a gratifying Jesuit life: "From experience we have learned that a life removed as far as possible from all infection of avarice and as like as possible to evangelical poverty is more gratifying, more undefiled, and more suitable for the edification of our neighbors" [FI 7]. Candidates for the Society are not expected to have the same conviction that poverty is helpful for progression, since the dimension of the relationship with the material world may not strike them as relevant. This aspect of the way of proceeding in the Society of Jesus has to be raised as the prerequisite of admission into the novitiate in the hope that it will be seen as an attractive ideal: "[the candidate should persuade himself that] his food, drink, clothing, shoes and lodging will be what is characteristic of the poor" [General Examen, ConsCN C 81]. A simple environment can only be helpful if it is perceived and freely welcomed as a dimension of Ignatian help. Unless novices can trust that the restriction of the satisfaction drawn from material objects will be helpful to them, and they try to make the best possible use of this situation for their progress, simple life conditions will appear to be a senseless burden. In this case, valuable objects of interest or convenience will appear as unjustly forbidden to them, and a dynamic that is foreign to the dynamic of progress on the Ignatian pathway to God will begin to install itself.

When a true dynamic of progress extends to the relationship with material objects, novices begin to reflect, based on their perceptions of themselves, about how they tend to use material objects for the purpose of relieving inner emptiness, for example to alleviate temporary boredom, bad mood or psychic tension. The aim of Ignatian help is to facilitate personal decisions that lead toward greater inner freedom and less dependence on the comfort, excitement or sense of achievement offered by material things. In accordance with the insight gained from the Spiritual Exercises, progress is helped by divesting oneself "of self-love and of [one's] own will and interests" [SpEx 189] that can be eminently realized through the moderation of the use and enjoyment of material things. More or less compulsive automatisms can thus be replaced by more conscious and responsible action that allows one to take a distance from the world of objects: "all should be taught that they must not have the use of anything as their own" [ConsCN C 254].

The purpose of progress in this area is to build up increasingly consistent habits, character traits and competencies in such a way that the beneficial effects of the virtue of poverty become part of the self-awareness of novices, and "they may begin to experience the virtue of holy poverty" [ConsCN C 254]. The virtue of poverty makes it possible to use material things with a certain ease, indifference and a sense of responsibility, and with a new taste of freedom. Poverty being qualified by the text as "holy" also reminds one that this virtue, far from being an isolated characteristic of the personality, is the capacity to establish a link between two, potentially split dimensions of human life: that of relating to the world of material objects and that of seeking God. Poverty as a virtue is founded in the experience that the intimate relationship with Christ and the attitude of remaining engaged in his mission can persist in situations of scarcity, not only helping to endure discomfort but potentially resulting in transformative experiences of Christ's presence. The virtue of poverty can grow through conscientiously undertaking everyday tasks of the novitiate, "such as working in the kitchen, cleaning the house and all the rest of these services" [ConsCN C 83], but also through occasional extraordinary incidents: "It will be helpful that superiors see to it that those who are in probation should sometimes experience [...] poverty" [ConsCN C 285]. One of these exceptional opportunities to experience some of the spiritual fruits of actual poverty is the pilgrimage without money: "Thus too the candidate, through abandoning all the reliance which he could have on money or other created things, may with genuine faith and intense love place his reliance entirely on his Creator and Lord" [ConsCN C 67].

Since the practice of poverty can be very different across regions and communities in the contemporary Society of Jesus, the novitiate can clearly not prepare for a life of poverty by instilling habits that could later ensure an almost automatic integration into a standard apostolic community. Tensions between apostolic needs and the ideal of a simple life cannot be solved in advance, and the role of formation is not to give fixed directives about such questions. The virtue of poverty as an inevitable dimension of personal progress should, however, prepare Jesuits for discernment that is well founded. To have made progress in the virtue of poverty means familiarity with personal tendencies and habits of gaining satisfaction from the material world, and some experience about going against these tendencies and habits by relying on the spiritual strength that can be found in the relationship with God. These capacities are a prerequisite for avoiding ideological discussions about poverty, where the concern about apostolic efficiency tends to exclude all other arguments, whereas ideas about a romanticized poverty can make one equally deaf to other opinions. Those who have made progress in the virtue of poverty will be able to hear arguments on both sides, but the desire to remain united with God will give them some inner freedom to weigh opinions carefully in such a way that their own spiritual and human good, the good of the Society as well as the need for adequate apostolic tools, are all taken into consideration.

## Values

In the relationship model of Ignatian anthropology, a third great dimension and motivational source is the world of intellectual, moral, aesthetic, religious and other value-based convictions that capture the attention and engage the intellect and the creativity of the human being. The novitiate places restrictions in this field as well: for example, novices who previously actively participated in political, professional, theological and other discussions and were engaged in important projects in these areas are asked to step back from what had attracted and occupied them before entering. Intellectual life as such is usually postponed until the subsequent phase of Jesuit life: "Generally speaking, there will be no literary studies in the house" [ConsCN C 289]. Restrictions are meant to serve better progress: to focus on academic studies in the novitiate could disrupt the progression in a manner very like the reading of heavy theological works while doing the Spiritual Exercises.

The environment that places restrictions on the "value dimension" of the life in the novitiate is likely particularly to challenge those who are intellectually gifted and like to ponder philosophical issues and the great questions of life, but also those energetic persons who like to identify and achieve attractive and valuable goals, who have good leadership qualities, who thrive when working for the good of others. The probation that is the novitiate will mean for such persons a chance to verify how their gifts can be integrated into a personality that is attuned to God before being attuned to formulating ideals and achieving attractive goals; in other words, what is eminently at stake for them is becoming contemplatives in action. If academic or leadership qualities turn out to be used to fulfill a self-centered need for success or intellectual supremacy, if they are habitually put forward to hide vulnerabilities or a narcissistic need to appear competent and potent, then they indicate a considerable fragility both in the relationship with God and in the world of interpersonal relationships. This is the reason why in the first phase of the Ignatian pathway to God, the desire to identify with and to work for the realization of organizationally or apostolically valuable projects is to be subordinated to the desire to progress on the Ignatian pathway to God, which in the specific context of the novitiate means entering the human reality of fraternal interpersonal relationships while seeking to find God in this specific context.

The restriction of otherwise valuable actions and occupations does not mean, of course, that the novitiate would be a place where values do not play a role. A striving for values needs to be kept alive, but priority should be given to values that benefit the community and enrich interpersonal relationships. In the particular context of the novitiate, a growing sensitivity can soon develop as to whether values such as reverence, patience, courage to be truthful and the like are present and sufficiently represented. Values are to be expressed in the daily living together; their role is to foster moral and general human growth and shape the community according to the Gospels. In other words, and using the preferred term of the *Constitutions*, values in the novitiate are expressed primarily by means of practicing the virtues. This is another way of understanding how the "progress [...] in virtues" [ConsCN C 243] contributes to a profound transformation of the personality. Virtues make it possible for values to penetrate not only individual acts but also habits, as well as the characteristic way of speaking and proceeding in the particular Jesuit community that is the novitiate.

As we have seen before, progress in virtues at the beginning of Jesuit life is a clear aim, but the *Constitutions* remain on an almost disappointingly general level without much further clarification: novices should be "applying themselves to the pursuit of the true and solid virtues" [ConsCN C 260]. The text hardly mentions any values or virtues that would be especially necessary in the first phase of Jesuit life. How can such a vaguely stated objective still influence everyday life?

First, there are the values implied in the community culture of the novitiate as embodied by the members of the formation community through their everyday behavior, habits, manner of eating and speaking, celebrating the Eucharist and feasts, and so on. Novices do not conform to abstract ideals but to an established, relatively firm way of proceeding. That is the primary way of assimilating values at this stage. This is one of the main reasons for maintaining a special formation milieu: "while they advance along the path of the spirit, they should deal only with persons and about matters which help them" [ConsCN C244]. The novitiate should be able to communicate a clear value system, but the values of Jesuit life should not take the form of abstract ideals. Novices should be able to resort to suitable persons to talk "about matters which help them". Values should be mediated by human beings rather that a formal insistence on values, even if such human mediation necessarily entails less than perfect moments. In fact, when a desire to make progress on the Ignatian pathway to God is present, the presence of human frailty tends to authenticate the values embodied by the community rather than disqualify them.

Since the way of proceeding mediated by a given Jesuit community is less than perfect, novices usually find it easy to formulate critical observations. Although such observations are probably made in the name of undeniable values or ideals, they should not be simply allowed to prevail in the community: "Even in judgment about practical matters, diversity [...] should be avoided as far as possible" [ConsCN C 273]. This instruction to avoid diversity, when taken out of context, may appear to be an obsolete, typically medieval way of imposing tranquility and unity by suppressing individual differences and freedom of expression. In the context, however, of making progress on the Ignatian pathway to God, it is to be implemented as a means of helping to progress. The question is thus not simply whether criticism is valid in the sense that it points out a value or a virtue that has been in fact neglected, and not even whether it has a potentially destructive effect on the conviviality of the community. These aspects need attention, but in the long-term perspective of progressing toward becoming persons who can be contemplative in action, a more important question is how to come to terms with the potentially judgmental and rigid communication of value statements, or, in other words, with possible tendencies of ideological thinking.

Those who tend repetitively to judge others at the expense of the peacefulness of the community or even of their own inner peace usually do so in the name of some idea that they value and cherish highly. Judgments imply a value, be it simplicity of life, justice, compassion, respect for individual differences, dignity of the liturgy, solidarity with the poor, the courage to go out and preach the Gospel, or some other such matter. That is precisely why it is practically impossible for the concerned individual to see what is "wrong" in the insistence on taking a value seriously. Ideological thinking, when an overly attractive value can trick someone into being blind to most other aspects of reality, is usually exceptionally difficult to integrate into self-knowledge, especially when it goes in tandem with a rigid personality. On the pathway to God that is Jesuit life, an "environment" that is able respectfully but firmly to resist the sheer force of visibly justified accusations is a necessary part of the Ignatian help given to such persons. The role of the superior is usually vital, but the support of other community members who in such cases usually experience uncomfortable feelings is also essential. Their benevolent, respectful, compassionate but also sustained and pertinent feedback—usually in a somewhat controlled setting like a suitable practice of "fraternal correction"—might be the only credible sign for the concerned individual that there is room for growth. At this point, empathetic yet purposeful accompaniment can help the individual to recognize the lack of inner freedom in his tendencies of "ideological" speaking, that is, the fact that he tends to seek security and strength in the identification with ideals rather than in a trusting relationship with God and with fellow companions. Awareness of what happens in prayer and what brings inner peace can orient the person toward recognizing how God can help him on the way to greater maturity, a capacity to establish trusting relationships and inner healing, which can for him progressively build up a solid basis for engaging in the mission of Christ.

The second way of imbuing the novitiate with values is familiarity with the Christian tradition and with general Christian literature. Authors of spirituality, theology, contemporary books on self-knowledge or community dynamics can be studied as far as they help to develop a healthy conception of spiritual life and nourish a dynamic of moving forward: "The study which those who are in probation will have in the houses of the Society should, it seems, be about what will help them *(lo que les ayuda)* toward what has been said on the abnegation of themselves and toward further growth *(para más crescer)* in virtue and devotion" [ConsCN C 289]. Among the things to study for their usefulness in progressing, we do not find such central themes of

Ignatian spirituality as indifference, discernment or even consolation and desolation. Instead, the *Constitutions* emphasize the need to be instructed about the sacraments and the basics of Christian teaching:

> On some days each week, instruction should be given in Christian doctrine, the manner of making a good and fruitful *(bien y fructuosamente)* confession, receiving communion, assisting at mass and serving it, praying, meditating and reading, in accordance with each one's capacity. [ConsCN C 277]

To the contemporary reader, this detail is not likely to sound like a revolutionary Ignatian insight that will renew Jesuit formation today, although one might acknowledge that, depending on the cultural background of novices, there may be a need for some additional catechism in some of these areas. One should, however, notice that it is a question not simply of the instruction of novices in doctrine and the sacraments but also of a fruitful practice. If the spiritual fruits of attending Mass or confession are wanting, then the interpretation of this paragraph of the *Constitutions* has remained unsatisfactory. And, as we have seen, the opposite is also true: unless a fruitful practice of the sacraments can be seen to transform the life of Jesuits, we will probably overlook the significance of this Ignatian instruction. In a cultural context where the practice of the sacraments, especially confession, is by no means evident, but where one can also see young people being attracted to congregations and movements where they do receive considerable help in these areas, a careful interpretation of the *Constitutions* could help Jesuit formation better to respond to the signs of the times in a postmodern culture.

The insistence on personal fruitfulness once again calls the Spiritual Exercises to mind. General, ready-made explanations are important in both cases but they can never replace patient and attentive personal reflection. In the Exercises, it "brings more spiritual relish and spiritual fruit" *(de más gusto y fructo spiritual)* to take the subject matter of contemplations or meditations "by reflecting on it and reasoning about it for oneself", and thus discovering "something that will bring better understanding or a more personalized concept of the history" [SpEx 2]. Among the themes enumerated by the *Constitutions*, we have thus a well-developed pedagogy, or rather a mystagogy, concerning "prayer

[and] meditating". Confessions, receiving communion, assisting at mass and serving it, as well as reading, are areas where neither the *Spiritual Exercises* nor the *Constitutions* give a similar pedagogy—or, rather, similar practices of mystagogy—probably trusting that Jesuit formators will be capable of developing them. Such creativity can certainly be expected, and formators can certainly learn from each other in these areas. It is also clear that given the diversities of cultural backgrounds and sensitivities, it would be difficult to give general instructions about how to proceed in these areas. Yet it is noteworthy, for example, that the *Constitutions* list the fruitful use of the sacraments together with "praying [and] meditating", possibly implying that a similar approach could apply to all of these areas of learning. In other words, formators can be expected to be creative because they can use the paradigm of the Exercises to introduce novices into a fruitful practice of confessions or into fruitfully assisting at the Eucharist. It seems that among the values that should characterize the novitiate, elements of Ignatian spirituality do not constitute an object, a "what" to be studied, but rather a means, a "how" to approach various elements of a common Christian heritage. Just as the *Spiritual Exercises* help primarily through helping to find a fruitful relationship with the Gospels, the *Constitutions* emphasize fostering the mystagogical dimension by helping to develop a fruitful rapport with the sacraments and with the basics of Christian teaching.

The third way of giving priority to specific values is by regularly reflecting upon the daily life of the community, which is the responsibility of each Jesuit but especially that of the superior. Such "evaluation" will show that the strengths of the community and also the deficiencies that affect the quality of community life keep changing, depending on the Jesuits who make up a community at a given moment. The objective of some sort of a community equivalent of the Examen is not simply to make an analysis but also to create a space for embracing new Gospel values. To speak about deficiencies in terms of values that need more emphasis can be helpful in this respect. Value language should not, however, be used to construct an ideal world that is painfully distant from reality. Personal accompaniment should provide help to individuals in the delicate question of what attitudes, activities and virtues will help them to contribute more fruitfully to the life of the community. Such an exercise of personalizing the evaluation of community life will entail acknowledging personal deficiencies, but when it happens in accordance with Gospel values and together with contemplating the life of Jesus Christ, it will turn the attention toward values and virtues that appeared important in the teaching and life of Jesus. The values and virtues that emerge in such a context will be perceived not only as relevant and desirable but also as a new means to know Jesus better, to follow him more closely and to love him more deeply.

The appreciation of Gospel values is a personal responsibility for everyone, yet it should not develop into some sort of individualistic competition. On the pathway to God, personal striving has to go together with the ability to talk authentically in a way that contributes to enriching the community culture:

> It is good that all [. . .] practice preaching inside the house [. . .] and express their good ideas for their own edification and that of their neighbors. They should speak often of what pertains to abnegation of themselves, the virtues and all perfection. [ConsCN C 280]

The word "edification" can sound obsolete today and if it is used at all, it tends to be used sarcastically. It is nevertheless not easy to replace the term with a more satisfactory one. It indicates a way of speaking or behaving that others find authentic and helpful for progressing in their own vocation. Edifying talk and behavior is indispensable if a community is to maintain a spiritual coherence and share common values not only rhetorically but also in reality. The reason why speaking in an edifying way has to be practiced from time to time is probably that edifying moments are not simply gifts of grace to be received in some privileged moments of community life but also the result of the progressively growing trust, attention and sense of spiritual communion among community members. Listeners can promote edifying talk by showing respectful attention and perhaps by giving feedback. Speakers can practice being well prepared while remaining composed and aware of their feelings and experiences. In a given community, instances of talking and behaving that are perceived as edifying are good indicators that the dynamic of progress is present and that the community as such is capable of supporting the progression of its members.

## Capital Sins and the Opposite Virtues

We have seen that capital sins in the relationship model of Ignatian anthropology can be regarded as inclinations that typify vital behavioral patterns of small children, who begin to interact with their environment during the early phases of personality development. In adulthood, however, the dominant and repetitive behavioral patterns implied in capital sins indicate the dysfunctional automatisms of an immature personality. Such patterns bring excitement or relieve tension in a way that threatens the inner coherence of the personality and hinders its fuller integration within a free and generous relationship with God. Capital sins thus do not simply indicate but also cause and maintain immaturity. As we have seen, the *Spiritual Exercises* suggest that both those without sufficient capacities to do the Exercises and those who are preparing to do them ponder the reality of capital sins [SpEx 18]. Meditation on the capital sins "which are to be avoided" [SpEx 244–5], together with other meditations, serves the purpose of "preparing" [SpEx 238] the soul for a deeper relationship with God.

Advancing on the pathway to God implies experiencing the effects of the capital sins—at least the ones most characteristic of one's personality—as temptations, that is, motivational forces which strongly influence thoughts and emotions alike, and are opposed to the movement of progress. In such cases the *Constitutions* call our attention to the "opposites" [ConsCN C 265] of temptations, namely, in the case of the capital sins, the "opposite virtues". There is nothing wrong with the manifestation of the signs of immaturity; they are expected to manifest themselves if transformation in these areas is to happen. But it is also expected that the person who desires to make progress will increasingly assume responsibility for these areas of immaturity. To be taught about how to "defend" oneself and how to "overcome" temptations [ConsCN C 260] can empower someone to go beyond knowing himself so that engaging in a struggle for inner freedom becomes possible. Yet the willingness to enter a struggle at the time of temptation has to go together with a positive striving that can lead to a long-term transformation, that is, novices "applying themselves to the pursuit of the true and solid virtues" [ConsCN C 260]. The text conveys the conviction that among the special conditions of the novitiate, and nurtured by intense personal prayer, real transformation of the personality can occur, and that even conditionings originating from the early phases of human development can to some extent be uncovered and modified for the better.

The firm instructions concerning temptations introduce novices to the theme of spiritual combat. This important topic of Christian spirituality can be analysed neither by relying on mere psychological categories nor by ignoring basic psychological caveats. For example, we are aware today that overly emphasizing "evil inclinations" [ConsCN C 265] and the need to fight against them can develop such a powerful super-ego that the person becomes fixated on imperatives about how Jesuit life "should" be lived. If such a development replaces progression on the Ignatian pathway to God with its rich affective dimension, then not only the liveliness of interpersonal relationships suffers but also the contemplative quality of prayer and Jesuit life. We are aware today of how a tyranny of the "should" can impede human and spiritual growth.

Psychoanalytic theories also emphasize that it is the father's role to forbid behaviors in the growing child that he considers immature. To interiorize fatherly "no's" and "shoulds" at successive levels of growth is a difficult but inevitable part of human development. Far from being a mere personal developmental challenge, the passage from immature forms of behavior to responsible adulthood is a vital condition for maintaining the well-being of any human society. The novitiate of a religious order can be understood as a period of initiation, a "rite of passage"[10] that helps and expects new members to develop personal maturity and a sense of adherence to the group. We have seen that capital sins are manifestations of immaturity that are normal in the case of young children but need to become the object of self-awareness in the case of adults. The *Constitutions*, by insisting on the virtues that are the opposites of capital sins, consider the novitiate as a culturally mediated transition to spiritual and human maturity. The transformation takes place in a psychologically balanced environment. The "fatherly" firmness in facing immature behavior is complemented by unconditional "motherly" acceptance in the privileged relationship with the novice master "whom all those who are in probation may love and to whom

10 G. A. Arbucle, *From Chaos to Mission: Refounding Religious Life Formation* (Trowbridge: Redwood Books, 1996), pp. 113–37.

they may have recourse in their temptations and open themselves with confidence" [ConsCN C 263]. As a result, the insistence on facing "evil inclinations" [ConsCN C 265] does not entail the suppression of desires or feelings. On the contrary, the possibility and even necessity to talk about these can facilitate the recognition of areas of the personality that could not be integrated before.

While proper psychological conditions are essential, the *Constitutions* regard progression in the greater context of Ignatian anthropology, insisting on the spiritual resources that can support growth in ways that psychology cannot. As we have seen, the *Spiritual Exercises* demand that with regard to capital sins, "opposite virtues" [SpEx 245] should be contemplated and asked for in prayer, as well as practiced so that they can become stable personality traits. The list of such opposite virtues was commonly known at the time to consist of chastity (the opposite of lust), temperance (as opposed to gluttony), patience and the ability to forgive (the opposites of anger), diligence (the opposite of sloth), neighborly love (the opposite of envy), generosity (the opposite of avarice) and humility (the opposite of pride).[11] The *Constitutions* present these character traits not as a simple list but in a variety of ways, always as virtues which can develop as soon as these areas of the personality are situated in some prayerful way within the relationship with God.

Chastity, the virtue opposite to lust, enables one to seek the fulfillment of the desire for love directly in a relationship with God and not in sexual pleasure. Being advanced in this virtue indicates a fine awareness of self that allows discernment over whether a relationship or sexual attraction is being used to fill in spiritual emptiness such as an infantile hunger for love. Over time, considerable stress or strong positive or negative emotions disturb less and less the capacity to find peace and fulfilment of the heart through finding God. Progress in chastity is fostered directly by exercises that channel the desire to love and to be loved toward God:

11 See for example: "Vertus et vices", in *Dictionnaire de spiritualité, Tome XVI* (Paris : Beauchesne, 1994), col. 503. As in the spiritual tradition the capital sins are listed with variations, likewise there are small differences in the terms that describe the opposite virtues.

> All should strive to keep their intention right, not only in regard to their state of life but also in all particular details, in which they should aim always to serve and please the Divine Goodness for its own sake and because of the incomparable love and benefits [. . .]. They should often be exhorted to seek God our Lord in all things, removing from themselves as far as possible love of all creatures in order to place it in the Creator of them [. . .]. [ConsCN C 288]

Temperance, the opposite of gluttony, also relates to a basic biological drive, namely hunger: "while eating they should be careful to observe temperance, decorum, and propriety both interior and exterior in everything" [ConsCN C 251]. As with virtues in general in the Ignatian vision, the virtue of temperance is rooted in prayer and frees one from trying to satisfy spiritual hunger and emptiness by eating. The pervasive contemporary problem of overeating is not simply to be faced, but is to be faced by creating a spiritually rich atmosphere that can help discernment: "While the meal is being eaten, food should be given also to the soul" [ConsCN C 251]. Related practical and spiritual instructions are detailed in the *Spiritual Exercises* [SpEx 210–17]. Interpreting the *Constitutions* in a contemporary context entails the development of viable practices that do not turn a blind eye to this area of potential growth while preserving the conviviality of common meals.

Patience and the ability to forgive, the opposites of anger, make it possible to restore or sustain the priority of inner peace even in the midst of conflicts. Patience and forgiveness differ from the repression of aggressive impulses. While repressed feelings extinguish the peace and the warmth of the soul, a patient and forgiving person will be able to manifest inner peace increasingly among the daily conditions and sometimes stormy periods of interpersonal relationships. Instead of passively enduring violence or aggressively bursting out in anger, he can use more creative, humorous or otherwise effective means for resolving conflicts. These competencies of the mature personality can grow through the practice of fraternal correction: "[The candidate] should be asked] whether he along with all the others will be willing to aid in correcting and being corrected, and to manifest one another with due love and charity, in order to help one another in the spiritual life *(para más ayudarse en spíritu)*" [ConsCN C 63]. Fraternal correction can be appropriated in an emotionally safe environment. Since the way of giving brotherly feedback is as important as the content, the novitiate should offer a variety of options for this exercise. Actual practices may vary greatly across cultural contexts, but there has to be a real choice of possible ways to handle disagreements. As we have seen before, the world of interpersonal relationships is the privileged place where the attitude of being contemplative in action can begin to develop in the novitiate. The relationship with God is to become the source of inner peace, which in turn can be reflected in human relationships. Signs of immaturity in this area should be taken seriously, and manifestations of raw or repressed anger are to be faced adequately, because unattended conflicts threaten the practice of contemplation in action, and risk perpetuating a limitation that can later impede apostolic life as well: "Passion or any anger of some in the house toward others should not be permitted. If anything of the sort arises, the parties should be made to reconcile immediately, with appropriate satisfaction" [ConsCN C 275].

Diligence, the opposite of sloth, is a further attribute of mature persons. Growth in diligence means reducing open or passive resistance when facing physical or intellectual work, and an increasing ability to engage in activities with ease, practicing charity in the midst of manifold responsibilities and spontaneous occasions. Lack of diligence is not merely seen as a bad habit in others but also as a likely source of other undesirable tendencies. In the long term, diligence enhances the quality of community life and boosts the apostolic thrust of those who want to remain united with God in the midst of action: "Generally, all those who are in good health should be busy with spiritual or exterior occupations [...] so that idleness, the source of all evils, may have no place in the house as far as this is possible" [ConsCN C 253].

Generous love is the opposite of envy and avarice. In the *Spiritual Exercises*, generosity is to be exercised as an attitude toward God: "The persons who make the Exercises will benefit greatly by entering upon them with great spirit and generosity toward their Creator and Lord" [SpEx 5]. The same attitude is no less important in the novitiate: "the more one binds himself to God our Lord and shows himself more generous toward his Divine Majesty, the more will he find God more generous toward himself" [ConsCN C 282]. The virtue of generosity and neighborly love can grow stronger in close personal relationships ("in all things they should try and desire to give the advantage to the others" [ConsCN C 250]) or in various activities: "it will be very specially helpful to perform with all possible devotion the tasks in which humility and charity are practiced more" [ConsCN C 282]. The emphasis on the attitude of generosity fosters a dynamic of progression in a way that is analogous to the Spiritual Exercises, and clearly differs from a culture that values the mere accomplishment of tasks and duties. In a contemporary context where innumerable electronic gadgets and other goods can trigger envy and avarice even in the life of Jesuits, the ability to be aware of such tendencies and inclinations and to be able to counter them with simplicity and generosity seems to become an increasingly important dimension of progression on the Ignatian pathway to God.

Humility is the opposite of pride, an essential attribute of mature love. While it presents itself in the *Spiritual Exercises* as God's free gift ("he or she should beg [our Lord] to be chosen for this third, a greater and better way of being humble" [SpEx 165–8]), we have seen that the *Constitutions* also emphasize personal responsibility in remaining in a state of humility: "all should take special care [. . .] to preserve themselves in peace and true humility of their souls" [ConsCN C 250]. In the daily life of the novitiate, humility is fostered by reverence toward others [ConsCN C 250], daily examination of conscience [ConsCN C 261], brotherly feedback [ConsCN C 63], and other tasks and activities "in which humility and charity are practiced more" [ConsCN C 282]. Obedience has a special role in creating circumstances where humility can be practiced: "they should obey entirely and promptly [. . .], with due fortitude and humility and without excuses or complaints" [ConsCN C 284]. In a contemporary context where obedience as one-way communication is often replaced by an open discussion between a Jesuit and his superior, the question of humility may remain more difficult to bring to the surface. Yet humility, the capacity to seek and find peace in the relationship with the Lord even among the sore emotions and the turmoil of thoughts that accompany a hurt sense of pride is a virtue that remains more relevant than ever.

The predominance of the virtues in the *Constitutions* is, of course, not to be interpreted in the daily practice of formation as a mechanical recommendation of "opposite virtues" whenever typical personal difficulties arise. The underlying vision is more important. Praying for the virtue of chastity and practicing it might well be helpful for someone with sexuality-related difficulties. Yet the same person might also discover that chastity-related temptations are aggravated when he feels worthless, not accepted or appreciated. He might also observe that his timidity at social occasions can rob him of inner peace. Such a novice can be encouraged to pray for courage, ask in advance for the Lord's help in "bearing" the occasional "reproaches and injuries" [SpEx 147]—instances of not being sufficiently respected and valued—and deliberately engage in challenging interpersonal situations with an attitude of openness to the Lord. Graces received in such exercises can help him to become more able to engage in healthy mutual relationships which in turn can alleviate his loneliness. In the protected milieu of the novitiate, virtues asked for in prayer and embraced through conscious practice can make relatively rapid progress possible. Relying on God for spiritual help while striving to develop more anxiety-free interpersonal relationships can help to cope with feelings of loneliness and to initiate relationships based on inner peace. The ability to create and maintain mature relationships will in this case prove to be an essential part of the virtue of chastity.

Since inclinations corresponding to the capital sins originate in the early years of human development and are thus deeply rooted in the personality of grown-up individuals, they can long remain hidden and unrecognized. Conscious and persistent practice of the Examen can help, but real change can be difficult to achieve. The novitiate can help by relieving novices of the heavy responsibilities of adult life and creating a milieu that is in some ways almost as protected as that familiar from childhood. In such an environment, immature forms of behavior can break out more easily. The person in probation can even perceive himself as "meaner" or "worse" than before entering, "in normal life". The advantage, however, of the less stressful yet well-structured environment is that it can make it easier to face painful experiences of the past, and to bring these—just like while doing the Spiritual Exercises—into prayer so that they can begin to heal. Novices who do not shift the responsibility to others, and do not blame the unusual circumstances of the novitiate but persist in an awareness of self and in seeking God, will be well disposed to receiving notable graces and to developing attitudes and virtues that stem from these graces within a surprisingly short period of time.

## Progress in Spirit

As we have seen, helping novices according to the *Constitutions* implies the consideration of a large array of seemingly small details. Meanwhile, the text refers to God in many ways and even the instructions concerning the "profane" dimensions, the world of material objects, other people and values, tend to demand that God be kept always in sight and Christ remain the focus. Still, precisely the large number of details could scatter the attention and overshadow the mystagogical aim, risking that the encounter with the mystery of the Trinity may remain superficial, consequently leaving one poorly prepared for later phases of Jesuit life. How is Part III of the *Constitutions* to be read as a mystagogical work? How do the manifold instructions help toward deeper unity with God?

Just as in the *Spiritual Exercises,* so in the early phases of Jesuit life it is important to recognize God as the giver of life, as a generous, compassionate and merciful Creator whose personal love for us is without limits. Beside personal prayer, in the milieu of the novitiate it is predominantly the manifestations of the "well-being" [ConsCN C 821] of the Society, for example, a sense of unity and peace among community members and the "bond of wills, which is the mutual charity and love they have for one another" [ConsCN C 821] that allow novices to experience this reassuring face of God. Unity, being a sign of God's love and a manifestation of the "glory" of God [cf. John 17:21–3], makes the presence of God obvious even for those who have not yet entered deeply into God's mystery. This is why the testimony of the authentic life of fellow Jesuits can be so helpful for the progress of novices:

> Within the house they should not converse with one another according to their own choice but with those whom the superior designates, so that they may be edified and helped by the others in our Lord *(edifiquen y se ayuden los otros en el Señor Nro)* through their good example and spiritual conversation, and not the opposite. [ConsCN C 247]

Especially the novice master, whose role in shaping the environment that holds the novices is decisive, has the responsibility of making this reassuring and caring face of God visible:

> It will be beneficial to have a faithful and competent person to instruct and teach the novices how to conduct themselves inwardly and outwardly, to encourage them to this, to remind them of it, and to give them loving admonition; a person whom all those in probation may love and to whom they may have recourse in their temptations and open themselves with confidence, hoping to receive from him in our Lord counsel and aid in everything. [ConsCN C 263]

Once the appropriate environment has been established, the second way of helping progression is by encouraging novices to seek, out of their own initiative, this same loving face of God:

> All should strive to keep their intention right, not only in regard to their state of life but also in all particular details, in which they should aim always to serve and please the Divine Goodness for its own sake and because of the incomparable love and benefits with which he has anticipated us rather than for fear of punishments or hope of rewards, although they ought to draw help from these also. They should often be exhorted to seek God our Lord in all things, removing from themselves as far as possible love of all creatures in order to place it in the Creator of them, loving him in all creatures and all creatures in him, in conformity with his holy and divine will. [ConsCN C 288]

To place God's generous and personal love at the center of attention is likely to be greatly helped by the first "experiment" in the novitiate:

> The first experience consists in making the Spiritual Exercises for one month, a little more or less; that is to say, in the person examining his conscience, thinking over his whole past life and making a general confession, meditating upon his sins, contemplating the events and mysteries of the life, death, resurrection, and ascension of Christ our Lord, exercising himself in praying vocally and mentally, according to the capacity of the persons, as he will be instructed in our Lord, and so on. [ConsCN C 65]

From the perspective of Jesuit formation, the main role of the *Exercises* is to help develop a personal practice of prayer that can bring "devotion", which, as we have seen, amounts to being able to find God:

> care should be taken both that they learn what is proper and not let it be forgotten, and that they put what they have learned into practice, all of them devoting time to spiritual things and striving to acquire

> devotion to the extent that divine grace imparts it to them. Toward this purpose, it will be helpful to give all or some of the Spiritual Exercises to those who have not done them, as may be judged expedient for them in our Lord. [ConsCN C 277]

If the environment of the novitiate is set up according to the *Constitutions*, one can anticipate that an initial period of enthusiasm will be followed by periodic changes of consolation and desolation. The analogy to the *Exercises* and the experience of formators confirm that continuous consolation cannot be guaranteed, and "endeavoring always to go forward in the path of the divine service" is to continue "whether with many spiritual visitations or with fewer" [ConsCN C 260]. The relationship model of Ignatian anthropology explains that as a consequence of using—even inadvertently—material things, personal relationships or cherished ideals and activities to cope with spiritual emptiness, one can expect resentment, emotional turmoil, even aggression—which can perhaps be projected onto God—when disillusioned by these "objects". Such experiences, although they can appear to novices like a challenge that they have never lived before, are as inevitable on the pathway to God as desolations during the Spiritual Exercises. One cannot break free from attachments—of which one is largely not even aware—without facing the emotional obstacles and the resulting doubts and thought patterns that oppose progression.

The probation can be expected to put to the test those who seek God with a right intention because they are repeatedly called to be "removing from themselves" [ConsCN C 288] all other affections. Before a trusting and nourishing relationship with God can become a solid basis for Jesuit life, the firm restrictions placed on the threefold "worldly" motivational sources will almost inevitably lead to periodically repeating painful and confusing emotional states like feeling bored, lonely or futile. Painful inner states can increase dramatically in the case of those who are strongly attached to objects of comfort, to friends with whom they could share moments of intimacy, to helping activities, or to rigid explanations and fixed beliefs. Psychologically, we might say that milder or stronger narcissistic traits and neurotic tendencies,[12] or else "life

12 K. Horney, *Neurosis and Human Growth: The Struggle toward Self-Realization* (New York and London: W. W. Norton & Co, 1950).

scripts",[13] determine the behavior of the person, but independently of the psychological assessment that one might make, the novitiate can be assumed to release enormous, previously unknown emotional energies. Impulsive, disrespectful behavior, suppressed aggression, compulsive self-observation can all indicate the initial fragility of consolation that can come from the relationship with God. Repressed feelings can often be recognized through the emotional difficulties experienced by other members of the community, or through the seemingly legitimate and rational arguments that the person puts forward in order to diminish the challenging character of the probation that is the novitiate. When personal attachments and preferences hide behind apparently rational propositions, it can be difficult for the superior to perceive that the conversation is in fact charged with emotional energies: one might simply find it difficult to answer with inner freedom although the request itself is seemingly innocent.

In such cases, discernment is necessary. Legitimate individual needs are to be respected, but the community should be maintained as a place fostering progression on the Ignatian pathway to God, even under emotional pressure or rationalizations by some of its members. Novices should persist in adapting to an environment that remains firm: "There should be someone to give the novices these or similar reminders every week or at least every fifteen days, or else they should be required to read them, lest they be forgotten through the condition of our frail human nature and so cease to be practiced" [ConsCN C 291]. Those who discover and begin to desire the spiritual character of progressing in the novitiate tend to perceive the firmness of the environment to be supportive, as one does during the Spiritual Exercises. To the extent that the relationship with God can become the milieu where the integration of other experiences can take place, where emotions and thoughts can be pondered and where inner freedom can be recovered, the daily schedule and other details of community life can begin to seem helpful. This is especially true at the times of desolation or distress when the observance of prayer times and other instructions can become difficult, but remains inevitable for facing desolation in such a way that it becomes fruitful from the perspective of progress [cf. SpEx

13 E. Berne, *What do you say after you say hello?* (New York: Bantam Books, 1972).

12–13, 318]. One of the beneficial effects of valuing firm structures can be that the tensions first manifesting themselves in interpersonal relationships including the superior (who personifies the novitiate milieu) can be discovered more easily within the relationship with God. Since the process of spiritual and human growth and personal transformation tend to provoke painful emotions and thought patterns, it can be extremely helpful if these are not projected onto community members or the superior but can be contemplated within the relationship with the person and the teachings of Christ. Again this dynamic is similar to that found in the *Spiritual Exercises*. Progress in the Ignatian sense is rooted in a living relationship with Christ who "is the way which leads men to life" [General Examen, ConsCN C 101].

To walk on the pathway to God according to the *Constitutions* means that sooner or later one will not only encounter the merciful, liberating and caring face of God but also the traits of God's firm and unyielding character. As with the Spiritual Exercises, such an experience is usually an inevitable, albeit not dominant, part of progressing. In the story of the Exodus from Egypt, which is a grandiose paradigm for subsequent processes of liberation by God, the pathway leading to freedom continues beyond a certain point only for those who acknowledge God as the giver of the Law, and who accept the Law and pledge to observe it. Jesus talked about his Father in an intimate and personal manner and preached a kind and merciful Gospel, yet did not hesitate to show the stern traits of God. He did not yield especially to scribes and Pharisees, who assertively vindicated their intelligence of things and their ways of proceeding, while, of course, also protecting their idealized self-images. Jesus' "Law", the Sermon on the Mount, is simultaneously meek, wise and firm to the point of harshness when it presents the commandment of love with a radical and universal authority.

To face the unfathomably exigent God is a distressing and potentially wounding experience, but it can also bring about extreme temptations. In line with the Christian tradition, the *Constitutions* predominantly refer to Abraham when interpreting trials that are decisive from the angle of trusting God but appear nonsense from all other, merely human, points of view. Such experiences are not typical during the time of probation yet sometimes they may prove beneficial. Moreover, in exceptional cases, and after careful consideration, the superior should trigger such situations:

> It will be helpful that superiors see to it that those who are in probation *(los que están en probación)* should sometimes experience their obedience and poverty, by testing them *(tentándolos)* for their greater spiritual progress *(para su mayor prouecho spiritual)* in the manner in which God tested *(tentó)* Abraham [Genesis 22], and that they may give evidence of their virtue and grow in it. But in this the superiors should as far as possible observe the measure and proportion of what each one can bear, as discretion will dictate *(como la discreción dictará)*. [ConsCN C 285]

Testing is not to be understood here in the sense of testing psychic or physical endurance but rather—as suggested by the Spanish *probación* and especially by the biblical expressions related to the verb *tentar*[14]—as a trial where perseverance in trusting God is at stake. Being tested means experiencing temptation and at the same time being asked to recommit oneself to God in a free decision of faith. The fruits of being tested can be abundant; to have persevered in a serious temptation may transform one's image of God and one's self-image radically. Those who can only live with an image of God who is kind and caring risk remaining ignorant of their—perhaps unconscious—weaknesses, compulsions and automatisms, or else risk perceiving these as realities that cannot be affected by grace. In contrast, those whose image of God corresponds to an uncompromising judge can hardly experience a truly liberating, intimate relationship with God. Persons who persevere in the test may go beyond one-sided images of God, and as a consequence experience greater inner freedom and love of God. If the test does not result merely in an uncontrolled explosion or an overly controlled repression of emotional reactions and thought patterns but the person can persist in seeking God even in the midst of the turmoil of extreme feelings and whirling thoughts, then the recognition may gradually dawn on him that the seemingly unbearable situation had been, in fact, a privileged passage where his freedom, progress and relationship with God were at stake.

Being put to the test can be helpful in learning to transform the question "Will I be strong enough to endure all that?" into the question

14 In Hebrew, *n$^{a}$sah*; in Greek, *peiradzein*.

of "How can I now seek to persevere in trusting God?" To recognize oneself as being put to the test rather than simply being in a difficulty implies precisely this change of perspective. Being put to the test implies that a difficulty is not avoided or downplayed but recognized as a difficulty. It also implies that the usual reactions of running away or demonstrating strength are also recognized as temptations. The paradigm of "having to cope with a difficulty" can thus be transformed into "facing a spiritual combat", where lucidity is important, and helpful means are not renounced, but more than anything else, trust in God is at stake.

The question of replacing the paradigm of coping with difficulties with that of being tempted becomes especially relevant when the difficulty consists in being caught up in the question of whether one will be strong enough to endure the hardships of Jesuit life. We know that this was a major temptation for Ignatius [Autobiography 20], and it clearly remains one for contemporary candidates to the Society, not to mention the dominant role it tends to play at times of vocational crises. Ignatius pursued this temptation with great inner force, but the long-term defense for him became the capacity to transform this question into "How can I now seek to persevere in trusting God?" The ability to make this shift of perspective, without which perseverance would become impossible, will be familiar to those who know by experience what it means to have been put to the test. The peculiar Ignatian exercise that makes reference to the temptation of Abraham seems directly to foster a capacity for such discernment, and is likely to prove vital for perseverance in Jesuit life.

The idea that a series of small crises is part of progressing and instrumental in avoiding a big crisis is not alien to Ignatian spirituality. Progression in the Exercises is never a smooth process without crises. Being put to the test during the novitiate, if the superior can "observe the measure and proportion of what each one can bear, as discretion will dictate" [ConsCN C 285], can be likened to being asked to return to a place of desolation during the Spiritual Exercises. While in desolation, the most diverse motivational drives can emerge into consciousness and become perceived tangibly as temptations. The extent to which these drives hinder "the divine service" can thus become manifest, and the moral judgment can be made that these drives are "evil inclinations" [ConsCN C 265], or else they can be simply said to be "thoughts [...]

which spring from desolation" [SpEx 317]. In the Spiritual Exercises, times of desolation are lived as times of small crises. Perseverance in a succession of such crises is not simply necessary for maintaining the dynamic of the Exercises but usually also becomes a source of new insights. Without an alternation of appropriately faced consolations and desolations, the Exercises can soon become monotonous and lose interest both for the director and for the person doing them. A succession of mini-crises, if dealt with according to the Rules for Discerning the Spirits, will foster the dynamic of the Exercises, deepen and strengthen the desire to continue, and the hypothetical big crisis of cutting the Exercises short can be avoided. It seems that mini-crises during Jesuit formation, if faced and accompanied according to the Ignatian instructions, can play an important role in avoiding the big crisis, which would be cutting Jesuit life short because the motivation to serve God in this apostolic body has vanished.

Similarities between facing temptations during the novitiate and while doing the Spiritual Exercises do not mean that it will be possible to maintain the same attention to detail in Jesuit apostolic life. Discernment usually needs time and a context of peacefulness, which are not necessarily given at any point in the midst of a busy apostolic life. Moreover, as the Rules for Discerning Spirits in the second week make clear, advancing in the spiritual life is likely to mean that discernment becomes a complex undertaking, where even more time might be necessary before one can see clearly. This is why the tools with which novices are to "defend themselves from all temptations" include the perseverance in "true and solid virtues" [ConsCN C 260]. Resisting temptations in Jesuit life is not only a matter of discernment and spiritual struggle, but also demands a capacity to resist, which in the Ignatian vision corresponds to being advanced in virtues, and which in more contemporary terms means having developed character strengths that help one to persevere in the good to which God calls human beings.[15] The novitiate has sufficient similarities with the *Spiritual Exercises* for novices to be able to strive to live in the presence of God in a way that can be said to be contemplative in action. The novitiate, however, does

15 See R. Dawson SJ and N. Austin SJ, "The Consolation of Character Strength in Ignatian Spirituality and Positive Psychology" in *The Way*, 53/3 (July 2014), p. 21.

not end after thirty days, so novices can begin to acquire or strengthen the personality traits that will enable them to remain contemplatives in action even in a busy apostolic life in the mission.

The expression "evil inclinations" [ConsCN C 265] suggests moral judgment, seemingly at odds with the approach that deficiencies tend to depend on instinctive childhood reactions that become rigid habits as a result of precarious, insufficient affective support. If inclinations like those expressed in the capital sins are the consequence of not having received sufficient help in childhood, then they could be said not to fall under moral categories but under that of healing. How could individuals who are victims of their past and perhaps not even aware of what exactly they are struggling with be held responsible for what they do? The Ignatian approach does not seem to allow much space for questions of healing; for example, the Gospel contemplations directly proposed by the *Spiritual Exercises* do not include any story of healing. While Ignatian spirituality certainly calls for respect and empathy toward wounded persons, and in some cases it seems possible to adapt the Exercises to persons seeking healing,[16] there is no reference to healing in the *Constitutions*, either. The Ignatian conviction seems to be that in the case of those who have been admitted to the Society, while vulnerabilities are to be acknowledged, they do not exclude responsibility. The example of the *Spiritual Exercises* could be helpful here again, since one often has the experience that during a spiritual battle, in a time of desolation, vulnerability and responsibility belong together like the two sides of a sheet of paper: "When we are in desolation we should think that the Lord has left us to our own powers in order to test us, so that we may prove ourselves by resisting the various agitations and temptations of the enemy" [SpEx 320]. Even in a spiritual battle where one feels that forces seemingly beyond the human scope, of an almost mythical scale, are at play, one might have the paradoxically simultaneous experience of ultimate exposure to temptations and a real responsibility to persevere with God. Although it would be difficult to describe what happens in the human soul during such times, periods of seemingly extreme vulnerability can be times of

16 See "Healing Mode" and "Calling Mode", in J. A. Veltri SJ, *Orientations* (Guelph Centre of Spirituality, vol. 2, part B, 1998).

exceptionally dynamic progress, when the Spirit of God can accomplish a powerfully transformative and liberating work. In the dynamic of this transformation, the appearance of moral categories is the sign of a new maturity that allows the person to assume responsibility for his own good as well as for that of others.

## Finishing the Novitiate

Over time, the rules that define the specific environment that is the novitiate may—depending on the progress that has been made—lose their relevance, since those who begin to rely on their relationship with God will develop behavior and thought patterns that gradually replace previous, possibly instinctive and arbitrary reactions: "Those who are proficient and doing well on their own in spiritual exercises *(corren en los exercicios spirituales)* and have a method for proceeding in them *(tienen forma para proceder en ellos)* [...] may be dispensed by the superior in whole or in part from the common rules in this matter" [ConsCN C 279]. The interpretation of the criterion of having "a method for proceeding in [the Spiritual Exercises]" will need thorough exegesis and a sharing of experiences among formators about how it can be fruitfully applied in practice, but it is clear that the mere fact of having done the thirty-day Spiritual Exercises or dutifully doing the daily meditation or the Examen are not sufficient for dispensation from the common rules that apply to spiritual matters in the novitiate. What is at stake is rather a live relationship with God that is expressed in the daily life of the novice. The clear priority and the integrated character of the spiritual dimension have to be coupled with a sense of personal responsibility for maintaining the exercises that can in fact foster the relationship with God.

Concerning the successful achievement of the purpose of the novitiate, the *Constitutions* give two more criteria, one in the First and General Examen and another at the beginning of Part IV. Both criteria could contribute to a complementary understanding of the novitiate.

The General Examen lists six "experiences" to be accomplished before the end of the novitiate: doing the Spiritual Exercises "for one month, a little more or less" [ConsCN C 65], serving in a hospital, making a pilgrimage without money, household works, teaching children, and preaching [see ConsCN C 64–71]. These experiments, which sometimes require several weeks or even months to be spent outside the house and would have been inconceivable as part of the novitiate before the foundation of the Society of Jesus are clear indicators of the apostolic character of the Society. The contemporary interpretation of this detail of the General Examen seems to be a good example of the general hermeneutical criteria that we formulated in the preliminary studies. Our way of understanding and practicing the novitiate experiments today tends to be meaningful in the light of all six hermeneutical principles that we listed above: 1. the novitiate experiments tend to help personal progression, 2. God can be found in new ways, 3. there is a sense of a growing incorporation into the Society and 4. increase in human maturity, 5. details are easily understood in the light of the whole, and 6. novices tend to gain an increased sense of being in agreement with Ignatian documents that talk about the ideals and the reality at the beginnings of the Society. As a consequence, novices and formators alike tend to find the preparation, accomplishment and evaluation of these experiments to be one of the most meaningful parts of the novitiate, and it is easy to understand why the General Examen calls these experiences "principal" and why it talks about them in detail.

Interestingly, however, these experiences in the Ignatian vision do not seem to have served the purpose of applying in real life whatever one has learned in the Spiritual Exercises and the secluded context of the novitiate community. According to the *Constitutions*, the experiments were to take place preferably in the first year, before joining the formation community in the strict sense of the word: "Before they enter the second year of their probation, which is made in the houses or colleges, all must spend six months in undergoing the six experiences just mentioned and six additional months in different ones" [ConsCN C 71]. It even seems to have been possible that a candidate could undertake these experiences before actually beginning the novitiate, "before he enters the house" [ConsCN C 64]. Basic spiritual dispositions must become visible during the experiments but instead of being presented as the fruits of the Exercises, these qualities seem to belong to the qualities that were necessary upon entering. For example, candidates to the Society should be such that they "are completely giving up the world with its pomps and vanities, so that in everything they may serve their

Creator and Lord, crucified for them" [ConsCN C 67], and the person doing the experiment "may with genuine faith and intense love place his reliance entirely in his Creator and Lord" [ConsCN C 67], able to work with "diligence and care in various low and humble offices" [ConsCN C 68]. Still, the emphasis on the "testimonies" and "reports" that have to be provided after each experience seems to indicate [ConsCN C 73–9] that the sheer fact of having undergone these experiences in a satisfactory way prevails over the spiritual attitudes that were to be at play. The vocabulary of progressing is absent in the paragraphs that describe the experiences, and so is the need to accompany the candidates with the same delicate care as during the time spent in the novitiate community. Although the experiments varied greatly in the lifetime of Ignatius,[17] and the text of the *Constitutions* is not silent about the tentative nature of the experiments ("These experiences may be gone through in whole or in part throughout the entire previously stated time of a candidate's probation; the sequence may vary in accordance with what is found expedient in our Lord" [ConsCN C 71]), it seems just to say that while the experiences appear to be characteristic and absolutely necessary components of the novitiate, they are not as tightly integrated into the Ignatian vision of helping progress as most of the other elements of the novitiate that we have discussed above.

The explanation is probably that the main purpose of the experiences is to test whether the candidates have the necessary human qualities such as endurance, humility, creativity and the like that will be necessary for apostolic life. The *Complementary Norms* describe a twofold goal: "[experiments] must place the novices in those circumstances wherein they can give evidence of what they really are" on the one hand, and, on the other, "show how they have made their own the spiritual attitudes proper to our vocation" [ConsCN CN 46 §1]. The *Constitutions* seem to underline the first objective, that of seeing who the candidates really are, and the extent to which they can work in a satisfactory way, although the experiments can certainly show the level of appropriation of spiritual attitudes that are necessary for apostolic life in the Society. But the ordinary time spent in the novitiate

17 Ph. Endean SJ, "Origins of Apostolic Formation: Jerome Nadal and Novitiate Experiments" in *The Way Supplement* 39 (Autumn 1980), pp. 57–82.

community remains the primary context where signs of immaturity can be dealt with, where reasons for not progressing have to be explored, and where a firm environment can play its role in confronting novices with some of the obstacles that make it difficult for them to progress on the Ignatian pathway to God. Experiments are not to be used automatically as a means to attain maturity as opposed to the "childish" context of the novitiate properly speaking. Although one may hope that a long apostolic experiment will help a novice to develop a sense of responsibility, and the person may in fact feel more mature and be happier among "normal" people, this could be simply the happiness of having avoided a difficult confrontation with oneself, like finding some interesting mental activity while doing the *Spiritual Exercises* in order to avoid a difficult experience of desolation. Experiences are thus of capital importance, but they should be used with prudence, because the fact of doing them well can say more about the human capacities of novices—for example, that they have the intellectual and practical talents to be a good teacher—than about the actual dynamic of moving ahead on the Ignatian pathway to God.

A final criterion for finishing the novitiate can be found at the beginning of Part IV, which mentions briefly the necessary qualities of those who are to begin their studies and who are thus allowed to move on to the next phase of Jesuit life: "once the proper foundation of abnegation of themselves and the needed progress in virtues *(abnegación de sí mesmos y aprouechamiento en las virtudes)* is seen to be present in the new members" [ConsCN C 307].

Progress in virtues has emerged as an important part of our reconstruction of the Ignatian dynamic of Jesuit life in the novitiate, but abnegation as a quasi-synonym for having laid solid foundations for Jesuit life demands further explanation. Our contemporary emphases in Ignatian spirituality would make it easier to understand if the criteria that had to be "seen to be present" in those who finish the novitiate included familiarity with God, the capacity for sound discernment, or love for the poor. Abnegation has not become a significant term in contemporary Ignatian spirituality, and there are hardly any discussions among formators about its contemporary interpretation and practice. Unlike, for example, novitiate experiments, where generally positive contemporary experiences indicate a fruitful reception of the *Constitutions,* abnegation remains a topic where bridging the gap between the Ignatian text and contemporary formation concerns remains a challenge yet to be faced.

The relationship model of Ignatian anthropology allows one to understand abnegation as the level of practical freedom that one has achieved vis-à-vis the three motivations that help human beings to be embedded in the created world. When there is no capacity for abnegation, the person has no other choice but to succumb to the influence of material goods that offer security and comfort, to the (presumed) approval and appreciation from others, or else to ideals and judgments that he cherishes for some reason. Someone who has made progress in abnegation can "negate" these motivations in order to choose the freedom inherent in a growing desire to love and serve God. While serving God—fortunately—is not necessarily opposed to the other three types of fundamental human motivations, one should be well prepared for incidents when there is a conflict. Abnegation is thus a spiritual and psychological quality, a character strength that allows one to persist in the service of God at times when it entails discomfort, disrespect or doing something apparently unreasonable: "the intention of the first men who joined themselves together in this Society was that those received into it should be persons already detached from the world and determined to serve God totally" [ConsCN C 53].

Abnegation is thus the human quality that allows Jesuits to live in such a way that the awareness of God does not remain a mere spiritual experience but can induce action. Together with discernment, it is a necessary prerequisite of being contemplative in action. The *Complementary Norms* clarify that self-abnegation is necessary for attaining a discerning attitude:

> If we are thus to hear and respond to the call of God in this kind of world, we must have a discerning attitude both individually and in community. We cannot attain this discerning attitude without self-abnegation, which is the fruit of our joy at the approach of the Kingdom and results from a progressive identification with Christ. [ConsCN CN 223 §4]

While the basic spiritual skills that enable one to recognize movements that come from the Spirit of God or from the "enemy of our human nature" [SpEx 135] can often develop within a few days while doing the Spiritual Exercises, abnegation necessarily entails the confrontation with and the slow transformation of personality patterns that had crystalized long ago and became fixed character traits. Abnegation demands time and appropriately conceived exercises, and Part III of the *Constitutions* repeatedly emphasizes that the novitiate is the favorable time for these [ConsCN C 258, 208, 284, 289 and so on]. A contemporary understanding of the *Constitutions* concerning abnegation will entail, beyond exploring how the word relates to other fundamental Ignatian expressions,[18] the development of a psychologically healthy yet purposeful Jesuit culture where this element of the pathway to God is valued and seen as a helpful exercise and a necessary condition for making progress. Abnegation can thus become a pertinent criterion for evaluating whether a young Jesuit can finish the novitiate. To the extent that a sense of obvious inner freedom is seen to be present in him that is maintained in the midst of stress, loneliness and varying group dynamics, he can be presumed to have the necessary basis for engaging in the dynamic of the second phase of Jesuit life.

The criteria for passing to the next stage of Jesuit life are, as we have seen, relatively well established. Yet the *Constitutions* do not give a checklist that would help to make the evaluation a mere automatism. A subjective aspect necessarily remains and it even seems to be the most important criterion when, for example, there is question of prolonging the novitiate: "if there is doubt on the part of the Society about [the novice's] talent or conduct, it will be safer to have him wait another year, or whatever time will seem wise later on, until both parties are content and satisfied in our Lord" [ConsCN C 100]. Whether the Society and, more specifically, the Jesuits who are directly responsible for the novitiate, will have doubts or be "content and satisfied", will depend on their conception of Jesuit life. When the dynamic character of Jesuit life is emphasized, then being content will not simply depend on the comparison of the novice to an abstract ideal but will also regard his capacity to progress within the specific environment that is the novitiate. If a capacity to progress is seen to be present, then the eventual prolongation of the novitiate can make sense, just as

18 "Abnegación", in *DEI (A–F)*, pp. 65–75.

the prolongation of the first week of the Exercises makes sense when the person giving the Exercises has the intuition that the person has "something more" to find in the context of the first week. If a novice has not engaged in the dynamic of the first week, prolongation does not make much sense. In other words, the criterion for finishing the novitiate is the intuitive conviction that the novice has made the most of the novitiate, and by engaging in a dynamic of progression, he has made good use of the firm environment and of the intensive spiritual and human support in order to face his disordered tendencies and immature patterns of behaving and thinking. Failure to have done so means running the risk that, although one can well imagine the person becoming a good Jesuit, for example, in the educational or the social sector, a "proper foundation" of Jesuit life is absent, and, perhaps many years later, difficulties will emerge that will be nearly impossible to deal with in later phases of Jesuit life. Being "content and satisfied" needs to imply a sense of satisfaction with the way the particular novice has engaged in the dynamic of progressing proper to the novitiate, and a sense that he has fruitfully and exhaustively used the possibilities for his own advancement, including the human, spiritual, interpersonal, apostolic and other dimensions of life that will all contribute to the apostolic fruitfulness of a formed Jesuit.

✠ 6 ✠

# Part IV of the Constitutions: Scholastic Years

## Relishing Spiritual Things or Studying?

The second phase of the Ignatian pathway to God is described in Part IV of the *Constitutions*: "It will be necessary to provide for the edifice of learning, and of skill in employing it" [ConsCN C 307]. These years require scholastics to invest themselves in philosophical, theological and possibly other studies that will provide them with the intellectual skills for engaging in the mission of the Society. Seen in the relationship model of Ignatian anthropology, the time of studies opens for scholastics a wide window onto the world of ideas and ideals, just as the world of interpersonal relationships became accessible to novices in a special way. The mutual exchange of "giving" and "receiving" happens primarily in the dimension of theories and ideas, which demand attention and effort but also yield specific satisfactions and joys. However, while in the novitiate the two dimensions of relating to God and to other persons could be relatively easily integrated within a single dynamic of progress, the sustained focus on studies may be in tension with the spiritual relish that can be found in God. Studying "in a certain way requires the whole person" [ConsCN C 340], and the pressure to engage the intellectual capacities may not always seem compatible with the desire to find God in all things.

The difficulty is not a theoretical one since studies are clearly a preparation for apostolic life, by no means foreign to the pathway to God that is Jesuit life. The challenges, as Ignatius noticed when he began studying seriously, are of a practical nature. After the deep, sensitive, emotionally rich relationship that he had been able to develop with God in Manresa and while traveling to Jerusalem, Ignatius was surprised to see that his spiritual experiences hindered rather than helped his studies:

> So, returning to Barcelona, he began to study with great diligence. But one thing was very much in his way: that is, when he began to memorize, as one must in the beginnings of grammar, there came to him new insights into spiritual matters and fresh relish, to such an extent that he could not memorize, nor could he drive them away no matter how much he resisted.
>
> So, thinking often about this, he said to himself, "not even when I engage in prayer and I am at Mass do such vivid insights come to me". Thus, little by little, he came to realize that it was a temptation. [Autobiography 54–5]

Later, during his theology studies in Paris, he encountered the same difficulty. As a solution, he temporarily gave up the affectively engaging, intense character of his relationship with God, settling for an emotionally less exciting, simpler practice of faith:

> As he began attending the lectures of the course [in Paris], the same temptations began to come to him that had come when he studied grammar in Barcelona. Whenever he was at a lecture, he could not pay attention because of the many spiritual thoughts that came to him. Realizing that in this way he made little progress in study, he went to his master and promised he would never fail to follow the whole course, so long as he could find bread and water for his sustenance. After making this promise, all that devotion which came to him out of time left him, and he went on quietly with his studies. [Autobiography 82]

It seems to be a characteristic of the Ignatian pathway to God that Jesuits who plunge into their studies after the novitiate can anticipate a conflict between studying and the interior savoring of spiritual things. Attention to this potential conflict is vitally important. The novitiate provides an environment in which everything is arranged to help progress in inner freedom and in the Spirit. Moving from the novitiate phase to the scholastic years, young Jesuits may perceive that the expectation or thrill of doing serious studies attracts their attention and energies more than the spiritual dimension that should be inherent in Jesuit life. This can destabilize them in their vocation. A sensitive balance is to be maintained:

> once they have satisfactorily completed [the novitiate] and are devoting themselves to studies, while care must be taken that they do not through fervor in study grow cool in their love of true virtues and of religious life, still they will not at that time have much place for mortifications or for long prayers and meditations. [ConsCN C 340]

Serious study would be no doubt impossible for someone who wanted to spend most of the day in long prayer and meditations. But studying and prayer can be incompatible the other way round as well: the excitement of studying, meeting deadlines and other expectations, or even the joy of learning, of responding to intellectual challenges, the satisfaction inherent in entering the world of concepts and theories can mean that—even though the person makes good progress in his studies and is apparently doing well as a Jesuit—the Ignatian pathway to God is forgotten, and the "love of true virtues and religious life" weakens. Studying with total dedication may result in spiritual dryness. Emotionally nurturing experiences of consolation can weaken or even disappear. A sense of emptiness of the heart can set in. Time dedicated to prayer may seem futile, and motivations contrary to the vows may become more intense. Without adequate help, motivations can become, almost without any noticeable sign, once again structured by what the "world" demands from any student who is eager to take the time of studies seriously. This means potentially increasing doubts about being on the right path, especially if in the novitiate affectivity was learned to be constitutive of the relationship with God, but sufficient generosity and character strength has not yet developed and the commitment to apostolic life is not yet firmly established.[1]

The scholastic years, the long second phase of the Ignatian pathway to God, can thus be characterized by a tension of the motivational system that can destabilize the person in his vocation. Progress accor-

1 For a lucid presentation of the tension between serious commitment to studies and the spiritual dynamism of Jesuit life, as well as how the Society at the beginning of the seventeenth century grappled with this core difficulty, see T. Bartók SJ, "L'Idéal intellectuel et ses pièges", in the doctoral thesis "Un interprète et une interprétation de l'identité jésuite: Le Père Louis Lallemant et sa Doctrine spirituelle au carrefour de l'histoire, de l'analyse institutionnelle et de la pensée d'auteurs jésuites antérieurs et contemporains" (manuscript, Paris: Centre Sèvres – Facultés jésuites de Paris, 2014), pp. 198 ff.

ding to the *Constitutions* can be helped by means of personal, prayerful consideration, and by making use of both dimensions of Ignatian help, that of creating an adequate environment to which scholastics adapt themselves and that of providing sufficient spiritual support: "The function of the rector will be first of all to sustain the whole college by his prayer and holy desires, and then to see that the *Constitutions* are observed" [ConsCN C 424]. To explore the facilitation of the progress of the scholastics in more detail, we once again use the fourfold relationship model of Ignatian anthropology to structure the material of the *Constitutions*.

## The Use of Material Goods

Dedicated and undisturbed studies require a solid financial background. According to the *Constitutions*, the need for good material conditions does not hold to the same degree for other phases of the Ignatian pathway to God since the experience of poverty is a vital part of both the novitiate and tertianship, while Jesuits with final vows are also to live a simple life. Although the "houses of the professed" where the sustenance of Jesuits depends on Providence alone [cf. ConsCN C 554–5] do not exist any more, life style in Jesuit communities "ought to bear credible witness to the countercultural values of the Gospel" [ConsCN CN 194]. For the scholastic years, however, considerable funds are necessary to guarantee the financial security which is necessary to maintain appropriate buildings, pay a competent faculty and sustain scholastics themselves.

This particularity of the scholastic years probably explains the surprising fact that the very first paragraphs of Part IV of the *Constitutions* give a detailed account of the manifold ways of expressing gratitude toward the benefactors. Chapters 1 and 2 [ConsCN C 309–32] call attention, for example, to the regular celebration of Masses for the benefactors but also to the wax candle which is to be presented to the founder or to the relative of the founder. In the light of the relationship model of Ignatian anthropology, these meticulously specified, concrete practices can be understood to express the concern for maintaining inner freedom vis-à-vis the unusually abundant material conditions established through heavy investments. The enjoyment of material goods and financial security is admissible to the extent that they serve the progress of scholastics on the pathway to God. However, unless this dimension is integrated into a sufficiently powerful vision of preparing for apostolic life in the Society, the uncritical enjoyment of material security can begin to weaken the inner freedom acquired in the novitiate. The instructions instill practices that can help Jesuits to regard material conditions from a spiritual perspective, which is a presupposition for keeping motivations ordered in accordance with what is necessary to move on the Ignatian pathway to God. The *Constitutions* make it a responsibility of the rector and the entire formation community to foster this spiritual perspective by remembering the benefactors, by helping to keep in mind the purpose of studies, and by presenting material goods in a way that they can be seen to be transparent to the "Divine Goodness" who acts through the benefactors, "employs [them] as ministers" [ConsCN C 309].

## Relationship with God

Instructions "in regard to spiritual matters" can be found in Chapter 4 ("The care and welfare of the scholastics in the colleges" [ConsCN C 339–50]). Accordingly, scholastics are to spend an hour daily in prayer: "they will have one hour, during which they will recite the Hours of Our Lady, examine their consciences twice each day, and add other prayers according to each one's devotion to fill out the rest of the aforesaid hour [...] by which [meditations and other spiritual exercises] the hour is filled out" [ConsCN C 342, 343]. The length of daily prayer is firmly set. Scholastics are to adapt to an expectation, to a characteristic of the milieu where they do their studies. This could be seen as a sign of putting expectations on individuals rather than trusting that they are sufficiently mature to set the time to be spent in prayer. In the perspective of the *Constitutions*, however, where Jesuits are to make progress in the complex Ignatian sense of the word, the insistence on the time to be spent in prayer evokes the Spiritual Exercises, where similarly firm instructions define the length of prayer times: "the one giving the Exercises should insist strongly with the person making them that he or she should remain for a full hour in each of the five Exercises or contemplations which will be made each day" [SpEx 12]). In both cases, one can recognize the first aspect of Ignatian help, that is, setting up the appropriate conditions to which those who are to progress will adapt themselves in order to be able to enter the space of inner freedom where growth can happen. In the Exercises, the expectation to pass a full hour in prayer even in the midst of not-so-enlivening spiritual movements will—at least in retrospect—be perceived as help received from a firm and not rigid, but purposefully established environment. The same is true for a scholastic who may find it difficult to set aside the daily prayer time out of purely spiritual motives when he is under the pressure of writing papers or passing exams or spending time with fellow students. The fact that the weight of responsibility for spending sufficient time in prayer is not uniquely on his shoulders will be perceived by him as a confirmation that the progress along the Ignatian pathway to God is maintained as a priority for him. As long as scholastics tend to find themselves alone with the responsibility for consecrating sufficient time to daily prayer, the contemporary interpretation of the *Constitutions* remains insufficient at this point. The individual responsibility of scholastics in this area is not to be considered as a self-evident consequence of their presumed maturity. It is a characteristic of the Ignatian pathway to God that the one-sided overemphasis of the intellectual dimension over an extended period can make it difficult to maintain spiritual maturity even for humanly mature scholastics. As with the Spiritual Exercises, where the occasional or sometimes repeated questions of the director concerning the actual length of prayer times provide an almost invisible yet fundamentally important support even to "mature" persons, scholastic life entitles one to the support of the formation environment, which is to result in prayer times becoming an obvious and steady part of one's daily schedule even in the midst of heavy academic challenges. Praying because the superior insists on the importance of daily prayer is not a highly sophisticated motive but, just as during the Exercises when someone may have no motive to sit down to pray other than having to talk about it during the upcoming accompaniment meeting, it does not hinder progress. Progress is hindered when prayer is given up.

The central role of progressing means that firm insistence on keeping prayer times is by no means the only quality requested from superiors. They are in the role of supervising a process of growth that necessarily entails a spiritual dimension. Firmness in upholding the value of sufficient prayer needs to be subjected to discernment, just as when accompanying the Exercises:

> for some persons the period of prayer could be lengthened or shortened. This will remain wholly within the discretionary power of the superior *(todo en la discreción del Superior)*. The specified hour will be taken, somewhat more or less, for the recitation of the Hours of Our Lady. [ConsCN C 343]

The need to consider individual abilities and needs is even more accented in the case of choosing the appropriate form and content of prayer:

> in addition to confession and Communion every eight days and daily Mass, they will have one hour, during which they will recite the Hours of Our Lady, examine their consciences twice each day, and add other prayers according to each one's devotion [...]
>
> [...] in the case of the scholastics who are not obliged to recite the Divine Office, the hour can more easily be changed at times to meditations and other spiritual exercises [...] especially with some who do not advance spiritually by one method *(que en el un modo no se aprouechan en spíritu)*, so that with God's grace they may be helped more by another. This is to be done [...] while keeping in view the genuine devotion of the subjects or of the founder, and also the circumstances of persons, times, and places. For those who do not have experience in spiritual things and desire to be helped in them, some points for meditation and prayer could be proposed to them in the way that seems best for persons of this kind. [ConsCN C 343]

In a contemporary context, the role of the superior can be certainly delegated to a spiritual director, but it remains noteworthy that the character of the spiritual direction seems to imply an authority relationship that is closer to giving the Exercises than to a casual spiritual conversation about freely chosen topics. The superior, or the spiritual director, needs to be able to discern what seems helpful, and has to see to it that the scholastic puts it into practice, as when doing the Exercises:

> They will do all this according to the order and judgment of their superiors, whom they oblige themselves to obey in place of Christ our Lord. [ConsCN C 342]

> This is to be done with the permission or through the order of their superiors, whose duty it will always be to consider whether, for certain reasons with particular persons, something different is more expedient, in order to carry it out. [ConsCN C 343]

Apart from daily prayer, the relationship with God can also be fostered by a periodic liturgical renewal of the commitment to Jesuit life:

> For greater devotion, and to refresh the memory of the obligation they are under and confirm themselves more solidly in their vocation, it will be good for the scholastics twice each year, at Easter and Christmas, to renew their simple vows. [ConsCN C 346]

As we have seen, there is considerable emphasis on elements of Ignatian help that do not depend on the personal discernment of scholastics but demand them to be in conversation with and to adapt themselves to the superior. Superiors are expected to pay personal attention to scholastics, including the length and the method of their prayer. This is quite surprising since young Jesuits can be expected to have had a solid introduction to prayer before becoming scholastics, and whether they became "proficient and doing well on their own in spiritual exercises" [ConsCN C 279] was a significant question in their formation. Ignatius' cautiousness might be explained by the fact that the studies which "require the whole person" place young Jesuits in an excessively unbalanced context, which drains their psychic energies to the extent that their spiritual senses can become unreliable.

Another aspect of Ignatian help is meant to support scholastics in maintaining attitudes and making personal decisions that serve their progress. Among these, "a pure intention of serving God" [ConsCN C 340] stands out. The theme of the purity of the intention recalls how much the regular preparatory prayer "for the grace that all my intentions, actions, and operations may be ordered purely to the service and praise of the Divine Majesty" [SpEx 46] can be helpful for progressing in the Spiritual Exercises. As with the novitiate, where keeping the right intention was a central attitude [ConsCN C 288], the time of study also requires one to keep this attitude alive. The scholastic years are not there to serve a one-dimensional development of intellectual competencies, but to contribute to the whole person's progress on the pathway to God. Purity of intention plays a central role in achieving this objective, but—as during the Exercises or in the novitiate—one cannot expect to possess it once and for all:

> In order to make good progress *(aprouechen)* in these subjects, the scholastics should strive first of all to keep their souls pure and their intention in studying right, by seeking in their studies nothing except the glory of God and the good of souls. [ConsCN C 360]

Personal responsibility in this area is of key importance, but individual effort is not the way to obtain purity of intention. Just as in the Spiritual Exercises, it can be prayed for and received as a grace: "they should frequently beg in prayer for grace to make progress *(aprouecharse)* in learning for the sake of this end" [ConsCN C 360]. One can also decide to exercise a certain discipline concerning thoughts. Since scholastic years can be poor in affective confirmations of the fact that Jesuit life is indeed a pathway to God, and consequently, intellectual doubts can also arise, faith-based convictions and resolutions become essential:

> Next, they should have a firm resolution to be genuine and earnest students, persuading themselves that while they are in the colleges they cannot do anything more pleasing to God our Lord than to study with the intention mentioned above; likewise, that even if they never have occasion to employ the matter studied, the very toil of study, duly undertaken because of charity and obedience, is itself a very meritorious work in the sight of the Divine and Supreme Majesty. [ConsCN C 361]

The importance of being motivated by "charity and obedience" can be understood in the light of the dynamic of this second phase of Jesuit life. The *Constitutions* suggest that a scholastic who is engaged in a dynamic progression on the pathway to God will probably find that the characteristic difficulty in his relationship with God is not the oscillation between consolation and desolation which was customary in the Spiritual Exercises and the novitiate [cf. ConsCN C 260], but rather a waning devotion and the lack of savoring God's presence. The risk of the progressive disappearance of one of the primary motivations to be a Jesuit and the diminishing satisfaction that one can find in prayer seems to be unavoidable at some point in the life of scholastics. The joy of studying may supplant these losses partially, but it can be anticipated that over time, studying becomes tiring and laborious and in this case "charity and obedience" may well remain one of the last sources of motivation for further progress. This characteristic of the second phase of Jesuit life has to be known to formators and scholastics alike so that they are not deprived of all the possible Ignatian help that the *Constitutions* envisage for this phase. Ongoing cooperation between the scholastic and his superior in observing the instructions of the *Constitutions* can insure that individual particularities and preferences can be respected but arbitrary ways of coping with this stressful phase of Jesuit life will not prevail in the life of the scholastic, and motivations in disagreement with the pathway to God can be resisted.

## Interpersonal Relationships

Although studying is basically intellectual work done alone, the *Constitutions* describe surprisingly rich and intense relationships among scholastics. Attention to one another, fraternal relationships and further advancement in virtues remain important [cf. ConsCN C 308, 424], given that a profound and lasting transformation of the personality will presumably take years even after the novitiate. As opposed to the novitiate, however, themes related to studies become a decisive part of conversations. Philosophical and theological questions are to be discussed daily in an institutionalized way: "an hour ought also to be designated each day for holding disputation within the college" [ConsCN C 379]. Disputes can simply give an opportunity to formulate freshly appropriated knowledge and confront it with other views, but from time to time they can go as far as stirring a "holy rivalry" [ConsCN C 383] with all the emotional energies that may imply. Interestingly, this seems to mean that human motivations belonging to the "world" are expected to contribute to creating a group dynamic that can help scholastics remain motivated in their studies not only individually but also as a group.

It would be, of course, anachronistic to revive scholastic disputations as they were practiced at the University of Paris at the time of writing the *Constitutions*, as a feature of the Thomist way of teaching philosophy and theology. These disputations reminded one old Jesuit who had witnessed them of clowns in the circus, who flex their muscles while pretending to lift colossal iron weights that in reality are hollow. Still, seeing how these disputations were supposed to engage scholastics in an activity that was intellectual and interpersonal at the same time, while also being a preparation for apostolic life, there may be room for contemporary creativity in this area. In a time when philosophical and theological studies are increasingly perceived as overly abstract and cut off from "real life", some form of disputations could both foster the motivation of scholastics and give more weight to studies. Sharing successful current experiences with disputations could be of much help in developing a relevant contemporary interpretation of these instructions of the *Constitutions*.

The *Constitutions* firmly restrict interpersonal relationships between scholastics and non-Jesuits. "Conversations", even if they are done with the purpose of helping souls, or as part of the "duties inside the house or outside it" [ConsCN C 362], may hinder focused studies: "In colleges of the Society, no curacies of souls, obligations to celebrate Masses, or similar duties should be accepted which greatly distract from study and impede the aim which is pursued in the colleges for the divine service" [ConsCN C 324]. Similar or even stronger restrictions apply to casual relationships between scholastics and non-Jesuits. While the rule of going to school in pairs has been abolished by modern general congregations, the interpersonal relationships that scholastics develop are to be subjected to the prudence of the superior:

> When they must go to schools open to the public (for they will not go to other places without requesting permission), they should go and return in pairs. [ConsCN C 349]
>
> our members in formation should have suitable contacts, arranged with prudence, with young people of their own age. [ConsCN CN 111]

Why are restrictions in the world of interpersonal relationships so firm? The answer might be found in the somewhat inconsistent anthropological situation of the scholastics. In a period where affective dryness can last several years and consoling experiences with God become scarce, scholastics may become unexpectedly and powerfully drawn toward persons from whom they hope to receive attention or empathy, or else who elicit empathy and a warmth of heart in them, offering a way out of the challenge of enduring emotional dryness for the sake of preparing for Jesuit life. Without sound Ignatian help, emotional attachments can easily develop, from which it is usually difficult to return to the dynamic of the pathway to God. A scholastic, since he is predominantly occupied by facing the immediate challenges that present themselves to him, does not have an overarching perspective of the pathway to God that is still ahead of him. Emotional attachments in such situations can develop quite unsuspectingly, since in the midst of affective dryness, an intimate relationship can catalyse the return of a liveliness of heart and a sense of inner freedom that could be previously savored in a relationship with God. If an affectively deep and nurturing relationship with an attractive person develops, a scholastic may think he has discovered the "better side" of his personality: instinctively, he will begin to perceive his life as more meaningful and joyful, and if he continues to pray, he can probably do so with a more spirited and sensitive heart. In such cases, even persons who have fine qualities of discernment tend to become convinced that God is calling them to leave the Society. What happens in reality is that the intimacy that has been found in the proximity of an attractive person becomes a more powerful motivation than the seemingly remote goal of "helping souls" as a Jesuit. Motivations return to what is characteristic of lay life: the promise of a fulfilled and integrated life appears to be realizable through the securing of intimacy in a privileged relationship, and progressing on the Ignatian pathway to God appears to be an abstract possibility without much appeal.

## The World of Ideas and Ideals

The primary characteristic of the "world" to which scholastics are exposed while studying philosophy and theology is that it appeals to the intellect. The *Constitutions* give detailed descriptions for creating a helpful environment: the program of studies and the authors to be read, the recommended methods of learning, and so on. Learning methods include library work, attending lectures, memorizing the material, and the practice of several forms of disputations [ConsCN C 369–85]. There is great emphasis on content: "those books will be lectured on which in each subject have been deemed to contain more solid and safe doctrine" [ConsCN C 464]. In the meantime, it is noteworthy that individuals are expected to be active in expressing both orally and in writing what they have learned, so much so that expressing the acquired material in various ways is almost as important as learning it. Routine-like daily practices vary with special occasions such as a festive disputation or sending exceptionally well-written papers to the provincial [ConsCN C 383].

The evaluation of our contemporary practice of formation in the light of the *Constitutions* and other relevant documents is an ongoing issue and too complex to be treated here. But it can be safely said that studies according to the *Constitutions* are not distinguished by some special content characteristic of the Society: "solid and safe" knowledge is required, and the areas where the specificity of Jesuit learning becomes manifest is the ample use of various pedagogical means. To be able to express well what has been learned is a condition for Jesuit apostolic life, and disputations bring home to scholastics that studying is in fact a direct preparation for a life in mission. The ability to express oneself in theological, moral, philosophical or other discussions where Gospel values are at stake belongs to the core competencies of a Jesuit, which will allow him to exercise ministry in a variety of contexts. In the light of the relationship model of Ignatian anthropology one can say that if a Jesuit can contribute to local or more universal discussions that directly or indirectly affect the good of individuals or communities, that is, if he can articulate his convictions while being receptive to values that others present, then he has become able to practice "mutual communication" in the dimension of values, ideas and ideals. To be active in this dimension is a characteristically Jesuit way of serving and of loving "more by deeds than by words", even if deeds in this case may mean well-founded words that in fact promote the good of others.

Towards the end of the scholastic years, the *Constitutions* shift the attention to the practical application of the learned material: "it is good for the scholastics to begin getting accustomed to the spiritual arms they must employ in aiding their fellow men" [ConsCN C 400]. Chapter 8 ("The instruction of the scholastics in the means of helping their neighbor" [ConsCN C 400–14]) lists issues such as the fruitful administering of the sacraments, thoughtful preparation and edifying delivery of sacred lectures, the practice of giving the Exercises to others, and so on. The apostolic purpose, the relevance and great usefulness of a practical preparation for ministry is obvious. Yet it also becomes clear that the objective is not a simple appropriation of pastoral skills that correspond to the teaching of the church or to sound pastoral principles, but doing ministry in a way that persons "may receive and frequent these sacraments well and fruitfully *(bien y frutuosamente)*, for the divine glory" [ConsCN C 406]. In other words, ministerial competences have to be appropriated in a way that the person can "help souls" while he remains open to God's action and the manifestation of God's presence. Acquiring ministry skills is not a matter of attending a few more workshops toward the end of theological studies but learning to engage oneself fully in the activities that comprise the mission of the Society.

By the time they actually begin apostolic life, Jesuits have spent many years as scholastics with a strong focus on intellectual life while having been submitted to the one-sided burden of intellectual accomplishments. Now they have to find a new balance in relating to God and to the world. Concerning interpersonal relationships, they will need to be perceptive and open, paying personal attention to the individual needs and desires of others. In other words, they will have to use all the interpersonal skills that they had appropriated in the novitiate, since they will be required to "associate with so great a diversity of persons throughout such varied places" [ConsCN C 414]. Concerning the intellectual dimension, they will have "to have prepared and have ready at hand the topics most useful for this ministry [of preaching]" [ConsCN C 402] so that their public speaking is rich in meaning. Jesuits will also need to learn to speak in an interesting, helpful and authentic way "to the edification of the people, which is different from the scholastic manner" [ConsCN C 402]. Moreover, all these competencies need to be exercised in a fashion that personal efforts are not in the forefront but are integrated seamlessly into a spiritual dimension: "all this can be taught only by the unction of the Holy Spirit and by the prudence which God our Lord communicates to those who trust in his Divine Majesty" [ConsCN C 414]. In the relationship model of Ignatian anthropology, this means that the interpersonal and the intellectual dimensions that may have developed up to this point to some extent independently from each other now have to be integrated with each other and into the contemplative dimension of human life so that apostolic activities can be lived as part of an ongoing relationship with God.

The maturity required at this level includes a high level of inner freedom. While a Jesuit has to be perceptive in his interpersonal relationships, he has to be able to bring forth a pure intention of serving God, distinguishing it from simply responding to expectations or enjoying intimate human relationships. Also, while he needs to be competent in shaping his environment according to Gospel values, he needs to be able to distinguish between the intention to serve God and the intention to be efficient and successful. Struggling to do good work and struggling to be accepted are necessary elements of apostolic work but both of them are to be subordinated to the struggle of remaining attuned to God. Depending on the character of each Jesuit, maintaining freedom certainly needs awareness and continuous vigilance in at least some of these areas.

At the end of the years of studies, it is not enough to have passed all the exams to begin a life of ministry. The manifold spiritual, interpersonal, intellectual and pastoral competences—"virtues" that one has developed—will need to be integrated in such a way that the person can remain attuned to God even in stressful situations, so that neither a perfectionist agitation nor the withdrawal into an ideal world nor the appreciation or admiration of a selected person or group become more important than the capacity to find peace and strength in the presence of God. This means that themes familiar from the novitiate come to the fore once again, this time as a direct preparation for apostolic life. The fruits of this final integration process are so decisive in Jesuit formation that they are to be fostered in a special phase of Jesuit formation, tertianship.

## Perseverance

Given the contemporary fragility of vocations and the apparent difficulty encountered especially during the period between the novitiate and tertianship in this regard, it may be helpful to summarize what has been said about the motivation of scholastics who make progress according to the Ignatian pathway to God at this phase of Jesuit life. As we have seen, the dynamic of progress is basically sustained by the harmony of two of the four basic motivational forces. Although facing intellectual challenges may become a major source of motivation, the intensity of this motive tends to vary greatly: scholastics can be in the "fervor in study" [ConsCN C 340] but later also experience the burdensome character of studying even to the point of doubting its usefulness. Conscious efforts frequently to rekindle a spiritual motivation, that is, to study "with a pure intention of serving God" [ConsCN C 340] can greatly help with persevering on the pathway to God. Scholastics who keep this personal objective alive will be greatly helped by the appropriately established environment and by the personal spiritual support that is available to them, so that they can preserve "their love of true virtues and of religious life" [ConsCN C 340].

Material goods and interpersonal relationships demand less attention during this period, even if these relationships are stimulated by regular disputations. To sustain freedom in these two areas is nevertheless important for maintaining a dynamic progression on the pathway to God. If attachments to material goods or persons develop while there is already a tension between investing oneself in studies and upholding the love for religious life, then the transformative character of Jesuit formation may fade away and motivations may be restructured according to what is typical in lay life. A sense of emptiness and lack of inner peace progressively alienate the person from his former commitment to become a Jesuit, spiritual strength and the determination to continue Jesuit life weaken, and the future will be increasingly imagined among the seemingly "real" challenges of lay life or in an intimate personal relationship.

In order to be able to give competent help, the rector or spiritual director will have to be aware of the difference between difficulties that are foreseeable during the years of studies and those that stem from significant attachments. Discernment will be greatly facilitated by contemplating scholastics in the light of the fourfold relationship model of Ignatian anthropology. When a scholastic is seen to be determined to persevere honestly in the intention to serve God, and he avoids enduring attachments to persons or material goods, then he can be encouraged to persist, because he will be well prepared to be consoled and fortified by God with ever new graces. In such cases, difficulties and doubts arising during the time of studies can be considered as "normal" as the times of desolation during the Spiritual Exercises. Lasting and serious attachments, however, or the loss of interest in making progress on the

Ignatian pathway to God, even if the crisis has not yet surfaced, should alert the rector and the spiritual director that motivations are being restructured according to what lay life demands, and consequently thoughts and emotions that cause apparent or hidden obstacles on the way to God may be expected to appear soon. Regaining inner freedom at this stage needs help that is both firm and trusting, but also respectful of the personal freedom of the scholastic in question.

In sharp contrast with our contemporary practice, the *Constitutions* do not recognize any scenario in which a scholastic's doubts about Jesuit life would justify doing the Spiritual Exercises in view of a new election, that is, engaging in another discernment process concerning one's vocation. This corresponds to the principle expressed in the *Spiritual Exercises*: "In the case of an unchangeable election, once it has been made there is nothing further to elect" [SpEx 172] and it is a logical consequence of the Jesuit formation being understood as a dynamic of progressing. If there is sufficient inner freedom and trust in God, and the person appears to be engaged in a dynamic of progression, then he can be helped to continue in the well-founded hope that his perseverance will bear fruit. If there are strong impediments or perhaps an attachment to the not even fully conscious longing that "God will come where this person desires" [SpEx 154], then sufficient inner freedom for a new election can hardly be present.[2] Discernment in such cases does not mean the weighing of the pros and cons of staying in the Society or leaving, but evaluating the question of why the progress so far on the pathway to God has been unsatisfactory. Dismissal from the Society is justified if, despite the initial commitment taken up in the first vows and adequate help to make progress, the scholastic cannot or does not want to take the decisions [cf. ConsCN C 819] that would allow him to continue to make progress on the pathway to God. Dismissal will also be necessary when he is willing to remain but the superior does not see any convincing signs of actual progression.

2 "I have had no real success in directing through the Exercises those who are trying to remake a decision about a permanent commitment already made, and have grown very disinclined even to try." J. Tetlow, *Choosing Christ in the World: Directing the Spiritual Exercises of St. Ignatius Loyola According to Annotations Eighteen and Nineteen* (Saint Louis: The Institute of Jesuit Sources, 1989), p. 187.

To understand Jesuit formation as a dynamic progress in no way means that Jesuits who want to leave the Society could or should be held back. Once again, the analogy of the Spiritual Exercises may help us to understand that if the superior is familiar with the characteristics of the dynamic of progress in the second phase of the pathway to God, then he can be more attuned to scholastics and so perceive potential difficulties more sensitively. A good director of the Exercises can sometimes be aware of an obstacle while listening to accounts of "successful" prayers, because, for example, the graces of the particular week may not have been received and there may be some false tone in the apparent success. Similarly, a superior who is knowledgeable about the Ignatian pathway to God can accompany scholastics in such a way that hindrances become manifest at a moment when the necessary time and relative inner freedom are still there, well before a major crisis breaks out. At this point, it remains primarily the superior's responsibility to discern how the person can be helped to re-engage in a dynamic of progress, but the superior is also responsible for terminating the formation process if there seems to be no hope that the person will be able to develop the skills necessary for Jesuit life. According to Part II of the *Constitutions*, a person must be dismissed from the Society if his remaining would be "against the good [...] of the individual" [ConsCN C 216]. If the dynamic of progress has come to a halt and the scholastic does not continue to grow in human and spiritual maturity, then—as with doing the Exercises—the person should not begin the next phase of progress. As in the Exercises, such a person needs to be helped to consider the graces received, but also to abandon, at least temporarily, the Ignatian way to God that has proved not to foster his actual progress. Depending on the evaluation of the person's Jesuit years, the separation from the Society can be interpreted in a variety of ways, from "having failed to respond to God's call" or "not having received sufficient help" to "having discerned the call to another way of life". Increasing clarity about the Ignatian pathway to God may yield an interpretation that is more just and more reassuring for both the person leaving and those who stay.

✠ 7 ✠

# Part V of the Constitutions: Tertianship

## Tertianship as Transformation

Part V of the *Constitutions* declares that after the completion of studies, before the final vows, a year of "third probation" must follow:

> if he ought to be admitted to profession, he will have another year after the completion of these studies to become still better known before pronouncing it. [ConsCN C 514]

> it will be helpful for those who had been sent to studies, upon finishing the work and effort of intellectual formation, to apply themselves during the period of final probation to the school of the heart, exercising themselves in spiritual and corporal pursuits which can engender[1] in them greater humility, abnegation of all sensual love and will and judgment of their own, and also greater knowledge and love of God our Lord. [ConsCN C 516]

What is the purpose of this phase of Jesuit life in the perspective of progressing on the pathway to God? Can one attempt to describe, as in the previous phases, the transformation that is to occur? The answer is not given readily in the *Constitutions*. Among the detailed instructions in Part V concerning the pronunciation of the final vows, the third phase of the Ignatian pathway to God is discussed only very briefly, almost marginally. In order to better understand the succinctly worded text, we may once again recall Ignatius' personal experience.

1 Here, the word "progress" occurs only in the approved Latin translation *(ad profectum in humilitate)* but not in the original Spanish text *(que más humilidad y abnegación de todo amor sensual y uoluntad y juizio proprio y mayor conocimiento y amor de Dios Nro. Señor puedan causarle).*

Having finished their studies in Paris, Ignatius and his first companions spent two or three months around Venice, among the sick and the poor: "they separated to serve in various hospices" [Autobiography 93]. Afterwards, they wanted to travel to the Holy Land, in order to follow their original plan and "spend their lives for the good of souls" [Autobiography 85]. However, the journey became impossible to make, and they decided to lengthen the expected waiting time of a few months to a whole year. They spent forty days in prayer and then carried on with various apostolic undertakings in extreme poverty:

> In that year no ships sailed for the East because the Venetians had broken off with the Turks. So, seeing that their hope of sailing was put off, they dispersed within the Venetian region, with the intention of waiting the year they had decided upon; and if it expired without possibility to travel, they would go to Rome. It fell to the pilgrim to go with Faber and Laínez to Vicenza. There they found a certain house outside the city, which had neither doors nor windows. They stayed in it, sleeping on a little straw they had brought. Two of them always went out to seek alms in the city twice a day, but they got so little they could hardly maintain themselves. They usually ate a little toasted bread when they had it, and the one who remained at home saw to its toasting. In this way they spent forty days, not engaging in anything other than prayer.
>
> After the forty days, Master John Codure arrived; and the four together decided to begin to preach. The four went to different piazzas and began to preach on the same day and at the same hour, first shouting loudly and summoning people with their caps. Their preaching caused a great stir in the city, and many persons were moved with devotion, and they received in greater abundance the material goods they needed. [Autobiography 94–5]

These months transformed Ignatius significantly and enduringly. When recounting his life shortly before his death, he evokes the remarkable changes in his spiritual life:

> During the time he was at Vicenza, he had many spiritual visions and many quite regular consolations; the contrary happened when he was in Paris. In all that traveling he had great supernatural experiences like those he used to have when he was in Manresa, especially when he began to prepare for the priesthood in Venice and when he was preparing to say Mass. [Autobiography 95]

These consolations marked the end of a long period of emotional dryness dutifully accepted by Ignatius at the beginning of his studies. The transformation proved to have been irrevocable. For the rest of his life, Ignatius "had always grown in devotion, that is, ease in finding God"; moreover, "every time, any hour, that he wished to find God, he found him" [Autobiography 99].

Although the intensity of his spiritual experiences at Vicenza and Venice is reminiscent of those in Manresa, there is an important difference. The great consolations and spiritual experiences in Manresa were received in a secluded environment of solitude, whereas the preparation for priestly ordination happened in the midst of travels and a variety of apostolic activities. Ignatius became skilled at finding God while being active, and this attitude became part of his life even while assuming heavy responsibilities as superior general of the newly born Society of Jesus.

Tertianship recreates for contemporary Jesuits the circumstances and activities that enabled Ignatius to go through this decisive period of spiritual and human growth in Vicenza. One can imagine that the progress that can be expected to happen in "knowledge and love of God" [ConsCN C 516] refers to a transformation that is equally similar to that of the first companions. Tertianship is not merely about refreshing one's knowledge of Ignatian spirituality, nor is it the equivalent of a spiritual renewal after the long years of study and demanding apostolic work, but rather a practical, supervision-like introduction to being contemplative in action, proposed at the threshold of entering active apostolic life. This relatively short but decisive period of Jesuit formation makes it possible for "a direct and ongoing sense of God's presence, practically the same thing as consolation"[2] to become the fundamental dimension of Jesuit life, according to what characterized the life of the first Jesuits: "this was what Jesuits hoped for themselves and tried to excite in others".[3] The Jesuit who enters the "vineyard of the Lord" [ConsCN C 603] has to have reached a high level of personal integration, which allows him the relatively free use of his practical, interpersonal, intellectual and apostolic qualities while focusing on the

2 O'Malley, *The First Jesuits*, p. 371.

3 *Ibid.*, p. 371.

service of God and the good of souls, and remaining fully perceptive to the manifestations of God's glory. The expected fruit of tertianship is thus a noticeable and lasting transformation, one that it should be possible to describe in anthropological and spiritual terms.

## Means of Helping Progress

When comparing the description of tertianship in the *Constitutions* to that of previous phases of formation, we notice that the characteristic Ignatian elements of help are more difficult to recognize here. There are hardly any references to either a suitable environment or to a specific way of offering spiritual support. Moreover, the text is not structured according to the relationship model of Ignatian anthropology. Progress in tertianship is not to be fostered—apart from the thirty-day Exercises done for a second time—by exercises made in a more or less artificially created environment but rather by making one's way through the challenges of real apostolic contexts.

Jesuits in tertianship can attain the objectives of this phase of the Ignatian pathway to God by engaging in activities that can engender "greater humility, abnegation of all sensual love and will and judgment of their own" [ConsCN C 516]. The issue of humility pinpoints the battle on the third step of the meditation on the Two Standards, where one's own capacity for purposeful action, the exercising of one's own will, is to be subordinated to the contemplative attitude of seeking God in all things, to acknowledging God's initiative and giving priority to it. The abnegation of "sensual love", a vigorous struggle for freedom from pleasurable self-centered motivations, is an obvious aspect of progress at this stage: "For everyone ought to reflect that in all spiritual matters, the more one divests oneself of self-love, self-will, and self-interests, the more progress one will make" [SpEx 189]. It is less clear, however, what justifies this mistrust of any "will and judgment of their own" even after the completion of many years of studies. What is the purpose of expecting an intellectually prepared and presumably prayerful Jesuit to "abnegate" the way he sees things? Why not trust his judgment and will?

The rules regarding the discernment of spirits may be of help in interpreting the transformation demanded by tertianship. A Jesuit who has conducted fruitful studies and eagerly awaits the beginning of his apostolic life is likely to have a vivid mind and a strong opinion about the challenges that await him. In most cases he will be full of plans and ideas which can make him thrilled or anguished or both at the same time as he begins the immediate preparation for assuming real apostolic assignments. This particular state of mind, although often seen by others as a "state of grace", makes it especially important not to follow one's own thoughts uncritically. Apostolic ideas, convictions and plans may be excellent in themselves yet not in harmony with God's intentions. As we know, the "evil angel" can take on "the appearance of an angel of light" and "brings good and holy thoughts attractive to [. . .] an upright soul, and then strives little by little to get his own way" [SpEx 332]. Newly ordained priests—not only Jesuits—can often be seen taking up apostolic work with great enthusiasm but then this very multitude of good ideas and intentions, the very expectations they tend to set before both themselves and their congregation, the idealism that is quite normal at this point, and, ultimately, the absence of a contemplative life style may quickly lead to the exhaustion of the initial energy and the development of disordered habits, sometimes as soon as within a year or two. The high level of studies does not protect from the temptations appearing under the disguise of good. Moreover, to have spent long years in studies may even foster a personal tendency to identify with one's own "good and holy" thoughts. A careful observer may well notice, long before the burn-out, how the priest left on his own in the first years of his apostolic mission, striving to meet expectations to the best of his abilities, starts to lose both the contemplative perspective centered on God and the inner freedom, the very preconditions for fulfilling his mission. The *Constitutions* envision tertianship as practical help for a better take-off in this characteristically difficult transition. As a prerequisite, one must learn to discern between these two motivational forces: on the one hand, the desire to realize one's own carefully constructed ideas and aims, and, on the other, the desire to realize the service and glory of God. The two are not the same; they may be in harmony with each other but they may equally be opposed to each other.

Such discernment can arise through the rules for discernment in the second week [SpEx 328–36] but, as we have seen while examining the third step of the meditation on the Two Standards, it is not merely a matter of applying a couple of rules. Beyond being a cognitive exercise where the affective dimension is also involved, discernment is also influenced by deeply rooted fixations and other personality traits as well as convictions, beliefs, ideals and cherished values, which can limit the capacity of the individual to apply the rules for the discernment of spirits. For example, the conviction that liturgical beauty or proximity to the poor has to have a central role in announcing the Gospel today can become the source of consolation in a community but also an ideological Trojan horse for introducing unproductive divisions and disintegration. Ultimately, it comes down to the new priest's personal and spiritual maturity whether he can fulfill his mission to God's greater glory by the wise and attentive use of his intellectual and leadership capacities or whether he begins to act in the name of an ideal or expectation which can make him rigid and unable to follow the guidance of the Spirit.

Along these lines it becomes clear that the goal of tertianship is to foster a possibly lengthy transformation. The capacity to recognize the temptation that can hide behind good thoughts and plans correlates with the progress made on the Ignatian pathway to God, that is, with the continuing transformation of the personality in accordance with the dynamic of Jesuit life. "Greater humility" here can be understood as learning to rely on the sense of security and quiet motivation that can be found in the prayerful, peaceful and inspiring presence of God as one acts contemplatively even while active. Humility thus presupposes the ability to distinguish a contemplative attitude from the sense of recognition and success that can be striven for when engaged in the flurry of responding to needs, forging plans and putting them through. Humility implies freedom vis-à-vis following one's own will more or less compulsively, and enables one to consider God as the primary actor, which in turn is a presupposition for acting "to the glory of God".

Tertianship thus means a vital part of the transformation demanded during Jesuit formation. Unless tertianship is proposed as a facilitation of the difficult passage from studies to apostolic work, young Jesuits risk remaining without appropriate support during the vulnerable early years of their apostolic life. Tertianship itself also risks losing its transformative character if it is done after many years of having assumed apostolic responsibilities, since it will hardly be possible to alter already fixed habits and attitudes even if a spiritually intensive tertianship awakens the desire to do so. The fact that the *Constitutions* present tertianship as the phase of the pathway to God which links the years of studies to apostolic life is a powerful confirmation of the insistence of the *Complementary Norms* that "for priests [tertianship] is not to be deferred beyond three years after priestly ordination except for a just reason in the judgment of the provincial" [ConsCN CN 125 §1]. In fact, even deferring tertianship for three years can in some cases result in young Jesuits coming back rich with a powerful spiritual experience, but unprepared to change the habits that had developed earlier, and thus poorly equipped to live a life that is contemplative in action even in the midst of heavy apostolic responsibilities.[4]

In a contemporary context, it may be the case that tertianship should not be conceived as a spiritually intensive sabbatical year after the first "real" apostolic mission or missions—a conception that does not seem to correspond to the *Constitutions*—but as a spiritually intensive, progressive introduction into apostolic life where the emphasis is on the enduring contemplative quality of the apostolic activity.

Tertianship therefore introduces yet another challenging phase of Jesuit life. Depending on individual persons and contexts, it can have the character of a "probation" in various ways, but its fundamental dynamic normally correlates with the third, last step of the meditation on the Two Standards. Abnegation of one's judgment and will for the sake of being purely motivated by the desire to be on the side of Christ can begin to happen through "spiritual and corporal pursuits" that correspond to simple acts of service, love and compassion. If the Jesuit will not do these out of his own initiative because he normally finds these "pursuits" less meaningful or of less importance, or else too easy or too difficult for himself, or if he is afraid of them or finds them unpleasant in some way, then he is well placed to discern the motivations that will help him move forward on the Ignatian pathway to God. Instead of activities that promise tangible results from an academic, sociological or even a faith and justice perspective, and which

4 For a fascinating elucidation of how the Society in the early seventeenth century faced the challenge of a need for a "second conversion" in Jesuit formation, see the chapter "L'Interprétation du troisième an dans la doctrine spirituelle", in Bartók, *Un interprète et une interprétation*, p. 297 ff.

tend to boost the idealization of the self-image and increase a sense of healthy or unhealthy pride, tertianship favors apostolic undertakings where no such quick results can be expected. The challenge in such a context boils down to how one can become aware of the tangible signs of God's actions and consoling presence while remaining active in the service of others. For example, at the bedside of a terminally ill person, the Jesuit who is already experienced in seeking God can relatively soon recognize—through smaller or greater crises, and preferably under the supervision of his tertianship master—how the effort of putting through his own possibly very pious or realistic convictions or interpretations differs from finding the inner freedom and sensitivity that is necessary for bringing consolation by remaining fully present to both the person and the often surprising inspirations of the Spirit.

The fact that the *Constitutions* present tertianship essentially as a series of experiences or activities where the emergence of the contemplative dimension is at stake can contribute to a better contemporary understanding of this phase of Jesuit formation. During the years of studies, the contemplative dimension has to be subordinated to some extent to academic exigencies. A Jesuit can, however, only be missioned on the condition that he has developed and can maintain a contemplative approach that will not fade away when apostolic challenges begin to multiply. This is why the experiments which recall the novitiate experiments constitute the essence of tertianship, the very context where progress can be made. Experiences that put a Jesuit in contact with distant cultures may be helpful in this regard since difficulties of adaptation to foreign customs and languages may help to develop a humble trust in God. But it seems more important that tertianship takes the form of an ongoing supervision with a special accent on the contemplative dimension of apostolic work. This implies that those in tertianship can regularly see the tertian master or a competent spiritual director during the apostolic experiment, helping to keep the focus of attention on God's activity. If tertianship experiments do not serve the objective of this phase of Jesuit formation, then the Jesuit in question risks missing the opportunity to engage in apostolic responsibilities with the support of competent supervision that can help him grow as a person who is contemplative even while active. This in turn can make it difficult for him to continue to make progress during the next phase of the Ignatian pathway to God, after having pronounced his final vows.

Supervision with a focus on being contemplative while active will necessarily take account of the affective dimension. If the role of tertianship is indeed to prepare Jesuits for the struggle on the third step of the meditation on the Two Standards where pride can be overcome by humility and a profound love of God, and pride is seen as a "natural", although partially unconscious function of the personality, then one can understand why affectivity and self-awareness play a significant role in overcoming pride. Knowing and loving God better, or recognizing and following inspirations coming from God all require sensitivity, intuition and a certain emotional intelligence: "the good angel touches the soul gently, lightly and sweetly, like a drop of water going into a sponge" [SpEx 335]. The contemplative, vigilant attention toward God and reality is different from the analytic thinking and attitude that is fostered during the studies. The progression that tertianship needs to facilitate can thus be called "the school of the heart" *(la scuela del affecto)* [ConsCN C 516]. The ability to recognize the subtle movements and eventual attachments of the heart, that is, the capacity to be attracted affectively by objects, persons or plans and projects becomes a crucial competence to be acquired before a full apostolic mission can be entrusted to a Jesuit. The emotionally and affectively intensive experiences and the intimacy brought forth by various pastoral or interpersonal relationships during tertianship foster the opening of the personality toward a deeper and more compassionate understanding and acceptance of reality. A spirited and sensitive heart is both an essential apostolic instrument in a multiplicity of pastoral and community life situations and the very area of the personality where the inspiration of the Holy Spirit can be recognized.

Contemplative persons do not merely alternate the analytical and contemplative ways of perceiving and understanding reality but instead learn to use their analytical capacities as an integrated part of their personality. A Jesuit going through the transformation required by tertianship is in possession of the competencies acquired during the scholastic years. He can rely on his ability to interpret situations in the light of theories and Gospel values. He can set goals and act accordingly, but he needs to learn to give priority to contemplating God's activity, which can confirm or refute his own ideas. The precondition of such a contemplative attitude is that the person is not a captive of his own constructions of goals and ideals but has sufficient inner freedom to find peace in God even at times when he is frustrated by the failure of his projects and goals. The Jesuit who tastes the fruits of tertianship can more and more easily return to a contemplative, vigilant state of attention to God and to reality, even in periods when apostolic successes are scarce.

The motivational system of the person who faithfully perseveres in the tertianship exercises is transformed step by step. As he again and again finds consolation in God among various apostolic works carried out with a readiness for the "abnegation of will and judgment of his own", he becomes less and less attached to his own ideas. He is no longer compelled rigidly to adhere to whatever option he had found good at the outset because he can taste the satisfaction of being attuned to God's activity, a gift that is not necessarily linked to the success of a particular project. Such re-examinations of *a priori* plans and ideas in the light of how God proves to be active will lead to greater freedom and generosity when accepting and engaging in new assignments. Thus, the "abnegation" of one's own judgment and will is not understood as the repression of intellectual capabilities but instead as a way toward growing freedom, a widening horizon, and an increasing flexibility of the intellectual and analytic abilities. The Jesuit in tertianship will presumably perceive the process as difficult yet also very rich in previously unknown insights and consolations.

## Suitability for Jesuit Life

The concise description of the final vows greatly emphasizes the requirement that before someone is admitted to the Society "more intrinsically" [ConsCN C 510] by means of the final vows, he needs "to become still better known" [ConsCN C 514] to the Society:

> those persons will be judged suitable for admission to profession whose life is well-known through long and thorough probations and is approved by the superior general, to whom a report will be sent by the subordinate superiors or others from whom the general desires information. For this purpose, it will be helpful for those who had

> been sent to studies, upon finishing the work and effort of intellectual formation, to apply themselves during the period of final probation to the school of the heart. [ConsCN C 516]

The insistence on fulfilling the criteria for final vows primarily serves the person's own benefit because—as this is familiar from the Spiritual Exercises—the dynamic of progress can continue in a consecutive phase only after the appearance of the previous phase's fruits. As we have seen, in the case of tertianship this means that Jesuits need to develop a contemplative attitude that can persist even in challenging apostolic situations. For this purpose an empathetic yet firm accompaniment will be necessary, just like in the Spiritual Exercises, where failure to receive the graces of a given week means that moving to the next week would not bring many fruits and it is better to terminate the Exercises. In the meantime, when evaluating the fruits of tertianship beyond the perspective of the given individual, special attention is paid to the apostolic body of the Society too, as the careful selection of professed members provides "much aid" toward "perpetuating the well-being of this whole body" [ConsCN C 819]:

> Thus it appears that care should be taken in general that all the members of the Society devote themselves to the solid and perfect virtues and to spiritual pursuits, and attach greater importance to them than to learning and other natural and human gifts. [ConsCN C 813]

In a contemporary context where vocations are scarce and young Jesuits who finish their formation are immediately needed in apostolic works, it may be difficult to propose tertianship as a time of final confirmation, that is, to consider a scenario where a person is not seen to be fit for Jesuit life after all as a realistic outcome. The Society could easily give the impression that after so many sacrifices demanded from a young Jesuit, there are now a set of lofty spiritual ideals with which he has to comply. Only a sufficiently characteristic articulation of the Ignatian pathway to God and a compassionate accompaniment of individual Jesuits will make clear that the progress demanded at this point is to the benefit of the individual as much as to that of the Society. It is thus important to see how tertianship serves both the good of the individual and that of the Society and what is at stake during this stage of formation.

The Jesuit who successfully completes his studies and is admitted into tertianship by his superiors is very likely to possess numerous promising qualities. Presumably, he is intellectually prepared, he can use his talents in the service of others, and so he appears to have the prerequisites of becoming a successful Jesuit, a competent teacher or preacher of the kingdom of God. He can be expected to work diligently and do his very best to face personal, organizational or intellectual challenges. Yet, as we have seen, all this is still not enough to be admitted to final vows: the fruits of tertianship are to be apparent, that is, the Jesuit must be able to seek God humbly, renouncing his self-love and his own will.

Why are the fruits of tertianship a *sine qua non* for Jesuit life? As we have seen, the Jesuit left on his own without the fruits of tertianship is in a vulnerable position because, immersed in the responsibilities placed on him by both his mission and his own desire to do valuable work, in need of all his strength and energies, attracted by pastoral, pragmatic or intellectual achievements, he may not perceive himself as someone who depends on God's Spirit. The person inexperienced in being contemplative in action yet driven by apostolic enthusiasm has a limited awareness of reality. Instead of engaging in the dynamic of "mutual communication" [SpEx 231] with God that engenders gratefulness, he may begin to feel that he gives disproportionally more than he receives. Upon giving thanks to God, his gratitude does not flow from the depth of his being since he is more strongly aware of the responsibilities and burdens of his own efforts than God's actions in his life. With time, his strained way of life may narrow his horizon even further. He will be prone to see phenomena that do not match his cognitive schemata as senseless, which in turn may make him judgmental and unable to appreciate those persons who appear "hopeless" in his eyes (that is, unfit for realizing some of his preferred values or convictions). When seeing his self-image or his work in jeopardy, a Jesuit without the fruits of tertianship is vulnerable to becoming aggressive or disappointed and disillusioned.

The Jesuit who lives without the fruits of tertianship is unarmed especially in the battle of the third step of the meditation on the Two Standards. His vulnerability is further increased by his reduced perspective, which may make him blind to his own condition. In this case pride is accompanied by a certain hardness of the heart, even though the person is probably unaware of this and may have only a faint sense of not progressing any more. Without a sensitive and spirited heart, such a person cannot perceive the Spirit's gentle movements, and he can easily be tempted "under the disguise of good" as he is incapable of discerning whether a particular idea touches his soul "gently, lightly and sweetly" or "sharply, with noise and disturbance" [SpEx 335]. The narrowed perception of reality will also result in a diminished spiritual sensitivity, which means that motivations rooted in prayer and in the relationship with God become progressively ineffective. Symptoms of burn-out may appear. The initial signs are barely noticeable: forced optimism, impatience, a relentless urge to redouble efforts, or, at the other extreme, feelings of incompetence and insufficiency, and a sense of being overburdened and constantly strained. In both cases, the person can display either insensitivity or oversensitivity to human suffering in a particular situation; friends and colleagues may be waiting in vain for a compassionate word, or a particular person in difficulty may become a predominant preoccupation at the expense of other responsibilities. Such signals may reveal the sensitive spot through which Lucifer's strategy can destabilize the personality of the Jesuit who has completed a long formation but has not yet developed a contemplative attitude that could lend him real inner freedom. Although unexpected changes in spiritual matters are not to be excluded, one can nevertheless say that there is little hope of change if coping with apostolic responsibilities remains the primary preoccupation. A life that is contemplative in action rarely develops in such conditions; on the contrary, progress on the pathway to God may easily come to a full stop.

If tertianship is seen as a distinctive part of a long transformation process that is the Jesuit formation, then the length of this phase will have to be considered with respect to the individual concerned: when and how do the fruits become manifest in his life? Doing the full thirty-day Exercises and other experiments for a couple of weeks or months does not automatically qualify someone to make final vows. The *Constitutions* say that "a whole year" [ConsCN C 514] is to be dedicated to tertianship, but "this period can be prolonged" [ConsCN C 514]. Such prolongation makes sense presuming that ongoing, purposeful practices can foster a lasting transformation that it is necessary to achieve before someone's final integration into the apostolic body of the Society, and the fruits of tertianship can be observed relatively precisely, somewhat like the fruits of a given week in the *Spiritual Exercises*.

Conceiving tertianship as a preparation for apostolic life could address a number of issues that sometimes manifest themselves a few years after final profession. Sufficient initial discernment and practice could help to prevent issues such as the appearance of stress-related avoidance patterns that are contrary to the vows; the development of a narrow, success-oriented mentality; the lack of appreciation for Jesuit life as a supportive way of being; or the possible diminution of Jesuit identity. The possibility of prolonging tertianship can provide additional time for the characteristic fruits of tertianship to appear so that typical blocks to ongoing development of a life that is contemplative in action can be addressed. Proper feedback from those who witness the period of tertianship will thus be as important for the concerned individual as for the superiors, who will need to decide whether the person can be "judged suitable for admission to profession" [ConsCN C 516]. Such feedback has to be given more accurately than tends to be our practice today, respecting due confidentiality, and taking into consideration how the criteria for being admitted for final vows [ConsCN CN 120] are emphasized in the context of a dynamic progression on the pathway to God.

If full incorporation into the Society is offered to Jesuits who have been helped to develop and also tested for an ongoing attitude of being contemplative in action in a variety of experiments, then Jesuits admitted to final vows will be characterized by a unique human and spiritual maturity, since the personal competencies they have developed in all three dimensions of their personality will work together harmoniously and subordinated to the capacity of seeking and serving God. An apostolic and contemplative personality is not quite the same as a hardworking Jesuit who is mindful about keeping his daily prayer times: "the whole personality of the contemplative, the entire reality of human existence becomes the holy place where the action of God reveals itself, so that we may engage in the work of human salvation".[5] The relationship with God becomes—beyond being

5 P.-H. Kolvenbach SJ, *The Road from La Storta* (Saint Louis: Institute of Jesuit Sources, 2000), p. 198.

a theological statement as described in the Principle and Foundation [SpEx 23]—a constitutive element of the personality, lending coherence to one's initiatives and reactions. The relationship with God becomes purified from illusions and revealed more clearly as a deep dynamic of giving and receiving. Such an experience of having received the salvation of the soul enables the person to act for the glory of God, fully attentive to the manifestations of God's glory, even in the midst of adverse or conflictive configurations of material things, interpersonal relationships or differing values and opinions. This is where the two metaphors of personal progression and incorporation into an apostolic body overlap, since the graces received while making progress on the Ignatian pathway to God enable one to rely on the same grace in the service of others:

> The end of this Society is to devote itself with God's grace not only to the salvation and perfection of the members' own souls, but also with that same grace to labor strenuously in giving aid toward the salvation and perfection of the souls of their neighbors. [General Examen, ConsCN C 3]

Sufficient spiritual and human maturity is a necessary condition for engaging in "spiritual and corporal pursuits" in such a way that the service of others, instead of becoming a matter of achievements more or less easily attained, or measured simply by the positive feedback from others, can lead a Jesuit again and again to "greater knowledge and love of God our Lord" [ConsCN C 516]. From the perspective of making personal progress on the pathway to God, this means that progress is no longer fostered primarily by ascetic practices and a favorable environment but by apostolic life itself. Moreover, at this stage of the Ignatian pathway to God, the vital role of personal progress in helping others becomes manifest. Personal progress and apostolic responsibilities become mutually supportive of each other: "so that when they themselves have made progress they can better help others to progress *(auiéndose aprouechado en sí mesmos, mejor puedan aprouechar a otros)* for the glory of God our Lord" [ConsCN C 516]. The dynamic of personal progress and the engagement in apostolic activities become closely tied. Activities can stem more and more from the relationship with Christ, who receives the person "under his standard" [SpEx 147], and they can lead to the observation of God's workings, stirring increasing awe. For the Jesuit who has pronounced his final vows, the contemplation of the fourth week of the Spiritual Exercises can illuminate his apostolic life as he becomes aware of how God can act through him: "how in this way he dwells also in myself, giving me existence, life, sensation, and intelligence; and even further, making me his temple" [SpEx 235]. Such openness of a mature personality to God means that the dynamism of apostolic life can rely on a powerful and ever-renewing source of motivation.

## ✣ 8 ✣

# Part VI of the Constitutions: After Final Vows

### Vows and Personal Responsibility

Part VI of the *Constitutions* ("The personal life of those already admitted and incorporated into the body of the Society") discusses the lives of Jesuits who have pronounced their final vows and are advancing in the fourth phase of the pathway to God. The text treats diverse issues such as ascetic practices, readiness to take up apostolic missions, refraining from civil court matters, and the support to be given to dying companions. Yet first of all, and with most detail, it discusses the three vows which become the prime means of seeking God: "Through the three vows, one intentionally creates emptiness in one's life, an emptiness not to be filled with gratifying human relationships, power or great pleasures. This emptiness, this intentional non-satisfaction by anything limited can become the springboard which keeps the impulse directed toward the infinite God in constant motion."[1]

It is somewhat surprising that the detailed discussion of vows is left to the final, fourth phase of the Ignatian pathway to God, given that the Jesuit who reaches this point has already been observing the vows for over ten years, from the moment of entering the novitiate. However, obedience in apostolic life is not the same as that of a scholastic,[2] and the same holds true in regard to poverty and chastity as well. The *Constitutions* address the detailed explanation of the vows to those who, after lengthy preparations, now strive "to employ themselves more

1 P. Nemeshegyi SJ, in manuscript.

2 Veale, "How the Constitutions Work", p. 12.

fruitfully according to our Institute in the service of God and the aid of their neighbors" [ConsCN C 547].

During the first phases of Jesuit life, especially in the novitiate, the *Constitutions* discuss poverty, chastity and obedience as virtues necessary for Jesuit life. Ignatius considers it a matter of fact that the competencies, spiritual and human traits required for living according to the evangelical counsels, are initially underdeveloped. By the time of the final vows, however, the essential virtues demanded by the Jesuit life are understood to have been established:

> Given the length of time and approbation of their life which are required before admission into the Society among the professed and also the formed coadjutors, it is presupposed that those so admitted will be men who are spiritual and sufficiently advanced that they will run in the path of Christ our Lord *(se presupone serán personas spirituales y aprouechadas ara correr por la uía de Christo N. S.)* to the extent that their bodily strength and the exterior occupations undertaken through charity and obedience allow. [ConsCN C 582]

An apparent trait of a professed Jesuit is that he is a "spiritual" man. Besides being spiritually sensitive, he is also able to "run" in the path of the Lord, that is, his life is characterized by an obvious dynamism that remains focused on seeking and serving God in everything. With reference to the relationship model of Ignatian anthropology, we can say that such a person is aware of his motivations, especially the manifestations of the three basic motivational drives, and he can relatively easily renounce impulses that risk undermining this dynamism ordered to the love and service of God, because in a certain intimate inner space of his being,[3] he can have access to the graces that stem from his relationship with God: "Give me love of yourself along with your grace, for that is enough for me" [SpEx 234]. This is how he can understand and cope with complex and possibly conflicting reactions and inconsistencies of

3 "a space of interiority is opened where God works in us, we are able to see the world as a place in which God is at work and which is full of his appeals and his presence." See "Decrees of the 35th General Congregation. Decree 2, A Fire That Kindles Other Fires", §8, No. 25, in *Jesuit Life and Mission Today: The Decrees and Accompanying Documents of the 31st–35th General Congregations of the Society of Jesus* (Saint Louis: The Institute of Jesuit Sources, 2009), p. 736.

his personality,[4] while striving to remain coherent in serving God and sustaining a personal and apostolic dynamic on the pathway to God.

Last vows constitute a special passage on the Ignatian pathway to God not only in the sense of being a point of no return but also because of the increased share of responsibility on the individual. While in earlier stages the superior was responsible for pronouncing the words of authority that maintained an environment suitable for progressing, final vows mean that individuals agree to carry the responsibility for creating the necessary conditions even in the absence of favorable external structures, wherever they go. Individual responsibility manifests itself first of all in keeping the vows, which makes it possible to keep God as the focus of a spiritual and human dynamic even where a propitious environment—such as an appropriately organized Jesuit community—is not provided.

The personally assumed responsibility expressed by the vows joins together the two fundamental dimensions of Jesuit life, that of personal progression and that of incorporation into the apostolic body of the Society. With regard to personal progression, we have seen that Jesuits who have made progress *(aprovechadas)* are understood to have a sense of responsibility for their own continuing progression to an extent that was not possible before. With respect to the vows as a public commitment to the way of life of the institutionally organized Society of Jesus, the vowed Jesuit assumes moral responsibility for the well-being of the Society of Jesus and its apostolic mission. These two ways of being responsible mutually illuminate each other. The manifold support received during formation is justified by the objective that the

4 "My self then becomes increasingly my *own*, even though it still remains in part a mystery to me. Human maturity does not therefore mean that I reach a state in my life where I am no longer aware of any tensions and conflicts in myself. Rather, I become mature precisely by engaging in the psychological and spiritual struggle between my conscious reality and God, and between my wishes and needs (including those that are unconscious) and my ideals, and by attempting to give a form to this struggle. That means that it is possible for me to grow rather than be blocked, in the ongoing tension between the poles—between the loosing of self and finding of self, between the self and others, between finitude and infinity." H. Zollner, "The Self—Its Nature and its Mystery" in H. Zollner (ed.), *Formation and the Person. Essays on Theory and Practice* (Leuven: Peeters, 2007), pp. 47–66.

person will use the fruits of his Jesuit formation as a member of the apostolic body. The apostolic body, in turn, can remain healthy when it incorporates persons for whom the vows are not simply the expression of the identification with the ideals of the apostolic institute but also the means to continue a joyful dynamic progression on the Ignatian pathway to God. The vows express the firm connection between the subtle spiritual responsibility of taking care of one's own good on the one hand, and the robust public responsibility of living in conformity with the spirit of the apostolic body on the other.

It is perhaps not by chance that this double responsibility inherent in final vows is reflected by the double meaning of the verb "observe (*observer*)" in the *Constitutions*. On the one hand, the vows as a voluntary submission to a set of publicly established requirements entail the moral obligation to observe these requirements. But on the other hand, the *Constitutions* also seem to use the word "observe" in the sense of paying attention to, being perceptive or aware of something. Without diminishing the significance of the first, this second aspect seems to be more important. What one has to observe after final vows is not so much a set of rules or expectations as an internal reality with a number of distinguishable elements:

> In order that those already admitted to profession or as formed coadjutors may be able to employ themselves more fruitfully according to our Institute in the service of God and the aid of their neighbors, they need to observe certain things in regard to themselves *(deben obseruar en sí mesmos algunas cosas)*. [ConsCN C 547]

The emphasis on conformity with an internal reality that can take the place of external rules is familiar from the Preamble to the *Constitutions*, which, like the First Principle and Foundation of the *Spiritual Exercises*, explains right at the beginning the objective which the rest of the text intends to help one achieve:

> On our own part what helps most toward this end [of preserving the Society] must be, more than any exterior constitution, the interior law of charity and love which the Holy Spirit writes and imprints upon hearts *(más que ninguna exterior constitutión, la interior ley de la charidad y amor que el Spíritu Sancto scriue y imprime en los coraçones, ha de ayudar para ello)*. [ConsCN C 134]

Pronouncing the vows with the desire to maintain inner freedom in loving and serving God can be understood as assuming the obligation to respect the interior law of charity and love, on the condition that the words charity and love are not simply used in their vague everyday meaning. Final vows mean a responsibility for discernment in this area. The interior law of charity and love written and imprinted upon hearts by the Holy Spirit differs from such inauthentic forms of loving as attaining achievements at the expense of disrespecting others, or pleasing people at the expense of neglecting one's mission. The vows, as we have seen, correspond to the three major elements of the relationship model of Ignatian anthropology and foster inner freedom concerning the use of material things, the engagement in interpersonal relationships and the choices about what seems worth doing. They thus provide criteria for distinguishing the inner dynamic of charity and love that develops within a relationship with the Lord [cf. SpEx 231] from the apparent good that can become a trap according to the logic of the various steps of the meditation on the Two Standards. This is how the relationship model of Ignatian anthropology can be helpful in understanding what "things *(cosas)*" Jesuits after final vows have to "observe in themselves", and why "the most important of these are reduced to the vows" [ConsCN C 547].

The vows therefore imply awareness of inner realities, which may indicate that attachments corresponding to any of the three steps begin to impede the spiritual man's "run" on the pathway to God. With regard to the relationship model of Ignatian anthropology, we can say that the vows protect and further reinforce the integrity of the person so that his binding to God and availability for mission can continue to increase. Observing the vows nurtures a disposition that enables the Jesuit to continue personal progress on the pathway to God even when actively involved in dealing with his environment in the turmoil of apostolic life. Poverty, chastity and obedience, once they have become established virtues, become the primary means for living Jesuit life to its full potentials.

## Chastity

Of the three vows, Part VI of the *Constitutions* talks about chastity first. The contemporary reader is almost disappointed by the text written so succinctly: "What pertains to the vow of chastity requires no interpretation, since it is evident how perfectly it should be preserved, by endeavoring to imitate therein the purity of the angels in cleanness of body and mind" [ConsCN C 547]. Without forcing the brief piece of text to say more than it actually does say, one can still make observations that may be helpful in interpreting the vow of chastity from the perspective of a dynamic progression on the Ignatian pathway to God.

First, purity is not to be understood here as an ideal in opposition to a presumably dirty sexuality, but rather as a constant attitude, a virtue, that applies to all three vows. Jesuits are to "observe obedience with great integrity *(con mucha puridad)*" [General Examen, ConsCN C 89]. Similarly, "Poverty, as the strong wall of the religious institute, should be loved and preserved in its integrity *(en su puridad)*" [ConsCN C 553], and the reason why the professed Society should not have access to the fixed revenues of the colleges is the "greater disinterestedness and a more spiritual attitude *(con más pureza y con mayor spíritu)* [...] for the greater service of God our Lord and for the good government of the colleges" [ConsCN C 419]. Purity is a characteristic of the desire and of the intention, and is almost always used with regard to God: for example, novices "should aim always to serve and please the Divine Goodness for its own sake *(puramente el seruir y conplazer a la diuina bondad por sí mesma)*" [ConsCN C 288]. Scholastics, as we have seen, "should strive first of all to keep their souls pure *(tener el ánima pura)* and their intention in studying right, by seeking in their studies nothing except the glory of God and the good of souls" [ConsCN C 360]. Scholastics are also required to give talks to each other in a way that leads hearers "to desire to grow in all purity *(desear augmento en toda puridad)* and virtue" [ConsCN C 484]. As to superiors, they should reflect before missioning someone with a "thoroughly right and pure intention in the presence of God our Lord *(intentión muy recta y pura delante de Dios Nro. Sor.)*", so that their judgment can reflect what is "expedient for the greater glory of God" [ConsCN C 618]. "Purity" in the Ignatian text has no sexual connotation but expresses the condition of integrity of a person fully attuned to God: "the means which unite the human instrument with God and so dispose it that it may be wielded well by his divine hand [...] are, for example, goodness and virtue, and especially charity, and a pure intention *(pura intençión)* of the divine service, and familiarity with God our Lord" [ConsCN C 813]. This Ignatian vision does not allow the gift of chastity to be treated as a separate entity. The purity of angels implies a "singleness of vision and readiness for mission which is the Ignatian understanding of the angels".[5] Chastity is the sign of a firm vision and a firm overall disposition. In other words, chastity is the fruit of the virtue that has begun to develop in the earliest moments of receiving the grace "that all my intentions, actions, and operations may be ordered purely to the service and praise of the Divine Majesty *(puramente ordenadas en servicio y alabanza de su divina majestad)*" [SpEx 46]. Those who have developed this virtue are "sufficiently advanced that they will run in the path of Christ our Lord *(personas spirituales y aprouechadas)*" [ConsCN C 582] and they are prepared to practice discernment in matters concerning chastity.

The anthropological precondition for observing the vow of chastity is the ability to distinguish between the spiritual experience of consolation coming from God and the satisfaction of receiving attention and affection from other human beings. The difference between the two is often apparent since God can provide powerful consolation without the involvement of human beings and likewise humans too can give plenty of joy which does not respond to a longing for spiritual consolation [cf. SpEx 316]. Yet the difference can blur when God is found in an encounter with an engaging person who not only attracts attention and affinity but also responds similarly. If the satisfaction found in an interpersonal relationship begins to undermine inner freedom and weaken the dynamic of making progress in Jesuit life, then relying on purely spiritual means, such as discernment of spirits, leads to the exploration of a confusing experience without solid criteria for seeing clearly. In such cases, observing the vow of chastity in the sense of a public commitment with concrete moral consequences can prove to be helpful in maintaining a tension where the difference between human consoling and consolation by God can emerge once again. Reviving the pure intention to love and serve

5 For an explanation see: "Decrees of the 34th General Congregation. Decree 8: Chastity in the Society of Jesus", §6, No. 233, in *Jesuit Life and Mission Today*, p. 577.

the Lord and to safeguard the supportive external conditions inherent in the vow of chastity can help to regain a sense of progressing in a dynamism of giving and receiving within a mutual relationship with God.

The vow of chastity evokes the second step of the meditation on the Two Standards, and its fruit is a certain spiritual quality of human relationships even in the absence of recognition received from the other person. The discernment that makes the vow of chastity possible is not primarily concerned with questions like the containment of sexual impulses or the development of affective attachments. Discernment, as we have seen, has to focus on the purity of the intention to love and serve God, and this has to be clearly distinguished not only from the dynamic of interpersonal relationships but also from being taken up in the dynamic of pursuing achievements—however important and good these may be—as well as from the dynamic of maintaining material comfort, however justifiable this may be from an apostolic perspective. Failure to engage in such discernment can result in a weakened sense of personal integration and identity, where symptoms of an extreme sense of loneliness begin to proliferate. Moreover, discernment can also remain superficial and of little practical use if it is not accompanied by the repeated practice of "divesting" oneself of the love of creatures, that is, "removing from themselves as far as possible love of all creatures in order to place it in the Creator of them" [ConsCN C 288]. In contrast, discernment practiced by those who have developed the virtue of chastity can reveal how the presence of God transcends human relationships, lending strength, a sense of security and compassion to those who persist in seeking God, as a late fruit of the exercise once practiced in the novitiate, "loving [God] in all creatures and all creatures in him" [ConsCN C 288].

While discussing chastity, the *Constitutions* reveal a concern about the experience of frailty, which explains the emphasis on the specific responsibility concerning chastity: "It is evident how perfectly it should be preserved *(constando quán perfectamente deba guardarse)*" [ConsCN C 547]. The *Constitutions* affirm succinctly that chastity can be safeguarded by means of the "cleanness of body and mind *(con la limpieza del cuerpo y mente)*" [ConsCN C 547]. Considering that *limpieza* is practically a synonym for *puridad* [see SpEx 32, 172, 278, 348], there seems to be a tautology here, as if chastity was to be safeguarded by practicing chastity.

By evoking the relationship model of Ignatian anthropology, one can go a step further. "Cleanness of body and mind" could be understood as an indication that chastity, which refers to the struggle of the second step of the meditation on the Two Standards, has to respond to a double challenge. As we have seen in the cursory presentation of the threefold lust in the history of spirituality, chastity is related to the sexual drive that evokes the longing of the infant for the mother, a longing that is present before consciousness develops and is written into the "body" of the human being. But in the meantime, chastity is also related to the longing for recognition and appreciation, "honor from the world" [SpEx 146], which is a common concern of grown-up persons. Chastity in this sense can be seen as "cleanness of mind". Experience confirms that the vow of chastity becomes very difficult to keep when attachments implying both dimensions develop, as in the case of an intimate friendship where there is also sexual attraction. "Cleanness of body and mind" can thus be understood as the result of ongoing discernment that specifically distinguishes between human attraction—whether sexual or not—and the love and service of God. Having made progress on the pathway to God does not make this ongoing discernment superfluous. On the contrary, increasingly heavy responsibilities will require increasingly subtle discernment so that the dynamic of making progress can endure.

Paradoxically, the near silence of the *Constitutions* on the practice of chastity can become a source of light in a contemporary context, where the temptation to regard the question of chastity as a problem to be solved in the course of religious formation looms so large. Although much has been written about celibacy and chastity, there is no straightforward methodology for living the vow of chastity. The reason why the *Constitutions* do not seem to respond to our contemporary questions may be that there is not much one can actively and directly do to achieve chastity. Chastity "is before all else God's gracious gift" [ConsCN CN 144 §2], and in case of eventual difficulties and even well before, one could start helping by asking whether the pure ordering of one's life to God's service has allowed one to receive this gift.

The *Constitutions* and the *Complementary Norms* mutually reinforce each other at this point. The *Complementary Norms* explain that chastity cannot be lived without practicing a number of other elements of religious life:

> Nevertheless, mindful of our frailty, which throughout our whole life accompanies the development of chaste love, we cannot omit observance of the ascetical norms confirmed by the Church and the Society in their wide experience and required by today's dangers to chastity. These include, above all, examination of conscience, spiritual direction, internal self-discipline, and custody of the senses, by which with the help of God's grace we diligently moderate desires and impulses that might lessen a just and wholesome dominion over our senses and affections. [ConsCN C 147, CN §4]

This enumeration of potentially helpful practices places chastity firmly into the larger context of Jesuit life. The *Constitutions* do the same, but the metaphor of progressing on the pathway to God implies an important benefit. Chastity in the *Constitutions* does not appear as a mere ascetical or apostolic necessity but also as a most helpful gift or virtue in maintaining a dynamic of progress. Those who make progress on a pathway to God can experience chastity as an increasingly personal and helpful means of support, as opposed to an obligation that one has to accept on top of other burdens of life. Awareness of the dynamic of progression can help us to understand how a sufficiently progressed Jesuit will begin to perceive chastity as a welcome aid in maintaining personal integrity, liveliness and focus on God while being fully active in apostolic life.

The idea that chastity is not a challenge to be faced on its own but an organic part of a multidimensional dynamic of growth corresponds to the legacy of the founders of religious orders. None of the great founders gave much practical advice about how to live chastely. More surprisingly, the extensive contemporary research reported by A. W. Richard Sipe also echoes the near silence of the *Constitutions*: "Often, the men who are the best examples of celibate achievement have the hardest time describing 'how' they do it".[6] The summary of a great

6 See the chapter "Essential Elements in Achieving Celibacy", in A. W. R. Sipe, *Celibacy in Crisis: A Secret World Revisited* (New York and Hove: Brunner-Routledge, 2003), pp. 294–320. Quotation from p. 296.

number of interviews conducted with priests is that although those who effectively practice celibacy can sometimes mention things that help them, for example, prayer or a hobby or the example of others, none of these is the primary explanation for how they live a celibate life: "somehow celibacy becomes for them a natural consequence of who they are, what they love, and what they are devoted to".[7]

Celibacy is not a grace randomly given to some but not to others. According to Sipe, those who can live celibacy have ten common elements in their lives: 1. work done with passion; 2. prayer or interiority; 3. some form of community life, with these three seen as 4. "service [...] on account of the Kingdom"; 5. their physical needs are met in the sense that they can savor food and drink while keeping a "quiet discipline"; 6. they can keep inner balance and restore it after deep internal struggles; 7. they have a sense of security, which, "Although mediated by others, [has a core that] is internal, secure in the commitment to the transcendent";[8] 8. they keep some order around them; 9. they are inclined to learning; and 10. they love beauty, for example, music or literature. Sipe summarizes these ten elements in support of religious celibacy by evoking the *Spiritual Exercises*, "a solid base for the transforming religious experience or orientation indispensable to celibacy", and by remarking that "it is from this base that [St Ignatius] founded his society, the Jesuits—a way of life that contains all the essential elements mentioned above".[9] The *Constitutions* say little about chastity but much about how one can be prepared to receive this gift and grow in this virtue.

One of the practical consequences of these considerations is that the difficulties concerning celibacy and loneliness which contribute significantly to departures from the Society could mean that the grace of chastity has not been received because the inadequate progress on the pathway to God did not lead to a sufficiently thorough transformation of the personality. Difficulties actually mentioned by those leaving the Society may well be symptoms of having abandoned the progression on the Ignatian pathway to God rather than inevitable causes for leaving. Beyond more pointed professional support in the area of affectivity and

7 *Ibid.*, p. 297.
8 *Ibid.*, p. 305.
9 *Ibid.*, p. 298.

the integration of sexuality, a better understanding of the *Constitutions* as a whole, as a handbook for fostering a dynamic progression on the Ignatian pathway to God, may prove to be necessary in order to better achieve the delicate personal and spiritual equilibrium that can allow Jesuits to be fully receptive to the grace of chastity.

## Obedience

Unlike the vow of chastity, obedience does need interpretation, as it did even at the time of writing the *Constitutions*. Difficulties in understanding obedience do not simply result from the mistrustful and critical attitude toward authority that has prevailed in Western cultures from the second half of the twentieth century. Obedience in the Society of Jesus is radically different from not only a *laissez-faire* attitude but also from the hierarchical subordination within corporate businesses or governmental structures. In the sixteenth century too, it was no less unique when compared to the common social or even religious understanding of obedience. The first companions were as aware of the possible dangers inherent in the vow of obedience as we are. They discussed the possibility of the pope forcing a foreign religious rule on them so that "all our desires which we have judged to be from Our Lord will be frustrated"; they knew that obedience had "unseemly connotations among the Christian people"; and they realistically saw that "not so many men will enter our company" [Delib. 7]. Obedience was far from being a self-evident reality for them: "Also others spoke to the point in other ways, a fourth, and a fifth, and so on, explaining the disadvantages which occurred to them as reasons against obedience" [Delib. 7]. They probably knew as much as we do that obedience can potentially promote a mentality of fearful conformity, passivity, disloyalty, fearful hypocrisy toward superiors, resentment about not being able to do what seems best, and so on. Thus, the contemporary tendency to oversimplify the issue by saying that the insistence on obedience that permeates the pages of the *Constitutions* reflects an authoritative cultural context where obedience was self-evident risks obfuscating the interpretation of the Ignatian text. A superficial understanding of obedience widens significantly the gap between the world of the *Constitutions* and our contemporary understanding of Jesuit life and formation.

Obedience in the Society of Jesus is to serve two purposes, the good of the apostolic body of the Society and the progression of the individual Jesuit on the pathway to God. The arguments brought up by the first companions in favor of the institutional need for obedience are easy to understand: "practical undertakings" can be carried out without the risk that "one would pass off the burden onto the other", and "if this Company were without obedience, it could not long endure and persevere" [Delib. 8]. Common sense says that some authority is useful, "any group is kept alive by obedience more than by anything else", and experience confirms that "This is especially true for us who have vowed perpetual poverty and are perennially preoccupied with unremitting labors, both spiritual and temporal; for these make it difficult to preserve fellowship" [Delib. 8]. The *Constitutions* perhaps capture this family-like atmosphere in which the *Deliberation of the first fathers* was undertaken when presenting obedience, far beyond a military-style attitude of taking and executing orders, as a state of being attuned to the superior, in a way that the two persons and consequently the entire body of the Society can act in an almost idyllic harmony: "All should strongly dispose themselves to observe obedience and to distinguish themselves in it, not only in the matters of obligation but also in the others, even though nothing else be perceived except an indication of the superior's will without an expressed command" [ConsCN C 547]. While it is easy to see how such obedience serves the unity and the apostolic availability of the institutional body of the Society, acknowledging its benefit for the individual can be more difficult. The common understanding today, just as at the time of writing the *Constitutions*, tends to be that obedience serves the good of the institution at the expense of the individual. At this point, analogies taken from civil life and habits appropriated outside the Society can be more of an obstacle than a helpful basis for understanding the Ignatian vision. Similarly, the *Constitutions* can also strike the contemporary reader as a resource that is not especially helpful since it offers no systematic elaboration of the various aspects of obedience, such as in the recent detailed and balanced document of General Congregation 35.[10] Instead, the *Constitutions*—as

10 "Decrees of the 35th General Congregation. Decree 4: Obedience in the life of the Society of Jesus", pp. 755–67.

we have seen before—immediately focus on those practical details that can be most helpful for the person who desires to maintain progress on the pathway to God after final vows, beyond the official conclusion of the time of Jesuit formation properly speaking.

Obedience in apostolic life can be difficult since it may imply moving to places where the comfort level is low, friendships are difficult to maintain, a sense of being appreciated may be wanting, and the meaningfulness of a new and unfamiliar project is far from being obvious. Such potential losses can generate profound anxiety and anguish since the prospect of a changed environment lays bare the core vulnerabilities of the human being, as spelled out by the meditation on the Two Standards. Obedience can expose one to temptations in the very areas where the "bad spirit" can be most intrusive and destructive. Subtle temptations in these areas differ greatly from fierce ones, but both can lead to spiritual desolation, that is, "darkness and disturbance in the soul [...], disquiet arising from various agitations and temptations [...] lack of confidence in which one feels oneself without hope and without love" [SpEx 317]. Unrecognized desolation will, in turn, give way to arguments and rationalizations that tend to help little in trying to find the will of God, because "in desolation it is the bad spirit [who guides and counsels us] and by following his counsels we can never find the right way forward" [SpEx 318].

Obedience cannot be mature without eagerly engaging in the discernment of spirits and in spiritual struggle. Recognizing and acknowledging the presence of anxiety and anguish is an obvious first step. The meditation on the Two Standards can help to move from a diffuse anxiety to acknowledging specific fears: which of the four fundamental dimensions of human life will be affected by an act of obedience? Which fears make it most difficult to trust the Lord? How am I to find spiritual consolation and the corresponding inner freedom and peace? The *Constitutions* depict the struggle involved in obedience as predominantly spiritual, and presuppose that engaging in this struggle will be similar to what had been previously experienced at times of temptation. In the midst of powerful spiritual and psychological movements, the crucial source of strength is the presence of the Lord as accessible through the experience of contemplation: "They should keep in view God our Creator and Lord *(teniendo entre los ojos a Dios Nro. Criador y Señor)*, for whom such obedience is practiced, and endeavor to proceed in a spirit of love and not as men troubled by fear" [ConsCN C 547]. The Ignatian practice of obedience repeatedly challenges Jesuits to re-engage in a dynamic of mutual giving and receiving within a personal relationship with God. Obedience presupposes that the Jesuit is ready to "let himself be carried and directed by Divine Providence" [ConsCN C 547] and that he can adapt to the new mission "with God's grace", trying to persist in the contemplative attitude of remaining "in our Lord" [ConsCN C 547].

In other words, the anthropological precondition of obedience is that the motivations resulting from the dynamic of mutual giving and receiving in a relationship with God can be distinguished from the three basic types of human motivations that originate in the created world, and that—to the extent that the desire to love, respect and serve God is fueled by the grace and consolation received—a deep-seated sense of peace and joy can set the individual free from being caught up in the potential threefold trap inherent in the context of human life. Generosity toward God and receptivity to God's graces can keep a sufficiently "advanced" Jesuit motivated even if the environment where he lives and works does not satisfy him immediately with a positive feedback from others, a sense of usefulness, or favorable material conditions. Such inner freedom means that the "desire to resemble and imitate in some manner our Creator and Lord Jesus Christ" [ConsCN C 101] can supersede other desires with relative ease.

The primacy of the spiritual dimension and the exigency to be free, as much as possible, vis-à-vis all other motivations do not mean that potential conflicts of motivations are neglected. The *Constitutions* focus on the particular conflict that arises when the mission received, or the Society's way of proceeding, does not coincide with what the individual Jesuit considers meaningful and worth doing. The tacit understanding seems to be that other possible opposing motivations, such as enduring material hardships or losing supportive friendships may be relatively easily overcome as soon as the person is convinced that he has good reasons for renouncing these for the sake of fulfilling a new mission. Yet exactly these good reasons are wanting when obedience introduces a Jesuit to the conflictive condition where he has to renounce his desire to do what he immediately perceives as meaningful, important or of value for the Kingdom, and rely solely on the spiritual motivation of "keep[ing] in view God our Creator and Lord". This conflict, which corresponds to that of the third step of the meditation on the Two Standards, can be deeply upsetting since it frustrates the single most valuable human motivation that the "world" can offer: upon being drawn to specific values and ideals, one may make plans and set goals in accordance with these, and as productive inner energies are engaged to accomplish one's "own will", a deep satisfaction and a sense of meaningfulness arise. The capacity to define what is worth doing is a key constituent of exercising human freedom, and consequently, when obedience entails renouncing one's own will, "we consecrate the chief and noblest part of ourselves to God".[11]

When discussing the obedience of Jesuits after final vows, the *Constitutions* propose three ways for diminishing this difficult and potentially destructive inner conflict by subordinating the motivations that result from one's own will to the chief motive of loving and serving God in all circumstances. Three different methods—two ordinary and one extraordinary—serve the ordering of motives with respect to each other in a way that the personal integrity and the dynamic of moving forward on a pathway to God can be preserved. By these methods, the mission can be fulfilled "with great alacrity, spiritual joy, and perseverance" [ConsCN C 547]; in other words, in a way that it radiates a sense of consolation that results from living and working in the presence of God.

The first and most obvious way of ordering one's own will to the primary desire to love and serve God in all things invites one to focus on the person of Jesus Christ. The mission received can be pondered as if the order was coming from Jesus Christ:

> Consequently, in all the things into which obedience can with charity be extended, we should be ready to receive its command just as if it were coming from Christ our Savior, since we are practicing the obedience [to one] in his place and because of love and reverence for him. Therefore we should be ready to leave unfinished any letter or anything else of ours which we have begun. [ConsCN C 547]

This "just as if" method relies on the person of Christ as a catalyst for connecting the mission received, in its concrete reality, to the spiritual

11 See the Preface of the *Constitutions'* first edition (1559).

conviction that it is the Lord who is engaging me in his vineyard. Most of the time, when a mission is received without particularly serious objections, the "as if" exercise should be enough for engaging one's own will to fulfill the mission: it can help me to see the particular mission received from the superior as important and worth doing since there is a firm conviction that the Lord is willing to be there for me and work with and through me.

The second, supplementary way of ordering one's own will to the spiritual desire—and to the vow—of loving and serving the Lord in all things in the apostolic body of the Society could be called the "backward perfection" or "logotherapy" approach.

> we should be ready [...] in the Lord to bend our whole mind and energy *(poniendo toda la intençión y fuerças en el Sor.)* so that holy obedience, in regard to the execution, the willing, and the understanding, may always be perfect in every detail. [ConsCN C 547]

> The command of obedience is fulfilled in regard to the execution when the thing commanded is done; in regard to the willing when the one who obeys wills the same thing as the one who commands; in regard to the understanding when he forms the same judgment as the one commanding and regards what he is commanded as good. And that obedience is imperfect in which there does not exist, in addition to the execution, also that agreement in willing and judging between him who commands and him who obeys. [ConsCN C 550]

Owing to the sense of meaningfulness being a fundamental human need, appropriate attention is to be given to instances when an act of obedience breaks the usual chain of causality that links consideration to action. Human actions normally imply three elements. First, one judges something as valuable and thus desirable and meaningful. Second, the willingness emerges to invent and realize a corresponding project. Third, the intended course of action is executed. Typically, execution takes place as a consequence of the two preparatory steps even though they often go unnoticed. Obedience, however, may mean that actions have to be executed without this natural preliminary process of creating a context of meaning. In such cases, activities appear to be meaningless, or meaningful only as an exercise of obedience. The spiritual motivation to serve God in the mission received—which one can suppose to remain valid—clashes with the human motivation of willing to do something more meaningful. The inner conflict will manifest itself progressively through resentment, lack of interest, lethargy or even bodily symptoms which in turn will disturb and easily get in the way of a consoling relationship with God. The *Constitutions* call this phenomenon "imperfect" obedience [ConsCN C 550].

Obedience is "imperfect" when a Jesuit feels obliged to act contrary to what he would personally find meaningful to do. This can, of course, happen not only to Jesuits but to anyone in the ordinary everyday context of professional and family life, or in case of a sickness, accident or environmental disaster. The specificity of the way the Society proceeds is that the urge "perfectly" to obey invites the person to alleviate this tension to the extent that it is possible. In other words, the person who is to obey is called to try to restore a context of meaningfulness to his activities even when an act of obedience interrupts the natural chain of causality that usually precedes his actions. The openness of the text of the *Constitutions* with regard to how this can be done allows the contemporary reader to be inspired by the work of modern authors like Viktor E. Frankl. Frankl, convinced that a sense of meaningfulness was a fundamental human need, was able to help many of his fellow inmates to survive even the absurd conditions of a Nazi concentration camp by helping them to find rational reasons for persevering.[12] Later, the therapeutic effects of focusing on values and goals that give meaning to courses of action that had not been freely chosen became manifest in less extreme conditions as well. Although logotherapy, the therapeutic method developed by Frankl, focuses on the dimension of values to such an extent that it risks overemphasizing a single aspect of the fourfold relationship model that characterizes the Ignatian vision of the human being, it can lend a powerful contemporary support to the Ignatian insistence that obedience, unless it becomes "perfect", cannot be done with "great alacrity, spiritual joy, and perseverance" [ConsCN C 547]. In the light of the findings of Frankl, the process of establishing a context of meaning by finding valid reasons to obey becomes not

12 V. E. Frankl, *Man's Search for Meaning: An Introduction to Logotherapy* (Boston: Beacon Press, 2006), first published in German as *Trotzdem Ja zum Leben sagen: Ein Psychologe erlebt das Konzentrazionslager* (Vienna: Verlag für Jugend und Folk, 1946)

only realistic but also profoundly healthy, liberating and beneficial for the human soul.[13] When we say that it is important for a Jesuit to be convinced about the usefulness of the mission that he is engaged in, we do not simply echo commonplaces of our individualistic societies but in fact approve the insistence of the *Constitutions* that obedience should be "perfect".

The third way of alleviating the inner conflict of opposing motivations applies when the first two methods fail to restore a fully peaceful heart and there remains "any contrary opinion and judgment of our own" as a result of an act of obedience: "we should be [. . .] renouncing with blind obedience any contrary opinion and judgment of our own in all things which the superior commands and in which no species of sin can be judged to be present" [ConsCN C 547]. The "blindness method" consists in moving ahead while being aware that reason, the primary and most natural means of directing human action, is not or not fully supportive of the course of action that one is undertaking. The analogy of blindness as a handicap or, for that matter, blind landing with an aircraft are helpful to the extent that they express the extreme discomfort but also the viability of making progress by not acting autonomously but trusting oneself fully to the word of others or to secondary sources of information like the electronic instruments in a cockpit. In the relationship model of Ignatian anthropology, such blind obedience corresponds to a state of extreme polarization of the basic

13 "Logotherapy is based on three tenets: [. . .] Life has meaning under all conditions; man has the will to reach out for meaning and feels frustrated or empty if this will is not applied; and man has the freedom, within obvious limitations, to find the meaning of his life. [. . .] Logotherapy sees man as a being whose life consists of a string of situations, each of which has a specific meaning for him, and him alone. His fulfillment, happiness, and even mental well-being depend on finding, to the best of his capacities, the meaning of each situation of his life. [. . .] What does make a difference, though, is his awareness that he is free to seek the meanings of his life, that he has the obligation to do so, and that no one can do it for him." J. B. Fabry, *The Pursuit of Meaning* (Boston: Beacon Press, 1968), p. 37. There are three areas in which man can find meaning: activities ("What matters [. . .] is not how large is the radius of your activities, but only how well you fill its circle"), experiences ("such as beauty, truth, or love [. . .] provide man with meaning by receiving") and attitudes (this way of finding meaning is "more difficult [. . . but] the deepest meaning can be found here"). *Ibid.*, p. 41.

human motivations, where pure faith and trust in God has to prevail over customary human motivations. In such cases, the more one can quieten the agitation caused by other motivations, the more easily one can proceed. An ultimate example of such a situation is the deathbed, where motivations that have helped until that moment are not relevant any more and can even become obstacles in trusting oneself fully to the mercy of God, who alone can continue to uphold and move the person. Therefore another image for illustrating the blindness method is that of a "lifeless body". Just as the lifeless body of a person who has fainted can be moved easily as opposed to a person who is not willing to go, or as a cane is utilized by a living person without difficulty, obedience can sometimes benefit—both for the sake of the apostolic body of the Society and for the progress of the individual—from stilling the urge to affirm who is right and why and what should be done:

> We ought to act on the principle that everyone who lives under obedience should let himself be carried and directed by Divine Providence through the agency of the superior as if he were a lifeless body, which allows itself to be carried to any place and treated in any way; or an old man's staff, which serves at any place and for any purpose in which the one holding it in his hand wishes to employ it. [ConsCN C 547]

As we have seen, such blind obedience is not "perfect" in the sense that without appropriate, personally meaningful reasons for undertaking a mission, perseverance will remain difficult and obedience will be reduced to being a strenuous task that can eliminate joyfulness. A permanent conflict of motivations would risk disintegrating the personality. However, while spiritual motivations can at times conflict sharply with common human motivations, the difficult choice in favor of the spiritual motivation can bring about unexpected, life-changing experiences of grace. This is why the *Constitutions* insist that paradoxically, even blind obedience that is imperfect in itself can promote perfection if the word is understood in the sense of becoming conformed to Christ down to the very desires of the heart. Obedience can arise from the desires of a Jesuit to be like Christ, and given that these desires are "so salutary and fruitful for the perfection of his soul" [ConsCN C 101], obedience can become a means of receiving new graces and making personal progress:

> Hence all of us should be eager to miss no point of perfection which we can with God's grace attain in the observance of all the Constitutions and of our manner of proceeding in our Lord, by applying all our energies with very special care to the virtue of obedience shown first to the sovereign pontiff and then to the superiors of the Society. [ConsCN C 547]

While purely spiritual reasons for obedience are understandable in the context of the Ignatian vision, they tend not to motivate contemporary readers of the *Constitutions*. For example, the idea that obedience makes it possible for the will of God to be conveyed through the will of the superior, an argument that seems to have been plausible up to the 1960s, rarely becomes a personal conviction today. Obedience understood as a privileged way to fulfill the will of God tends rather to appear like a touchstone of an irredeemably medieval way of thinking that has little relevance in a modern society, where all good is not seen to descend from God in a hierarchically ordered social structure. Even the contemporary emphasis on personal discernment, a fundamental aspect of Ignatian spirituality, can provide the unintentional side effect that while personally discerned options are readily accepted as the will of God, obedience to a superior who does not necessarily approve the result of such personal discernment may appear to be all the more alien to the highly valued spiritual motivation.

A thorough reading of the *Constitutions* reveals a number of details that can help the contemporary reader to see these issues more clearly. First of all, conformity with the will of God is placed into a wider context that has several interrelated elements:

> We ought to act on the principle that everyone who lives under obedience should let himself be carried and directed by Divine Providence through the agency of the superior as if he were a lifeless body, which allows itself to be carried to any place and treated in any way [. . .] For in this way the obedient man ought joyfully to employ himself in any task in which the superior desires to employ him in aid of the whole body of the religious order; and he ought to hold it certain that by so doing he conforms himself with the divine will more than by anything else he could do while following his own will and different judgment. [ConsCN C 547]

A Jesuit thus does not "conform himself with the divine will" simply by executing the order of the superior. Consequently, the will of God is not simply equated with what the superior orders. The *Constitutions* mention three conditions that can be used as criteria for discerning whether one is acting in conformity with the will of God. The first concerns choosing the primacy of the relationship with God which is expressed in the attitude of letting oneself be "carried and directed by Divine Providence" even while following the word of the superior in an act of obedience. God is thus acknowledged as generous and caring in all circumstances, and obedience becomes an expression of the desire to love and serve God in all things. The second criterion consists in allowing oneself "to be carried to any place", that is, not showing resistance to the movement of trust initiated by Providence. These two criteria mirror the Ignatian conception of human maturity as analysed among the hermeneutical principles for interpreting the *Constitutions*: the primacy of God and the resulting inner freedom are intrinsically connected. The third criterion for doing the will of God, joyfulness, is equally related to the previous two. It indicates independence from the satisfaction of desires or potential motivations offered by the "world"—such as enjoying material comfort, personal attention coming from others, or doing what one finds important to do—and expresses the liveliness of the relationship with God.

Doing the will of God is thus not to be thought of simply as the equivalent of engaging in a well-discerned project or course of action. Conformity with the "divine will" is rather a dynamic state of keeping oneself indifferent as much as possible, while seeking to sustain with God a joyful, generous mutual relationship of giving and receiving, and remaining perceptive and prompt in following the movements of the Spirit. This general sense of acting in conformity with the divine will is to be translated into concrete service through engaging in projects either under obedience or in consequence of a discernment process. Doing the will of God thus presupposes the ability to distinguish between the satisfaction of realizing projects competently and taking specific courses of action, and the more general spiritual attitude of openness and promptness to the ever surprising new incentives of the Spirit. Failing to make this distinction may result in pushing one's own will rather than acting in conformity with the will of God, something that Ignatius too was confronted with during his pilgrimage to the Holy Land. The idea of the pilgrimage originated in the very first discernment that Ignatius made while convalescing in Loyola [cf. Autobiography 8]. As he acted upon the desire that he discerned to be coming from the Spirit of God, he traveled to Jerusalem, and by the time he arrived there, the discernment transformed into a "firm resolution" [Autobiography 45] to stay in the Holy Land. Only the threat of excommunication persuaded him to obey the Franciscan custodian and leave the Holy Land, and he needed plenty of time afterwards to be able to "understand that it was the will of God that he does not stay in Jerusalem" [Autobiography 50].

Seen from the perspective of the relationship model of Ignatian anthropology, doing the will of God presupposes the inner freedom that is a consequence of a spiritually live relationship with God and the competent activity in the "worldly" dimension of relating to human beings, as well as the ability to unite these two dimensions. An important Ignatian metaphor articulating the connection of the contemplative and the active dimensions is that of being an instrument in unison with God. The famous passage often quoted as the interpretative key to the *Constitutions* describes how the body of the Society depends on individuals who can remain united with God while being active in helping souls:

> For the preservation and growth not only of the body or exterior of the Society but also of its spirit, and for the attainment of the objective it seeks, which is to aid souls to reach their ultimate and supernatural end, the means which unite the human instrument with God and so dispose it that it may be wielded well by his divine hand are more effective than those which equip it in relation to human beings. Such means are, for example, goodness and virtue, and especially charity, and a pure intention of the divine service, and familiarity with God our Lord in spiritual exercises of devotion, and sincere zeal for souls for the sake of the glory of the one who created and redeemed them and not for any other benefit. [ConsCN C 813]

Coming back to obedience, we have seen how the *Constitutions* provide help for the person who desires to obey in a way that obedience does not hinder his personal progression toward God and does not diminish his apostolic dynamism in the service of souls. So far, the question of what particular mission is being conferred has not received any attention. The steps helping one obey in a "perfect" manner do not depend on what the Jesuit has been actually asked to do. One of the reasons for this silence about the subject matter of the mission is that determining the "task in which the superior desires to employ [a Jesuit] in aid of the whole body of the religious order" [ConsCN C 547] is such a central theme that it is treated separately in Part VII. For the time being, from the perspective of the one who obeys, the single criterion for obeying is that "no species of sin can be judged to be present" [ConsCN C 547].

Another issue related to obedience is the dialogue between a Jesuit and his superior that precedes and accompanies the actual act of obedience. Here as in many other places, the *Constitutions* emphasize the account of conscience as the privileged channel of communication "once a year and as many times more as [the] superior thinks good" [ConsCN C 551]. In a contemporary culture where dialogue is highly valued, the insistence of the *Constitutions* on mutual dialogue should not be difficult to put into practice, considering also that numerous letters of Ignatius give practical details about how he conceived this.[14] In the meantime, ongoing difficulties indicate that more could be done to benefit fully from the possibility of dialogue between a Jesuit and his superior, and exchanging good formation practices or other similar measures could enhance the contemporary reception of this insistence of the *Constitutions*.

Another aspect related to obedience is the quality of the relationship between a Jesuit and his superior, an issue that receives surprisingly strong attention. One might think that the question of whether a Jesuit was on good terms with his superior or not was irrelevant in the medieval cultural context when the *Constitutions* were written, given the great emphasis on obedience in no matter what circumstances. In reality, the quality of the relationship between the individual Jesuit and his superior appears to be of crucial importance:

> Likewise, it should be strongly recommended to all that they should have and show great reverence, especially interior reverence, for their

14 St Ignatius of Loyola, "On the Method of Dealing with Superiors", IX, 90–2, Letter 5400a, in *Letters of St. Ignatius of Loyola*, selected and translated by W. J. Young SJ (Chicago: Loyola University Press, 1959), p. 390.

> superiors, by considering and reverencing Jesus Christ in them; and from their hearts they should warmly love their superiors as fathers in him. Thus in everything they should proceed in a spirit of charity. [ConsCN C 551]

The spirit of charity evokes the "interior law of charity and love" [ConsCN C 134] which is, according to the Preamble, more helpful in making progress than the written letters of the *Constitutions*. Similarly, the attitude of reverence toward the superior is highly valued, and Jesuits are invited to contemplate Jesus Christ in the person of the superior. While this can be easily interpreted as a remnant of an exaggerated medieval piety, the *Constitutions* in fact invite one to consider the superior in the same way as any fellow Jesuit in the novitiate, where each should "grow in devotion and praise God our Lord, whom each one should strive to recognize in the other as in his image" [ConsCN C 250]. Obedience appears to be presupposing the same spiritual quality of interpersonal relationships that novices are invited to aim for in their mutual relationships and also toward their superior. This exigency can considerably challenge the human and spiritual maturity of the Jesuit who obeys since acts of obedience tend to be stressful situations where psychological self-defense mechanisms like projection can easily arise. A Jesuit who in the novitiate did not learn to recognize such reactions and to deal with them competently will be poorly equipped to "proceed in the spirit of charity" while obeying in a difficult context. In such cases, the relationship with the superior is bound to suffer, since impulses of overt or repressed aggression against the superior will make his real weaknesses appear exaggerated to such an extent that alienation can easily set in. In such moments, taking projections back by practicing charity and respect is a precondition to finding inner peace anew, which in turn can allow one to enjoy a sense of the enlivening presence of God once again.

## Poverty

In the relationship model of Ignatian anthropology, the vow of poverty concerns the third basic motivation in human life, the dimension of material goods. The subject matter is of special importance since according to the meditation on the Two Standards, the question of poverty precedes the other two steps in some way. Human freedom can be undermined primarily at this point: "first [the devils] should tempt people to covet riches (as [Satan] usually does, at least in most cases)" [SpEx 142]. In accordance with the meditation on the Two Standards, the *Constitutions* attach the utmost significance to the vow of poverty in the sustenance of the dynamic of religious life. Actual poverty puts an edge on the question of whether a basic sense of security, an essential aspect of everyday life, comes from the use of material goods or is rooted in God:

> But the Society, relying on God our Lord whom it serves with the aid of his divine grace, should trust that without its having fixed revenue he will cause everything to be provided which can be expedient for his greater praise and glory. [ConsCN C 555]

Such direct use of actual poverty to elicit trust in Providence is obviously a risky enterprise. Poverty can efficiently enhance the importance of non-material motivations, like fraternal relationships, firm commitment to "higher" values and even a trusting and selfless relationship with a generous God. When, however, an enforced poverty indicates a voluntarism that is detached from the delicate task of making progress along a pathway to God, the results can be devastating. Grumbling and anger, a spirit of discord in interpersonal relationships, an ideological interpretation of events instead of the graciousness of seeking to find God in all things can be but some of the signs that something is going wrong. In the perspective opened by the *Constitutions*, actual poverty is presented to be helpful to those who are truly engaged in a dynamic of progressing on the Ignatian pathway to God. Its fruits can be expected to manifest themselves on the condition that there is clarity about what such progress means, and poverty is integrated into a complex set of Ignatian means in support of a delicately yet firmly applied mystagogical approach. In other words, poverty will appear to make sense when the personality begins to be structured according to the dynamic of growth that is characteristic of religious life, where not fulfilling one's material and security needs beyond an elementary level frees up energies to move forward in an ever deepening trust in God.

Giving up the security and comfort provided by material goods can, as with the vows of chastity and obedience, lay bare an inner emptiness and consequently—by provoking a series of mini-crises—lead to stronger reliance on God. The sections that have been conserved from the *Spiritual Diary* demonstrate the weight that Ignatius attributed to this spiritual dynamic. This is why, during his deliberations about implementing poverty in the Society, he finally ended up renouncing the potentially practical and apostolic benefits of fixed revenues for the maintenance of houses and churches: "In the houses or churches which the Society accepts to aid souls, it should not be licit to have any fixed revenue, even for the sacristy or building or anything else, in such a manner that any administration of this revenue is in the control of the Society" [ConsCN C 555].

The presentation of poverty in Part VI of the *Constitutions* strikes the reader as an issue that pertains first and foremost to the Society as a whole. Individual responsibility is obviously implied in the very vow of poverty, yet the text emphasizes the crucial importance of an appropriately crafted common life style. Within a purposefully ordered physical, spiritual and ethical environment, individual decisions can become more transparent in terms of making progress on the pathway to God. Individual poverty needs to be able to rely on a sufficiently firm common way of proceeding and cannot be seen as a substitute for it. Everyday individual decisions are important, but attention to long-term tendencies is crucial:

> Poverty, as the strong wall of the religious institute, should be loved and preserved in its integrity as far as this is possible with God's grace. The enemy of the human race generally tries to weaken this defense and rampart which God our Lord inspired religious institutes to raise against him and the other adversaries of their perfection. Into what was well ordered by their first founders he induces alterations by means of interpretations and innovations not in conformity with those founders' first spirit. [ConsCN C 553]

The rest of Chapter 2 of Part VI of the *Constitutions* ("What pertains to poverty and its consequences") discusses an abundance of practical aspects with keen attention to detail: the case of professed Jesuits, the prohibition of possessing any stable property without a direct apostolic purpose, the use of fruits harvested in the gardens, details of when and how to accept or decline alms, the question of perpetual alms or stipends, the prohibition of placing collecting boxes in the church, and other similar matters. The seemingly endless list of instructions indicates that Ignatius did not entrust these details to the discernment of individual Jesuits or even superiors who in other areas of Jesuit life tend to receive much more room to exercise personal responsibility. The reason is perhaps that the relationship with material things is not just one of the most sensitive areas where Lucifer can intervene. According to the meditation on the Two Standards, the issue of poverty is the very first step where things can go wrong. This is where the difference between the dynamic of religious and lay life can become blurred the most easily, and a significant precondition for engaging a dynamic of progression can be lost inadvertently. While lay life presupposes a basic sense of material security as a fundament for the further unfolding of a meaningful life, and consequently the acquisition and the proper management of material goods is a serious personal responsibility, a similar sense of self-reliance can radically weaken the dynamic of religious life, including its spiritual vitality and its credibility in witnessing the Kingdom of God. Although in theory this distinction is probably quite clear, in practice the use of material goods can induce almost imperceptible ambiguities, which in turn may result in an impairment of the religious life's characteristic dynamic of progression to the point that a sense of loving and serving God becomes hard to maintain. If chastity necessitates an overall human and spiritual balance, and obedience presupposes considerable conscious reflection and discernment, then poverty implies a sound common practice of a simple life. The routines and procedures that embody poverty as a common characteristic of the body of the Society constitute the necessary background for poverty to become a criterion for individual discernment, preventing a Jesuit to abandon the dynamic of progression on the pathway to God in ways usually less dramatic but no less real than incidents associated with the vows of chastity and obedience.

## The Relationship with God

Part VI of the *Constitutions* talks about the relationship with God, the major motivational drive of a professed Jesuit, by way of a new metaphor: a lively relationship is depicted as the elevated temperature of the spirit. The expression evokes an image familiar from the *Spiritual Exercises* (the soul is "inflamed with love of its Creator and Lord" [SpEx 316]), but also allows for a relatively stable, ongoing sense of consolation that can be understood to be less influenced by affective surges, such as in the final clause of the definition: "Finally, under the word of consolation I include every increase in hope, faith, and charity, and every interior joy which calls and attracts one toward heavenly things and to the salvation of one's soul, by bringing it tranquility and peace in its Creator and Lord" [SpEx 316]. There is no indication that the spiritual life of a professed Jesuit is expected to go through similar fluctuations as that of a novice ("whether with many spiritual visitations or with fewer" [ConsCN C 260]). It seems as though the relationship with God has become calmer and more reliable over time. Although the warmth of the spirit is a sign of the presence of God, which clearly there is no guarantee of attaining by any prayer method or relaxation technique, the *Constitutions* explain that by means of practices of self-denial learned earlier, the warmth of the spirit can be quite reliably fostered. The way of doing this appears to be as simple and practical as the fireplace tools that are waiting to be used when the fire needs to be rekindled:

> Therefore in what pertains to prayer, meditation, and study, and also in regard to the bodily practices of fasts, vigils, and other austerities or penances [. . .] they should be vigilant that these practices not be relaxed to such an extent that the spirit grows cold and the human and lower passions grow warm. [ConsCN C 582]

Practices of self-denial are thus significant because they have an effect on the fire within. Their immediate goal is not to extinguish passionate affections. Instead, self-denial can play a role similar to the vows in the sense of enhancing a certain inner emptiness and composedness which allows one to turn toward God with a more sensitive and emotionally involved attention. Practices of self-denial are not presented as weaponry to fight against inordinate attachments or some other evil, but as an instrument to open oneself more fully to the light and warmth of God's love.

The practices that are suitable for rekindling the warmth of the spirit are not defined by generally valid instructions: "It does not seem proper to give [to Jesuits with final vows] any other rule than that which discreet charity *(la discreta charidad)* dictates to them" [ConsCN C 582]. The expression "discreet charity", which has earlier been used in the *Constitutions* only in regard to the responsibilities of the superior, is applied here for the first time to Jesuits taking decisions about themselves concerning "what pertains to prayer, meditation, and study, and also in regard to the bodily practices of fasts, vigils, and other austerities or penances". Although "the confessor [must] always be informed", and "when a doubt about advisability arises, the superior [too]" [ConsCN C 582], Ignatius trustingly relies on the discerning abilities of the Jesuit who is "spiritual and sufficiently advanced" [ConsCN C 582]. The awareness of having the responsibility to maintain the flame of loving God and being loved by God is the precondition for remaining engaged in the dynamic of progression on the Ignatian pathway to God, and it is thus a foremost priority. Good health and aptitude to be missioned, together with the ongoing concern for rekindling the inner fire, characterize the Jesuit who after final vows wants to serve others with the spiritual depth, integrity and energy that are characteristic of the Society. Ascetic means for reviving an affective union with God are, however, to be used with moderation and in view of the apostolic goal of the Society, that of living and working for others:

> they should take care that the excessive use of these practices not weaken their bodily strength and take up so much time that they are rendered incapable of helping the neighbor spiritually according to our Institute. [ConsCN C 582]

By covering the fourth, final phase of the pathway to God—the life of Jesuits with final vows—the *Constitutions* have accomplished the first objective of their writing: helping the personal progression of individual Jesuits from the moment they had joined the Society until their final incorporation and beyond. The *Constitutions* can now turn to considering the second objective, the good of the apostolic body, which is the "end eminently characteristic of our Institute" [ConsCN C 603]. Four areas of concern—mission, union, governance and preservation of the Society—remain to be discussed in Parts VII–X of the *Constitutions*, but the interpretation of these parts is beyond the scope of this book.

# Looking Forward: Inculturation

## Theory and Practice

How to help personal progression and growth in Jesuit life? This question has been the focus of our attention as we have interpreted the *Constitutions*. How do the Ignatian instructions foster the spiritual and human maturity of those joining the Society? What characteristics need to develop so that a full apostolic mission can be entrusted to a formed Jesuit? Our interpretation of Parts III to VI has not broken with the contemporary tendency of reading the *Constitutions* as a text of spirituality,[1] yet it has opened new perspectives by using the essential Ignatian concept of "progress" as a primary interpretative key. Within the successive phases of formation, tangible sub-goals and practical methods for helping to reach them have become recognizable, and the organic unity of the movement of progression across these phases has also become more understandable. We have seen how the Ignatian vision embodied in the *Constitutions* can be helpful to Jesuit formators, offering both an overarching perspective and many practical details for supporting a complex process of growth in a grace-filled manner.

We have considered Ignatian formation as a dynamic of progression with emphasis on human growth, mystagogy and incorporation into the apostolic body of the Society. This vision is hopefully sufficiently attractive to inspire further research and a deeper understanding of our way of life. In the meantime, the practical consequences of our reflections may seem limited and somewhat elusive. If this is indeed the case, it hopefully confirms the thesis that the question of personal progression in Jesuit life cannot be understood in a purely theoretical manner. Our interpretation of the *Constitutions* is certainly in need of

1 Coupeau, *From Inspiration to Invention*, pp. 49 ff.

further theoretical clarifications but these alone will not bring about understanding, since interpreting a handbook of formation means actually making use of it. The conception of the pathway to God as implied in the *Constitutions* needs to be confronted with the practical experiences of Jesuits, especially formators and superiors. Those who have first-hand experience of the reality of a dynamic of progress will need to contribute to interpreting the *Constitutions*. Since current channels for sharing such experiences—community meetings, formators' gatherings or occasional articles about Jesuit life—are only locally relevant, the present understanding of the *Constitutions* on the level of the Society remains inevitably unsatisfactory.

Poor input from the actual users of the *Constitutions* means that the contemporary interpretation of this primary Ignatian text lacks an essential prerequisite. Seemingly small details about how individual elements of the Ignatian pathway to God can be explained, how misunderstandings can be cleared in conversation with actual Jesuits in formation, how these persons can be helped to take responsibility for actually moving ahead are indispensable constituents of understanding the text today. Such details can only emerge by evaluating the actual practice of those helping others to progress. Without in fact seeing and touching the graces and lasting gifts that can be received when a young Jesuit is more purposefully helped to make progress on the Ignatian pathway to God, all the talk about pathway and progress can seem like trying to enforce an overly idealistic "method" which focuses on the details of the *Constitutions* in a fundamentalist spirit and thus raises suspicions rather than sparking further interest. The *Constitutions* will gain the ongoing attention of Jesuits only to the extent that we acknowledge the practical fruits that emerge. Jesuits who feel better helped as well as superiors who can discern and trust themselves to the movements of the Spirit more sensitively and courageously will contribute significantly to the contemporary reception of the *Constitutions*. The Society as a whole will embrace this text more fully as soon as it can rely more extensively on the generosity, availability and competence of its members when it comes to mission.

As happened in the case of the *Spiritual Exercises*, where understanding the text went hand in hand with learning to apply it in practice, it is hoped that the interpretation of the *Constitutions* will gain momentum if the familiar signs of consolation and "divine power" begin to appear in Jesuit formation as a result of the more attentive use of the Ignatian text. When in the 1950s small groups of Jesuits began to study the book of the *Spiritual Exercises,* asking questions about method, key concepts and spiritual dynamic, they did not merely engage in scholarly research but also started using the text while accompanying persons who came to do the Exercises. Early experiences in giving the personally guided exercises propelled these Jesuits further in exploring and understanding the succinct, and at times enigmatic, text, because they discovered how the precise yet in themselves not always inspiring terms and instructions of the *Spiritual Exercises* could help in receiving consolations by being given a desired grace, admitting a secret sin, being set free from a paralysing fear, or desiring to follow Christ more closely. The reception of the Ignatian heritage was catalysed by the synergy between scholarly research and actual ministry: the practice of giving the Exercises helped to interpret the Ignatian words while the Ignatian text helped with giving the Exercises more effectively.

In other words, the paradigmatic story of rediscovering the Exercises leads us to consider the contemporary inculturation of the *Constitutions.* The *Constitutions* promise relevant and important answers to formation questions but the full richness of these answers will only be revealed to us when feedback from actual usage begins to support theory, and vice versa. Closer interaction between theory and usage would mean that a process in many ways similar to the one that led to a profoundly renewed way of understanding and giving the *Spiritual Exercises* could get under way, and now that the inculturation of the *Exercises* has become pervasive in our personal reflections and in our ministries as well, a deep, effective and transformative reception of the *Constitutions* is also becoming possible. Such a prospect will, of course, turn into reality on the condition that productive time and collaborative work will be invested in refining our understanding of how Jesuits can be better helped to progress on the Ignatian pathway to God. The treasures waiting for us are similar to the ones that were revealed to us in the second half of the twentieth century, but we can also expect serious obstacles on the way. In order to be able consciously to face these challenges, it will be opportune to discuss them briefly.

## Contemporary Challenges in Interpreting the *Constitutions*

If indeed a deeper sense of the helpfulness of the *Constitutions* is necessary for the contemporary understanding of this document, if the Ignatian criterion of considering the usefulness of the text is not to be disregarded,[2] then the contemporary reception of the *Constitutions* will depend on our ability to learn from our experiences of applying the text in practice. This unique process of understanding will necessarily include, beyond the expertise of scholars of Ignatian spirituality, formators who are willing to share best practices and experiences in helping actual Jesuits move along the Ignatian pathway to God. The hermeneutic principle of helpfulness presents an opportunity to take up a number of formation questions and unresolved issues in Ignatian spirituality through a collaborative exploration of the *Constitutions*.

At the same time, the very imperative to collaborate constitutes one of the major challenges ahead. Evaluating, sharing and systematically organizing our formation experiences in relation to the text of *Constitutions* would mean, theoretically, simply extending the work that has been done in the past fifty years with regard to the *Spiritual Exercises* to an additional area of our Ignatian heritage. In reality, however, hitherto unknown difficulties can be expected to appear. While the *Exercises* imply a process that arrives at completion and can be evaluated after a few days or weeks, the fruits of engaging in the dynamic of Jesuit formation may sometimes only become visible several years later, thus making the evaluation rather difficult. While in any particular retreat house there are usually more Jesuits who give the Exercises simultaneously, the novice masters, college rectors and tertian masters live and work at long distances from one another and can only meet in yearly get-togethers at most. While a Jesuit can usually give the Spiritual Exercises throughout his life, continuously re-evaluating and refining his approach, formators tend to be assigned to a given task for a few years only, which means that by the time they develop a mature

2 "We need a fundamental hermeneutical reflection [...] According to Ignatius the texts do not exist alone and apart from their usefulness, from a 'profit' to be drawn from them." Goujon, *Pilgrims of Research*, p. 52.

vision of how they can best help Jesuits in formation, they risk being assigned to some other task, normally without having the opportunity to contribute to reinforcing a common formation culture of the Society through writing articles or books.[3]

The ongoing evaluation and accumulation of formation experiences is also hindered by the fact that the *Constitutions* do not tend to play an explicit role in structuring the information that is shared at formation meetings and workshops. While we quite naturally and habitually use the notions, categories and implicit structures of the *Spiritual Exercises* when sharing our experience about having done or given the Exercises, formation experiences are usually not evaluated in the *Constitutions'* framework but rather, for example, in the context of attending to the pressing need to solve a current problem. In such cases, we usually quote short sections of contemporary documents of the Society, try to appropriate good practices used elsewhere, or rely on our own former experiences and general spiritual or psychological knowledge in the hope of coming up with helpful insights. Such an approach, while often helpful in solving short-term problems, barely contributes to a contemporary inculturation of the *Constitutions* and to the emergence of an overall vision of Jesuit formation within which particular details could be discussed with more clarity. Part of the challenge is thus not merely to strive for a more resolute sharing of formation experiences but also to arrange our experiential knowledge in line with the conceptual framework of the *Constitutions*. This Ignatian text is not primarily a set of instructions but a context of meaning. Interpreting the text has to imply interpreting our experience according to the text.[4]

Three more obstacles to a contemporary inculturation of the *Constitutions* became apparent in our preliminary studies. The most obvious is the incomprehension resulting from the cultural distance between the world of the text and our modern way of thinking. We have seen, for example, that the *Constitutions* expect scholastics to go to school in pairs, and not go anywhere else without prior permission [ConsCN

3 See for example: W. Au SJ, *By Way of the Heart* (New Jersey: Paulist Press, 1989)

4 See Lukács SJ, "A Next Generation of Questions for Ignatian Spirituality" in *Ignaziana* <www.ignaziana.org> 17 (2014), pp. 171–87.

C 349]. This instruction has, of course, been abolished by a recent general congregation, because enforcing it to the letter would correspond to the "heresy" of Jesuit fundamentalism.[5] At the same time, does the superior not overlook an important aspect of the Ignatian vision if he just mechanically labels this regulation as a mere instance of an outdated approach? Cultural differences, unless they inspire creativity, obstruct understanding. We have seen that scholastics are expected to make progress on the Ignatian pathway to God in a fragile psycho-spiritual balance where competent help is necessary. Since the dimension of interpersonal relationships becomes especially sensitive at a time when affective warmth and consolations can be scarce, creating firm structures for continually helping scholastics to keep re-entering into real, intellectually and to some extent affectively engaging contacts with each other remains an important responsibility of the person who is in charge of helping scholastics to make progress. Simply to drop Ignatian practices without inventing culturally adequate and realistic alternatives would risk resulting in a loss of momentum and stoppages in the lives of Jesuits in formation.

We have seen that terminology can also hinder the contemporary inculturation of the *Constitutions*, since a number of Ignatian expressions have lost their rich original meaning over the almost half-millennium that has gone by. Moreover, solid prejudices stemming from superficial understanding make it difficult for Ignatian expressions to be renewed and imbued with appealing contemporary meanings. These blockages will be impossible to dissolve without vigorous further research. How to make relevant some of the fundamental terms of the *Constitutions* in a contemporary context? Only the future can tell whether such basic expressions as *virtue* can break free from the net of negative cultural associations and acquire vivid present-day connotations, as has happened in the case of many key expressions of the *Spiritual Exercises*. If this can happen, then today's Jesuits can engage in a more personal, in-depth relationship with the text of the *Constitutions*. Otherwise the use of synonyms will be necessary. For example, we may find it more helpful to speak about human abilities

5 P. Endean SJ, "Who do you say Ignatius is? Jesuit Fundamentalism and Beyond", *Studies in the Spirituality of Jesuits* 19/5 (1987), pp. 1–53, at p. 22.

or skills instead of virtues, just as we adjust the vocabulary of the *Spiritual Exercises* according to a variety of cultural contexts, replacing possibly too heavy Ignatian words with somewhat imprecise yet easily comprehensible synonyms. The important thing, regarding virtues, is to become able to talk about how some of the grace-filled moments of contemplating Christ or other biblical personalities are expected to bear fruits through repeated practice and the progressive development of stable character traits, changing the person in ways that enable him to become more like the Lord and become better prepared to be sent on the mission.

Thirdly, and perhaps most profoundly, the inculturation of the *Constitutions* is thwarted today by the radical and ongoing changes in our way of understanding the human being. One of the reasons why the Ignatian text feels distant and unfamiliar to our postmodern thinking is the strong influence of scholastic philosophy and anthropology, the typical conceptual framework of the time of its origin.[6] To stick with St Thomas's synthesis of ancient Greek philosophy and Christian spiritual tradition, which was an extraordinary intellectual accomplishment in the thirteenth century, would be as anachronistic today as trying to calculate the motions of the planets using the brilliant yet from our perspective unnecessarily convoluted Ptolemaic system. One of the major reasons for moving to a different paradigm of philosophical anthropology is that since the sixteenth century practically all fields of science—such as physics, astronomy, biology—evolved from a descriptive, static approach into a dynamic vision which integrates time and change as a constitutive dimension of these theories. Phenomena in all these areas are to be understood today in the context of their emergence and progressive development.[7] In the

6 "Commonplaces such as interior/exterior, memory/understanding/will, soul/body or poverty/chastity/obedience, and so forth serve two purposes: they reveal the Scholastic sources of this ideology and insert this discourse into the Western tradition of religious life." Coupeau, *From Inspiration to Invention*, p. 177.

7 "In just the last 150 years, Wells says, nearly every social and natural science has made this transformation from a taxonomic, entity-oriented perception of the phenomena of investigation to a developmental, process-oriented perception: in astronomy with La Place (1832); in geology with Lyell (1833); in logic with Hegel (1892) and Feuerbach (1846); in history and political economy with Marx (1931);

unusually complex area of understanding the human being, a similar paradigm shift began relatively late, with the work of Sigmund Freud, and it is still in progress. Despite the exponentially growing quantity of theoretical and practical findings, the outlines of a comprehensive, commonly and practically applicable anthropology are not yet emerging. About a century into the advancement of the psychological movement, we consider it natural that our approach is defined by not necessarily matching mosaic tiles of competing psychological theories. The lack of a coherent and comprehensive anthropological framework not only causes enormous difficulties in the formation of the religious but tends to undermine more general discussions of education, society, moral values and the like.

Part of the anthropological challenge in understanding the *Constitutions* today is that psychological models do not provide sufficient room for understanding the human being's relationship with God. Even though a more or less vague notion of spiritual needs is beginning to make its way even into mainstream psychology, it remains a far cry from the rich and transformative relationship with a living God known to Christian theology. Therefore, common contemporary anthropological concepts can offer only modest help in understanding religious life, unlike in Ignatius' time, when Jesuits were supposed to be familiar with the comprehensive and at the time widely accepted vision of St Thomas Aquinas. The merits of having a sophisticated Aristotelian philosophical and anthropological system integrated with Christian theology used to be obvious, and so is the difficulty today of not having a comparable integrative vision. This is why we have opted to bridge the anthropological gap that is standing in the way of a more thorough inculturation of the *Constitutions* by means of the fourfold relationship model of Ignatian anthropology. Presenting the human being as both active and receptive in the fourfold dimension of relating to the environment that is "worldly" and divine at the same time is, in itself, a rather unsophisticated model in comparison with contemporary psychological and motivational theories. The simple model, however, turns out to be surprisingly robust because it does not aim to replace

in biology with Darwin (1889)." Kegan, *The Evolving Self*, p. 13. See H. K. Wells, "Alienation and Dialectical Logic" in *Kansas Journal of Sociology 8* (1972/1), p. 9.

existing models but rather to offer a framework within which spiritual and psychological approaches can mutually complement each other. The reader who is familiar with Ignatian spirituality will recognize how deeply this model is rooted—through the uncommonly important meditation on the Two Standards—in the *Spiritual Exercises* and also in the long line of thought of "the threefold lust" in the history of spirituality, while also offering striking resonances with a number of modern psychological theories.

The Ignatian vision of the human being can thus help us avoid two impasses, the naïve confusion of the spiritual and psychological approaches on the one hand and their artificial and sterile separation on the other. Ignatian anthropology can help to maintain the relationship with God as the foremost lens when contemplating a human being, while also considering the psychological, developmental challenges that one has to face in order to enter more fully into a relationship of praise, reverence and service of God. André Louf, a spiritual writer in the Cistercian tradition, uses the evocative images of the "Inner Mirror" and the "Inner Policeman" to discuss the spiritual challenge of facing two powerful and generally present psychological phenomena, narcissism and super-ego.[8] While some of the emphases would be put differently in the Ignatian tradition, a similarly detailed contemporary elaboration of the nature of the spiritual struggle at the third step of the meditation on the Two Standards would be a significant exercise of creative fidelity. A vivid explanation of how the spiritual and psychological aspects interfere with each other—for example, how a novice with low self-esteem can find freedom in loving and serving the Lord while being lured or harassed by the inner Mirror and the Policeman—could be helpful in understanding the novitiate as a place where spiritual combat on the one hand, and human growth and healing in the area of interpersonal relationships on the other, belong together as two sides of the same coin.

8 A. Louf, *Grace Can Do More: Spiritual Accompaniment and Spiritual Growth"* (Michigan: Cistercian Publications, 2002).

## Some Fruits to be Expected

It would be hard to foretell how a purposeful contemporary inculturation of the *Constitutions* might affect life and formation in the Society of Jesus. We can assume that the serene yet apparent transformation of our way of life that began with the renewed understanding and use of the *Spiritual Exercises* in the middle of the twentieth century would continue in the significantly different cultural context of the twenty-first century. A more profound awareness of the pathway to God as presented by the Institute of the Society would influence the way Jesuits consider their goals and each other, and how they make themselves available to the praise, love and service of God. Outsiders, for example those interested in joining the Society, could see the current unceasing attractiveness of the Spiritual Exercises flow over more easily into Jesuit life itself. A more purposeful use of the *Constitutions* would have powerful bearings on our sense of identity, allowing the recent, theologically accurate and beautifully poetical elucidation of our Jesuit identity[9] to be endowed with a more directly practical dimension. Improving the help given to fellow Jesuits in their progression on the pathway to God would strengthen our individual and collective sense of identity, quite like how moving ahead in the *Spiritual Exercises* strengthens a sense of general Christian identity.

A possible paradigm shift concerning Jesuit life and spirituality, comparable to that in the 1960s, but fueled by the *Spiritual Exercises* and the *Constitutions* together as opposed to narrowing the focus to the *Exercises*, thus appears on the horizon. The future of the Society will depend on how each generation of Jesuits can help younger companions to make progress on the Ignatian pathway to God, and how the art of helping others to progress will be passed on. Facing this challenge today will not only turn us toward the future but also revive an element of our Jesuit identity that was very much present at the beginnings of the Society:

> These are the matters which we were able to explain about our profession in a kind of sketch [. . .]. We have now done this, that we may

9 "Decrees of the 35th General Congregation. Decree 2: A Fire That Kindles Other Fires", p. 733.

> give succinct information, both to those who ask us about our plan of life and also to those who will later follow us if, God willing, we shall ever have imitators along this path *(imitatores vnquam habebimus huius viae)*. [FI 9]

Familiarity with the Ignatian pathway to God is predominantly a practical wisdom, a capacity to live a fruitful life as a Jesuit and to introduce others into it, without, of course, excluding theoretical reflections. This is why the most immediate fruits of a deeper contemporary reception of the *Constitutions* could be expected to appear in the field of formation. Novice directors, superiors and tertian masters will be empowered to support Jesuits in formation more consciously, since much of the helpful dynamic usually taking place between the exercitant and the giver of the *Exercises* will begin to develop in everyday formation settings, giving new meaning to such details as the choice of words, meta-communication and concrete interactions. Companions at earlier stages of formation will be able to see more clearly why they submit themselves to the authority of a superior or a formator. Joining empathy and firmness while exercising authority—in the manner that is familiar from directing the *Spiritual Exercises*—will be more easily attainable since a Jesuit in formation who desires to make progress on the pathway to God will be less inclined to perceive the superior's instructions as unwelcome intrusions into his personal sphere, and more capable of perceiving the assistance of the superior as help intended to foster his progression.

During each phase of formation, more personally and accurately defined short- or mid-term goals will reduce diffuse anxiety ("how am I going to be able to persevere in this life?") and provide reliable support for the preparation for subsequent phases. As genuine motivations which stem from the love of God grow stronger, compensatory acts arising from anxiety or aimlessness and behaviors in opposition to the vows can recede. Formators can learn to rely on a road map similar to the one they already possess while giving the *Exercises*. Signs indicating that a particular phase of formation can be considered as completed will be easier to discern, once again in a manner analogous to recognizing the indications during a thirty-day retreat that one can move into the next week. All in all, instruments that are both deeply rooted in a coherent

Ignatian heritage and perceived as helpful by contemporary companions will be more readily at the disposal of formators and superiors.

The evaluation of specific formation issues, such as the disappointingly high departure rates mentioned in the Introduction, will become more pertinent as a result of a better understanding of the *Constitutions*. The strengths and weaknesses of a given formation context can be analysed and accountability can become a reality. Discernment becomes possible in the perspective of the Ignatian pathway to God. Does the Ignatian pathway to God receive the high priority—second to God—requested by the Formula of the Institute? How does one verify that those entering the novitiate have the necessary qualities and dispositions so that they can begin to make progress? Which elements of a supportive formation environment have been implemented and which ones need to be improved? How do Jesuits in formation receive spiritual support so that they can make the right decisions and become responsible for their own progress? What are the typical areas of resistance and how do formators face these? These and other similar questions can guide reflections concerning formation in the same way as their equivalents commonly help to evaluate the giving of the Spiritual Exercises. As to the perplexing case of the Jesuit novitiate in Hungary in 1989, one can conclude that insufficient awareness of the Ignatian pathway to God made it impossible to evaluate responsibility issues. While seemingly many elements of Jesuit formation were present, they were neither presented nor discerned as exercises aiming at helping novices to progress on the Ignatian pathway to God.

A deeper contemporary inculturation of the *Constitutions* promises to bring forth yet another fruit for the Society itself, that of responding more flexibly and effectively to recent transitions concerning religious sensitivities in Western cultures. Young adults who choose a religious life today tend to differ from previous generations in desiring to receive more definite and tangible help to live a good life. Preferred choices of religious communities express an increased need for security.[10] Our

10 "Although these [vocation promotion] practices can have a positive impact on attracting and retaining new members, the research suggests that it is the example of members and the characteristics of the institute that have the most influence on the decision to enter a particular institute. The most successful institutes in terms

current Jesuit corporate culture easily groups together such tendencies under the label of a conservative trend that hardly corresponds to the cherished values of individual responsibility, maturity and inner freedom that we have been highlighting to describe the ideal of Jesuit life in the recent past. In the light, however, of the Ignatian pathway to God, which also emphasizes the importance of tangible and concrete support especially at early phases of formation, such persons with conservative preferences can be more easily recognized as potentially outstanding candidates for the Society.

One of the main areas where responsiveness to new cultural needs will entail noteworthy changes is the use of authority. An authority crisis prevalent from the 1960s onward has made many traditional practices of Jesuit formation appear childish and pointless. In response to that cultural transformation, it seemed helpful to break away from a cold institutional atmosphere and to implement an extremely cautious style of practicing authority so that life in the Spirit may be preferred to the mere emphasis on authority. Half a century into this changed perception of authority, a critical attitude toward authority is still present, but at the same time one can perceive an increasing longing for genuine authority figures. Those who grew up in fragmented social contexts without the support of a safe family background or a reassuringly strong faith community often discover how much they lack either the criteria for setting goals or the strength to achieve them. To such persons, rigid institutions and impersonal structures do not necessarily appear to be the primary obstacles to personal freedom. Awareness of one's own inadequacies can even lend attractiveness to communities that show firm leadership and resolute purpose since they can promise to help

of attracting and retaining new members at this time are those that follow a more traditional style of religious life in which members live together in community and participate in daily Eucharist, pray the Divine Office, and engage in devotional practices together. They also wear a religious habit, work together in common apostolates, and are explicit about their fidelity to the church and the teachings of the Magisterium. All of these characteristics are especially attractive to the young people who are entering religious life today." M. E. Bendyna RSM, and M. L. Gautier, *Recent Vocations to Religious Life: A Report for the National Religious Vocation Conference* (Washington: Georgetown University, Center for Applied Research in the Apostolate (CARA), 2009), p. 127.

overcome an inner chaos by instilling an ordered way of common life that is also expressed in visible formalities and firm structures. The risks of a merely compensatory safety-seeking are obvious, and it is also obvious that seeking security in institutional structures—while psychologically understandable—can lead to painful disappointments. Yet, while the immense cultural pendulum is gaining a reverse momentum in Western Christianity and the resulting phenomena are seemingly opposed to the strivings of the 1968 generation, careful discernment can reveal similarly mixed ambitions. Naïvely idealistic forms of behavior where appearances not only express but also distort deeper realities are undeniable, but they should not make us blind to the signs of a genuine desire for God and for inner freedom as a precondition for living a fruitful life.[11]

In the midst of sweeping cultural transitions, a religious community either adapts to the changing environment by adopting new cultural values or takes its distance from the surrounding culture by emphasizing the values that have traditionally constituted its identity. Both options entail advantages and risks, and neither of them guarantees that the community will successfully survive the crisis. While deliberating possible responses to the cultural challenges that we are facing at the beginning of the twenty-first century, it may be helpful once again to consider the transformation of mainstream spirituality in the Society of Jesus during the second half of the twentieth century. Jesuits at that time understood that their contemporaries, Jesuits and laypersons alike, were seeking God and personal freedom simultaneously, and that they needed help because they felt more and more alienated from traditional and institutional forms of support, whether in the Society or in the church in general. In the midst of immense sociological changes, the answer of the Society was neither mere adaptation nor closing in on traditional values and ways of proceeding. Instead, a collaborative initiative of Jesuits dedicating themselves to the understanding and the

11 "Les problèmes qui se posent ne sont pas dus uniquement à une crise de la foi. La question est plutôt de savoir comment vivre la foi après le choc culturel considérable et assez radical que l'Europe a vécu à la fin des années 1960 [. . .] dont les conséquences ne sont pas encore terminées." P.-H. Kolvenbach SJ, *Faubourg du Saint-Esprit: Entretien avec Jean-Luc Pouthier* (Paris: Bayard, 2004), p. 112.

application of the *Spiritual Exercises*—the rediscovery of the personally accompanied Exercises—resulted in establishing a viable and authentic option for those seeking God with contemporary cultural sensitivities. As a result of this effort, the Society of Jesus was able to avoid both the temptation to hold on to lifeless structures that were quickly becoming anachronistic, and the risk of losing its unique character through forced compromises with the surrounding culture. Spiritual progress according to the *Spiritual Exercises* was reinvented as a cornerstone of Jesuit identity in the changed cultural context, both anchoring the Society to the best of its spiritual tradition and providing uncommonly helpful tools for maintaining the spiritual well-being of the Society and its ministries alike.

How to give a similarly providential and creative response to contemporary cultural challenges? Neither a disdainful or indignant denunciation of conservative tendencies nor mere conformity to them by, for example, emphasizing liturgical or ministerial formalities will do. The *Constitutions* offer a viable way out of these two impasses. Formators can acknowledge the need for more tangible and visible structures without opening the door to endless controversies. The entire issue can be placed in the context of a dynamic progression on the Ignatian pathway to God, where a firm formation environment—especially in the early phases—is an obvious means of support. Within this favorable context for making progress, authority can appear to be simultaneously firm and helpful, and elements of the general Christian and specific Jesuit tradition can be used freely to set up a safe and supportive formation environment. Awareness of the Ignatian pathway to God allows one to use particular practices creatively, without giving in to nostalgia or traditionalism, just as the awareness of the dynamic of the *Exercises* inspires creativity without bringing back obsolete forms of religiosity. Ideological issues can be relatively effortlessly dealt with once a person is engaged in the dynamic of the Exercises. One can anticipate that the usually barren tensions between liberal and conservative opinions will similarly diminish among Jesuits who begin to walk more consciously on the Ignatian pathway to God. Jesuits of "different judgments" would thus find the "unobstructed way" along which they can walk together [Delib 1].

Another beneficiary of a more in-depth contemporary reception of the Ignatian vision of Jesuit life would be religious life in general. The

Second Vatican Council, by emphasizing the universal call to holiness, removed the theological foundations for regarding religious life as a superior choice in comparison to lay life. In the absence of the theological ideal of the state of perfection, criteria of an anthropological nature have begun to prevail in evaluating religious life. Since contemporary reflection on the human being is dominated by psychological models that do not integrate the relationship with God as a constitutive element, even the religious tend to have a hard time explaining how their life form is a valid and helpful one. For instance, how can the nearly complete exclusion of some of the greatest challenges of human life—such as decisions concerning financial independence, sexuality, intimacy, family life and career options—lead to human and spiritual maturity?[12] Just as the Council placed lay life in an adequate theological context, religious life needs to be placed in an adequate anthropological framework so that spiritual or theological considerations can be solidly founded. As we have seen, the Ignatian pathway to God, beyond offering an entirely practical introduction to the mystery of God, also implies strong anthropological foundations. Ignatian anthropology allows one to understand how fundamental human motivations develop and are integrated into a mature personality in a way that is fundamentally different from the developmental trajectory of lay life, given that the primary and decisive relationship is that with God from the outset. The ability to distinguish between the anthropological challenges involved in religious life and those of lay life is an important basis for discernment when accompanying our contemporaries in religious life. Facing more resolutely the theoretical and practical challenges inherent in our Institute would also enable us Jesuits to offer more pertinent contributions to discussions about religious life, which has so many unexplored potentialities in a spiritually hungry world today.

As to the question of how Jesuits in formation could be better helped to respond to their calling, more emphasis on the Ignatian pathway to God would certainly help but it would not solve all the difficulties that we encounter day by day in our agitated postmodern cultures. Yet instead of being carried away by our divergent and multiplying

12 For a characteristic illustration see Richard A. Blake, "The First Word ...", *Studies in the Spirituality of Jesuits* 43/2 (2011), pp. iii–viii.

questions about prayer, community life, affectivity issues, perseverance, sufficient maturity for undertaking challenging ministries and so on, we could begin to see these issues as organic parts of a single dynamic leading toward God while profoundly challenging and transforming the human being at all significant areas of his personality. Providing help to twenty-first-century Jesuits who carry their culturally conditioned wounds, ambitions, fears and desires could be placed, instead of patiently and dutifully managing an endless stream of difficulties, into a dynamic Ignatian framework reminiscent of that of the *Spiritual Exercises,* where the focus is on God, on the relationship with God and on the complex spiritual and human dynamic of progress, understood in reference to the Ignatian text describing this dynamic. Our contemporary cultural context makes the almost half-millennium-old book of the *Constitutions* well worth taking off the bookshelf, and placing on our desk, right next to the *Spiritual Exercises.*

www.ingramcontent.com/pod-product-compliance
Lightning Source LLC
LaVergne TN
LVHW101321110826
845152LV00011B/26

* 9 7 8 1 7 8 1 8 2 0 4 3 8 *